Ideology and Form

in Eighteenth-Century Literature

Ideology and Form

in Eighteenth-Century Literature

Edited by
David H. Richter

Texas Tech University Press

This book was set in Kuenst 480 and Futura Medium Condensed. The paper used in this book meets the minimum requirements of ANSI/NISO Z39.48-1992 (R1997). ∞

Design by Melissa Bartz

Printed in the United States of America

Library of Congress Cataloging-in-Publication Data
Ideology and form in eighteenth-century literature / edited by David H. Richter.
p. cm.
Includes bibliographical references and index.
ISBN 0-89672-415-8 (cloth : alk. paper)
1. English literature—18th century—History and criticism. 2. Politics and literature—Great Britain— History—18th century. 3. Literature and society—Great Britain— History—18th century. 4. Fielding, Henry, 1707-1754—Political and social views. 5. Fielding, Henry, 1707-1754—Technique. 6. Literary form. I. Richter, David H., 1945- .
PR448.P6I34 1999
820.9'358—DC21 99-13130
CIP

99 00 01 02 03 04 05 06 07 / 9 8 7 6 5 4 3 2 1

Texas Tech University Press
Box 41037
Lubbock, Texas 79409-1037 USA

800-832-4042

ttup@ttu.edu

Http://www.ttup.ttu.edu

Contents

Preface

While many anthologies of critical essays are notoriously gatherings of jumped-up conference papers, the present collection has the superlative indignity of having begun as a single conference paper on Henry Fielding at the 1991 MLA Convention in San Francisco, given at a session that owed its very existence to the MLA's failure to publish then division leader Terry Castle's call for papers.[1] There I argued, with what I thought at the time was all manner of qualification, that many of the canonical texts of the eighteenth century were endangered and needed to be saved from our ideological readings of them. That conference talk, revised and sent to *The Eighteenth Century: Theory and Interpretation*, generated sharp controversy among its editors. One of them wanted to publish it, the second to reject it outright, while the third thought that, whatever its quality in itself, it might make an effective nucleus for a special issue of the journal, particularly if its author could get some of the critics whose marxist and feminist interpretations he had attacked to respond with equal candor and verve.

I took up this challenge, and the result was the September 1996 issue of *TECTI*, which brought together not only cogent and challenging responses by John Richetti and Patricia Meyer Spacks, but new and equally provocative essays by Michael Boardman, Gerald J. Butler, Carol Houlihan Flynn, and J. Paul Hunter. Texas Tech University Press then extended an invitation to enlarge the reach of the project into further areas of contemporary theory and interpretation, and the result is before you. These new essays include a wide-ranging feminist approach by Laura Brown, a Bourdelian analysis of the Augustan cultural field by

Trevor Ross, a neoformalist essay on Fielding by Ralph W. Rader, a cultural studies approach to the genre of the agricultural tour by Ina Ferris, an analysis of the eighteenth-century elegy via queer theory by George E. Haggerty, and a trenchant defense of the marxist approach to literature against my *jeu d'esprit* by historian of the novel Lennard Davis. All these essays are freshly written for this collection.

The history of this project is important because the essays are not the product of a particular moment but span nearly a decade, a period that has witnessed enormous changes in the structure of higher education in general and in the work of scholars in the eighteenth century in particular. Indeed, my own contribution to this volume—which stands to the rest of the essays as does the gritty irritation within the body of the bivalve to the precious pearl produced—was itself written in reaction to essays by Richetti, Spacks, and other critics published in the late 1980s. So one end of the arch described by this book extends back into what has been called the Era of Grand Theory, while the other lies in the present posttheoretical age when epic poems, manuals of midwifery, and scholarly essays about either genre may all be viewed as potentially comparable cultural practices. I shall be discussing some of the implications of this development in my afterword.

The title of the book, *Ideology and Form in Eighteenth-Century Literature*, has been cleverly designed to obscure as much as it reveals. Readers will note that no two contributors use the terms "form" or "ideology" exactly alike, that the eighteenth century has been quietly extended back into the seventeenth and forward into the nineteenth, and that "literature" is used to cover almost any text deploying the medium of language. But the heaviest work is performed by the tiny but powerful word "and," which deserves to be paid extra for its ability to describe the manifold possible ways in which form can be related to ideology, from parallelism and parataxis to outright opposition, and a good many hypotactic positions in between, as the popularity of those Jamesonian terms "the form of the content" and "the content of the form" may indicate.

Those who peruse the contents will find essays like J. Paul Hunter's, suggesting how poetic elements, like Pope's lists and closed couplets, that one might suppose purely formal in their implications may nevertheless bear the weight of social, even political ideology; and, on the other side, essays like Michael Boardman's, questioning whether the peculiar structure of Inchbald's *A Simple*

Story should be ascribed to feminist ideology or (as he rather thinks) the desire to write an innovative novel within an existing tradition. And we even find metapositions regarding this dichotomy: Trevor Ross's essay bears witness to a declining locus of contact over the course of the eighteenth century between artistic form and social ideology, and the rise of what we think of (with favor or with condescension) as the doctrine of the autonomy of the realm of art, an ideological shift that is itself viewed as the product of deep social and economic changes. Where my own venture into the realms of ideology had consisted of claiming that Fielding had been considerably more politically correct than his marxist and feminist readers wished to suppose, Gerald J. Butler trumped my ace by insidiously suggesting that mine was only the latest venture into the corridors of cant, and that the pleasures of Fielding depended precisely on the impossibility of reducing the vivid life he reproduces to an example of any system whatever.

All of the writers who responded, whose pieces are here included, will be gratified that I have grown wiser than I was eight years ago, and would think twice before asserting the sort of blanket opposition between "form" and "ideology" that my provocation piece assumes. Unless we are to take form as a purely mechanical device (a device "primarily of repetition," as Lennard Davis would have it, like the rhyme scheme of a sonnet), literary forms cannot exist outside and apart from the ideological. The form of a poem within any stable system of genres, like the elegy, necessarily proceeds through a prescribed sequence of moves with prescribed ideological meanings—the announcement of death, the mourning around the body from which the spirit has departed, the consolation of the survivor—although as George Haggerty shows, the cultural significance of each of these moves may metonymically bear the strains and tensions of the homosocial bond it celebrates. Similarly, the form of a fictional plot necessarily engages the desires and expectations of its readers; those desires presuppose that one state of affairs must be found preferable to another; those expectations presuppose that we understand the world of the fiction and the world we live in tolerably well, and the probability that the desires that shape the arch of plot will be fulfilled in the real as well as the virtual world.

The aesthete who reads for the tang of aesthetic beauty alone is thus committed to accepting along the way notions of goodness and notions of truth, sometimes mediated in the service of other ends, but sometimes even as ends in themselves. In the most explicitly neoformalist essay in this volume, Ralph Rader in effect argues that R. S. Crane failed to do the highest justice to the form of *Tom Jones* because Crane, adhering to a theoretical commitment to the autonomy of the literary masterwork, and to the incompatability between mimetic and didactic literary genres, was forced to view Fielding's norms in abstraction from their historical setting and to treat Fielding's latitudinarian beliefs about the nature of divine providence in the world and his sentimental views of sympathy as inspiring virtuous action as accidental, rather than essential features of the structure of that novel. Rader in effect shows how *Tom Jones* can be seen as no less a masterwork for being contemplated not as a timeless classic but as a text that lives in the history of its ideas.

Few formalists today, I think, would disagree that form cannot help but engage the ideologies of its day. The issue that might legitimately arouse the ire of formalists is our need to make texts live within the history of our own ideas, to claim—for example—every eighteenth-century novel written by a woman for contemporary feminism. Michael Boardman's analysis of Elizabeth Inchbald's novel, *A Simple Story*, is driven by a desire to defend Inchbald as a realist who used all her art to tell "a complex, gripping, and therefore profitable story" rather than an allegorist out to attack the institution of patriarchy. Inchbald's literary form is inflected in the ideology—in the sense of false consciousness—of her day, and her achievement as an artist is not necessarily improved by making her the innocent bearer of our political imaginary. To put it another way, it deprives Mary Wollstonecraft of her rightful place in history, of her revolutionary originality as a feminist thinker, when we pretend that every other woman of her era thought much as she did and figurally worked such thoughts into her writings.

A similar reaction against the workings of the political imaginary is what I suspect lies behind Laura Brown's "feminist formal history of the eighteenth century." Whereas practitioners of cultural studies such as Nancy Armstrong are willing to move directly from the positioning of "the household as a specifically feminine space" to the notion that "modern culture has empowered middle class women," Brown is not. For a cultural materialist like Brown, power is more than just a discursive space, and her history of feminism flows through considerably less amiable territory than the annals of domesticity: It takes account of the deep, often cruel misogyny of the Augustan Age the commodification of sex, and the deep ambivalence of men toward the feminization of the masculine ideal in the age of sentiment.

Not every essay in cultural studies merely reproduces the ideology of the perceiving subject; it is possible to evolve a liberating approach to literary and quasi-literary texts focused strictly on the ideology of the object. Such an essay is Ina Ferris's discussion of Arthur Young's agricultural tour of Ireland. Ferris adopts a stance of engaged but disinterested inquiry, seeking out the relation between method and purpose, trying to understand the rifts within Young's ideology—both his notions about scientific discourse and his conceptions of political economy—and the difficulties Young had in the process of confronting and trying to represent the stubborn world, which could not be made to conform in every respect to his preconceptions about it. My own effort in this line discusses some of the biographies of Jonathan Wild, the self-styled "thief-taker general" of Great Britain, that were published within a short time of his execution. Whereas Young ended up telling a complex truth that did not correspond to his ideological stance, I found that fact and fiction had in effect traded places. Many of Wild's biographers were so deeply responsive to the demands of genre, here the Tyburn biography, that they were forced to fictionalize the life of England's first important organized criminal, while paradoxically, writers like Gay and Fielding, who explicitly fictionalized Wild, presented a view that was in some ways closer to our present sense of the significance of Wild's career than those who purported to recount the facts of his life.

In gathering together a dozen extraordinary essays from all regions of the ideological spectrum, this collection aspires to represent for the current decade what the Laura Brown/Felicity Nussbaum anthology *The New Eighteenth Century* was for the last decade: a sampler and an emblem of where the intellectual currents of our time have taken our profession.

This book came together with a great deal of help from a great many people. First and foremost let me thank the contributors, who have been uniformly wonderful about submitting their essays, revisions, and tiny corrections on time and in readable form, making my own editorial work a breeze. Thanks are due also to Bruce Clarke, who was editor of *The Eighteenth Century: Theory and Interpretation* when the special issue was conceived and published.

And I have greatly enjoyed working with the folks at Texas Tech University Press: with Virginia Downs, the house editor, and Mary Maddox, freelance copy editor, with Melissa Bartz, who designed the book, and Marilyn Steinborn, who was in charge of production. Carole Young, the Director of Texas Tech University Press, deserves a sentence all to herself: there's nothing like working with a publisher who believes in your project and working with Carole was like a dream. Passing through New York, she also allowed me to realize my weirdest authorial ambition: that of taking my publisher out to lunch. Any virtues this book has are theirs: its faults are probably mine alone.

This book is dedicated to another freelance editor, my kid sister Bernice, who is probably wondering how old we have to get before I stop calling her my kid sister.

Notes

1. Castle herself believed this a mere inadvertency, but the Modern Language Association has been notoriously stingy in its treatment of the eighteenth century at its annual convention. At the 1997 convention, for example, only three panels, out of the grand total of 745 events, were scheduled in English literature 1660–1730, all three sponsored by the Division—that is, no special sessions in the field were approved—and two of the three were scheduled to meet at the same time. Several prominent eighteenth-century scholars have taken to boycotting the MLA convention (even when it is sited in their home towns) and presenting their work at the regional and national chapters of the interdisciplinary American Society for Eighteenth-Century Studies instead.

Ideology and Form

in Henry Fielding

The Closing of Masterpiece Theater: Henry Fielding and the Valorization of Incoherence

David H. Richter

In an essay on *Joseph Andrews* published in *Studies in the Novel*, Brian McCrea calls the text "a kind of literary endangered species—a text that critics have dared to 'close.'"[1] McCrea's notion implies that texts live, not so long as they are admired, but rather as long as they continue to generate controversy, to raise questions that students of literature feel called upon to solve. Fielding too represents an endangered species, one in danger of being understood too well, or so we may suppose when even his devotees think of him as an ideological dinosaur, "marvelous but outdated, possessed of latent conflicts whose importance and scope later writers will limn."[2]

McCrea's specific issue is the slick and tidy way in which Fielding manages to dispose of the issues of class and gender in *Joseph Andrews*. Unlike *Pamela*, in which Richardson was forced to make as credible as he could the misalliance central to its plot, in *Joseph Andrews* Fielding evades the issue by a sleight-of-hand, revealing that Joseph is by birth a gentleman, the son of Wilson, while Fanny is the sister of the newly elevated Pamela. An Althusserian might find McCrea's point exactly backwards. Fielding's need to evade the class issue—of the sexual politics of the old regime—speaks even more eloquently about the split in mid-eighteenth-century ideology than does the way Richardson met the problem head-on.

Whether or not McCrea gets his Marx right, he points to a general problem about Henry Fielding, who in an age of canny criticism is in danger of being thought an easy read. For the case of Fielding is perhaps only emblematic of the literature of the

Table 1

Statistics from the MLA Bibliography for Recent Years

Year	1971	1981	1989	1990	1980-90
Grand total	39511	47006	46699	43888	520,723
Total Eng/A	8414	9397	10341	12598	182,910
17 Century	670	570	653	655	8015
18 Century	676	465	467	723	6950
Defoe	34	27	29	25	459
Fielding	40	30	19	22	421
Richardson	13	19	19	23	538
Smollett	18	10	10	9	142
Sterne	21	19	40	22	407
Gothic	9	9	17	21	811

Figures for 1971, 1981, and 1989 are taken from PMLA; figures for 1990 and the period 1980–90 are taken from MLA Online Bibliography.

eighteenth century in general, which has already become a casualty of the growing interest in literary theory. Or so the statistics would suggest—see Table 1.

The figures tell us that, whereas twenty years ago critical interest in Fielding was stronger than any other eighteenth-century novelist, today Sterne and Richardson have either caught up to Fielding or surpassed him in total studies. But these total figures hide even more devastating trends, for the 421 books and articles contain a high and growing proportion of items on Fielding's work as a playwright and as a political journalist. Richardson scholarship, to the contrary, is almost entirely concerned with his three novels and Sterne scholarship with his two, to the point where essays concerning *Clarissa* and *Tristram Shandy* well outnumber those on *Tom Jones*. Although there does not seem to be the sort of question of Fielding's place in the canon that there may be coming to be about Smollett's—any semester course in the early English novel is bound to include at least one work by Fielding—one may wonder whether Fielding has not arrived at the edge of what Barbara Herrnstein Smith has called a "trajectory of extinction."[3]

Fielding has been in trouble before. In the nineteenth century, "healthy, hearty, Harry Fielding" was a little too hearty not to suffer eclipse. Today Fielding's relative eclipse is the result of the conflict not of sexual moralities but of aesthetic ideologies. Fielding's Georgian valorization of tight economy of plot, coherence of tone, and elegance of expression are likely to prove progressively less in tune with an age whose aesthetic ideology valorizes incoherence, disjunction, and *différance*. The three most inventive and productive critical methods coming into common use in the 1980s were structural marxism, feminism, and deconstruction, and their characteristic modes of operation involve searching for and exploiting loose ends, gaps, and incoherencies within texts. Given this characteristic mode of operation we should not be surprised at what small purchase such methods give on texts of enormous formal intricacy, like the novels of Fielding. Perhaps it is poetic justice that Fielding, who profited from the prevailing formalism of the 1950s and 1960s, should suffer from our current impatience with masterpieces of form and our attraction to texts with considerably looser formal economies.[4] The suffering is found not only in diminished interest—the 50 percent drop in the attention of critics catalogued by the MLA—but in distortion by friends and foes alike. In this ideological age, these distortions often take the form of crude readings of Fielding's ideas about politics and society, readings that frequently arise from presuming that every artistic choice must be ideologically motivated. While no one would deny that novelists convey beliefs within their texts, my own position is that some artistic decisions are ideologically charged, that others are made on the basis of purely formal considerations, and that a third group is overdetermined. But as long as the second group exists, there is always the possibility of drawing false conclusions from a novelist's practice.

In limited time I can concentrate on only a few readings and I shall begin with Carl R. Kropf's "*A Certain Absence: Joseph Andrews* as Affirmation of Heterosexuality," because it is the only thing describable as a deconstruction of a Fielding novel I am aware of in the recent literature. [5] Kropf's position is that the absence of homosexuality in *Joseph Andrews* is the most certain sign of its presence. Kropf notes that homosexuality was present in Fielding's society, that it was notoriously attributed to John, Lord Hervey, the probable model for Beau Didapper, who was called by Pope "Lord Fanny," which is significantly the name of Joseph's sweetheart; and that Joseph himself is a pupil of Parson Adams, and that pupils and masters have at times been involved in homosexual relations. For Kropf, homosexuality is the dog that did not bark in the nighttime, but his conclusion is *not*, as one might think, that Joseph, Fanny, Adams and Didapper are all covertly involved in a gay romp, but rather that *Joseph Andrews* by suppressing its homosexual theme thus affirms heterosexuality all the more.

One might think that this is merely what Michael Boardman has called the "mechanical operation of *différance*." Kropf's question is this: Why, if it had been Fielding's intention to satirize his enemy John, Lord Hervey, did he choose to make Beau Didapper heterosexual? This may indeed be no question at all, since whatever Lord Hervey's sexual orientation was, it was certainly not exclusively homosexual.[6] If there is a question, though, Kropf may be seeking the answer in the wrong place. If you assume from the start that Didapper's sexuality is an ideologically charged artistic decision, your answer is going to be found in Fielding's sexual ideology—and it is odd that Kropf draws the tamest possible conclusion from his evidence. But if you are willing to entertain the possibility that Beau Didapper plays a major structural role in a narrative comedy—specifically, that he plays the role with respect to Fanny that Lady Booby does with respect to Joseph, as a potential lover who is rich, wellborn, and sexually unattractive—then Didapper must be interested in women to fulfill this role. It is probable that Fielding first conceived of Didapper's role relative to the comedy and only then decided to shape his mannerisms to parody those of Lord Hervey.

Kropf's was not, of course, a serious attempt to apply deconstruction to Fielding. Nevertheless, even a serious attempt is likely to be difficult, partly because Fielding is not the sort of dialectical thinker commonest since the romantic revival, and many of the rhetorical antinomies pioneered by Derrida and de Man on poets and philosophers since Rousseau operate less showily on nonbinary thinkers like Fielding.[7]

Let us turn quickly to a recent feminist critique of Fielding by Patricia Meyer Spacks, "Female Changelessness; or, What Do Women Want?"[8] Spacks's "exemplary texts" are *Memoirs of a Woman of Pleasure*, better known as *Fanny Hill*, by John Cleland, and Fielding's *Amelia*. "*Fanny Hill* details, with repetitive and often pornographic specificity, the stages of a whore's career, from rural innocence to urban prosperity and marital bliss. . . . *Amelia*, on the other hand, rich in realistic social detail, virtually canonizes a heroine apparently devoid of erotic impulse, who cares only for her family, happily endures poverty, and rarely deviates from perfect goodness. Fanny is woman-as-sinner; Amelia, woman-as-saint. But both characters, equally the products of male fantasy, are defined by unchanging structures of feeling."[9] "Things happen to Amelia without changing her. . . . She . . . grows—but only to become more unmistakably what she was from the beginning."[10] Spacks's point is that "ideal women," as constructed by eighteenth-century men, want "whatever men want them to want. The naughty woman differs from her virtuous counterpart in the number of men each chooses to satisfy and in the ways she is willing to provide satisfaction." The connection is made in the minds of men like Cleland and Fielding who, despite their own "complex, ambivalent, contradictory" behavior, "imagine women as existing in a condition approaching stasis."[11]

The facts Spacks points to are there, but they need her eloquence, for they don't really speak for themselves. The choice to have a heroine-protagonist resolve the instabilities of the narrative by her constancy is viewed as purely ideological, a matter of sexual politics. But it can be more than that, or less. If we glance at the Jane Austen canon Spacks knows so well, we find that Austen wrote comedies about women changing, like *Pride and Prejudice* and *Emma*, and she wrote comedies about women remaining the same despite temptations to change, like *Mansfield Park* and *Persuasion*. This was a formal issue—or at least I am not aware of any evidence that Austen changed her sexual politics back and forth over the last five years of her life. Women have written novels valorizing men who remain constant (like Eliot's *Daniel Deronda*), and men have written novels valorizing men who remain constant (like Scott's *Ivanhoe*). Men have written novels about other men who are tragic because they *cannot* change (like James's *The Beast in the Jungle*). Women have written novels about men *and* women remaining the same despite the tidal flux of experience (like Woolf's *The Waves*). Cleland and Fielding taken by themselves may appear to point to a universal truth about the construction of gender; add Austen and Scott and Eliot and James and Woolf and the truth universally acknowledged turns into a morass.

Though it seems initially more plausible, Spacks's argument has the same problem as Kropf's. Her inquiry about Amelia's constancy has been designed so as automatically to find the rationale within Fielding's sexual ideology. But as before there may be ideologically neutral reasons why Booth changes and Amelia does not. One might posit that Booth changes not because Fielding was writing a male bildungsroman—a form he never attempted—but because Fielding needed to end a plot that was in danger of becoming too serious. Booth needs to change because his moral attitudes (including attitudes about gender) are seriously awry, but this change is a conversion experience, based on his reading of Barrow, rather than on reflections about the errors of his life, and the change has no real consequences within the novel except allowing those of us who are able to suspend our disbelief in it to accept with equanimity the possibility that the virtuous Amelia will spend the rest of her life with him.

Spacks—who assures us at one point that she doesn't think Fielding is a bad guy—is not the only feminist to have trouble cracking this nut. Both Margaret Lenta and Angela Smallwood have defended Fielding by demonstrating that, as the "woman question" was defined in the 1740s, Fielding stood on the side of the angels (and against mere "angels in the house").[12] But such defenses have seemed irrelevant or unconvincing to other feminists because those contemporary issues, like women's education, are not their own. On the other side, attacks on Fielding like those of Katharine M. Rogers or Mary Anne Schofield usually involve quite a bit of selective quotation in their arguments.[13] Judicious quotation can make Fielding seem either the most chauvinistic or the most liberated of eighteenth-century novelists because, as a conservative, he approved of the system of female subordination and wished only that it were administered intelligently and humanely, while, as a realist, he depicted women like Sophia Western as exquisitely balanced between heart and head, hormones and appetites, and as able—like most of Fielding's women—to get the lion's share of what she wants despite that system. Fielding would doubtless have a better reputation today if, like Richardson, he had portrayed patriarchy as a coherent and unified system of oppression, but he had a lawyer's awareness that, in the real world, systems leak and that people can reshape principles as well as principles people.

I shall need to take a little longer with the Althusserian approach of John Richetti in "Representing an Under Class: Servants and Proletarians in Fielding and Smollett."[14] The crux of Richetti's argument that Fielding uses form to negate or nullify proletarian characters in his fiction appears in the following passage which I must quote at length:

> [Pierre] Macherey's "deficiencies of reproduction, seen as such from the point of view provided by historians like [E. P.] Thompson [the reference is to *Whigs and Hunters*], seem defiantly inherent in the literary tradition to which Fielding turns when he fashions plebeian characters and their world as we now choose to understand them. Promising a richly totalized social representation, Fielding retreats while advancing, making his "indirect figuration" a synthesizing abridgement of an actuality that otherwise yields no knowledge worth having. What *Tom Jones* makes clear is that to represent the lower orders so they can be properly apprehended, made part of a moral and social order, the novelist must necessarily reconstruct them, extract the universality that is their truth from the temporary historical difference that merely serves to obscure them as knowable subjects. In so doing, Fielding is overtly canceling history in favor of a recurrent "natural" order, openly producing what a modern critic might want to call ideology. What *Tom Jones* offers its readers is, to adapt one of Terry Eagleton's formulations, an object "which is inseparable from its modes of fashioning it—which is an *effect* of those modes rather than a distinct entity." Eagleton's rendering of ideology, like Macherey's appeal to a reality that literary expression cannot reproduce or even know, insists upon an order of experience (history, a Marxist critic would want to call it) that is coherent and, potentially, at least, available for reproduction. . . . But this "distinct entity" is visible in *Tom Jones* only as a raw material now no longer present, as circumstances necessarily transformed by ordered representation. Given Fielding's obtrusive fashioning, his avoidance of representational directness, history in this special Marxist sense is by no means denied, but openly and comically negated. (91)

The burden of this attack is directed at Fielding, who explicitly promises in *Tom Jones* "a richly comprehensive social representation" but who "undercuts that promise by . . . recurring moral equivalences that reduce or even nullify social distance and difference." An example of what Richetti is specifically addressing is Fielding's use of the mock-heroic in describing the Somersetshire mob's attack on Molly Seagrim, who has transgressed against class sumptuary rules by dressing in one of Sophia Western's discarded gowns. The mock-heroic, for Richetti, shifts the cultural register away from a specific instance of plebeian folkways (what the cultural historian Robert Malcolmson describes as "rough music") and toward a comic universal. The argument is that if A is seen in the context of B, then A is negated or nullified, while B is represented. Some of us may not be ready to admit that such vivid cameo roles as Jemmy Tweedle, Echepole the sow-gelder, and Goody Brown are negated as proletarian individuals by Fielding's parody of Greco-Trojan combat.

But even were one to concede the point for the sake of argument, the fact would remain that Fielding is an equal-opportunity nullifier whose genteel characters disappear, as a result of his heroic similes, into proletarian ones. For Fielding shifts registers or representation down as well as up: in Book Sixteen, chapter two, "Western beheld the deplorable condition of his daughter with no more contrition or remorse than the turnkey of Newgate feels at viewing the agonies of a tender wife, when taking the last farewell of her condemned husband. . . . Or to hit the case more nearly, he felt the same compunction with a bawd, when some poor innocent, whom she hath ensnared into her hands, falls into fits at the first proposal of what is called seeing company."[15] Richetti himself cites the passage in which Square is discovered in Molly Seagrim's minuscule closet in a posture which Fielding compares to military prisoners or to the London poor squatting to beg—or perhaps to defecate—in the open streets. For Richetti this is "a graphic rendition of the raw material Fielding normally transforms." A less slanted reading would acknowledge that there is no "raw material" within literary representations, that the Somerset folk are no more negated than the genteel tutor or the Westerns, and that the beggars are as much the objects of representation as the heroic world of Fielding's parody.

All this confusion ultimately proceeds from Richetti's unexamined assumption that social historians provide "direct or unmediated experience" as opposed to the "ordered representation" of the novelist. This is of course a reification of history that neither Macherey nor Eagleton in his high-Althusserian phase would have countenanced. In effect, Richetti privileges one historical representation of the poor—the viewpoint of Thompson and Malcolmson—in order to decenter another—that of Fielding. But if Althusser has taught us anything, it is that "history" is a text like any other, with all the antinomies entailed by textuality.

The reason a critic of immense learning and sophistication like John Richetti might be drawn into this indelicate procedure is that Fielding does not present the sort of surface in which structural marxists like Macherey take delight. Macherey sought out the rifts within social ideology within gaps and incoherencies in the texture of representation, areas of paradox, confusion, evasion that betoken the author's attempt to paper over contradictions between what the novelist sees and the way the novelist's society has agreed to describe it. You don't need to go far into a text with a relatively loose formal economy—like the Gothic novel—before you run across incoherencies whose semantic dysplasias suggest the operation of what Fredric Jameson has called the political unconscious.[16] But with texts that sport relatively tight formal economies, scratching the surface isn't enough. Even drilling at random into Fielding's polished surfaces can lead to a lot of dry holes. By sleight of rhetoric, Richetti may momentarily make comic figurations seem ideologically motivated—Fielding's way of making the underclass disappear—but even a short perusal of the novel as a whole suggests that such figurations may be governed by prior formal choices (such as Fielding's need to give us comic reassurance that Molly's vanity and pride are not going to result in more than temporary discomfiture), and thus may well be ideologically neutral.

The problem with ideological readings like Richetti's, like Spacks's, like Kropf's, is that they degrade the Fielding text; they substitute a raw, crude vision of sexual, social, political life in Georgian England for the subtle and complex vision that Henry Fielding represented. One should admit at once that Fielding was not politically correct; by today's agenda he was neither a radical nor a feminist. Nevertheless, a Fielding who held that women cannot undergo moral growth, or that the working classes ought to disappear, isn't convincing either. And Fielding is surely not the only canonical author made monstrous by ideological readings of his works.

But what can be done in defense of a rich and pluralistic tradition? One remedy would be to abandon ideological criticism entirely, and I am sure there are many scholars who would welcome the prospect of putting the genies of deconstruction, feminism, and structural marxism back into their respective bottles. But it seems foolish to abandon the valuable tools contemporary literary theory has created merely because they can be abused. And in any case, genies are too smart for that these days. Perhaps the only genuine remedy for crude reading is better reading, a reading more responsive to the text as a whole, a reading sensitized by the awareness that artistic choices can be made for formal as well as ideological reasons. Ideological criticism can be valuable when it proceeds in tandem with formal criticism, tempering its tendency to read Fielding too easily. Without this sort of dialogue, we may witness the final closing of masterpiece theatre.

Notes

1. Brian McCrea, "Rewriting *Pamela*: Social Change and Religious Faith in *Joseph Andrews*." *Studies in the Novel* 16 (summer 1984): 137.

2. McCrea, 147.

3. See Barbara Herrnstein Smith, "Contingencies of Value," in *The Critical Tradition*, ed. David H. Richter, (Boston: Bedford, 1989): 1320–43.

For the statistics, the base year is 1971, well before the theoretical revolution. The fragmentary data available for 1990 from the Wilsonline computer system suggest that the trend lines are continuing. Besides Sterne, the other really bullish area is the Gothic novelists, up to seventeen items, with nine for Radcliffe alone . . .

Whether the shortening figures for the eighteenth century as a whole denote real shifts in interest or are just a statistical artifact would require more analysis. It is possible that critical studies once placed with general eighteenth-century categories (e.g., fiction, drama, criticism) are now placed with articles on theory. It is also possible that all periods have suffered equally with the eighteenth century by the growing interest in theory.

4. The distinction between "tight" and "loose" formal economy is an intuitive one that applies to artistic texts of all types, not just to literary ones. For example, Wagner's *Meistersinger* (arguably his masterpiece) is sufficiently loose of formal texture to permit Hans Sachs's closing *lied* to include a politically motivated warning against the Walloons (i.e., the French under Napoleon III); the finale of Mozart's *Marriage of Figaro* (arguably his masterpiece) is too tightly engaged with resolving the lines of plot that any extraneous comment would be insufferable. Some composers (like Bach and Berg) cut themselves even less slack than Mozart, though the initial choice of text (*the Gospel according to St. John* or Buechner's *Woyzeck*) can have obvious ideological implications. Some genres (like the baroque three-part invention, or the sestina) are so tightly form-bound that a small number of initial parameters (in the case of the fugue, the theme itself, and the measure and the register at which the subsequent entries of the theme will be made) determine the fugue so thoroughly that writing the music out was thought unnecessary (see for example the MS of Bach's *Musical Offering*). No Fielding novel could be as formally tight as a Bach invention, but it seems intuitively clear that

the degree of formal patterning is far greater in *Joseph Andrews* than in *The Romance of the Forest*.

5. Carl R. Kropf, "A Certain Absence: *Joseph Andrews* as Affirmation of Heterosexuality." *Studies in the Novel* 20 (1988): 16–26.

6. Hervey was married to the beautiful lady-in-waiting Mary Lepell and had at least three sons by her; he quarreled with Frederick, Prince of Wales, because of their rivalry for the favors of Anne Vane; his quarrel with Pope was occasioned by his relationship with Lady Mary Wortley Montagu (Fielding's cousin); and he was of course rumored to have been Queen Caroline's lover. Pope's attack on Hervey in "Epistle to Arbuthnot" ("Now master up, now miss / And he himself one vile antithesis.") specifies sexual ambidexterity, not homosexuality as such. And as Eve Sedgwick (following Foucault) has pointed out, the very concept of "homosexuality" dates only from the late nineteenth century. Eve Kosofsky Sedgwick, "Introduction: Axiomatic," *The Epistemology of the Closet* [Berkeley: University of California Press, 1985].

7. Fielding's characteristic rhetorical move is to establish an "either-or" situation and then deconstruct it with an "unless . . ." or "except . . ." An early example is in *Tom Jones*, chapter three of Book One, Mrs. Deborah Wilkins's fright at seeing Allworthy without his pants on is either ridiculous, in the view of "sneerers and profane wits" or admirable in the view of "my graver reader" unless "the prudence supposed to attend" women of Mrs. Deborah's age "should a little lessen his admiration." See Henry Fielding, *The History of Tom Jones, A Foundling*, ed. Fredson Bowers, with an introduction and commentary by Martin C. Battestin (Middletown, Conn.: Wesleyan University Press, 1975), 1, 3, 40.

8. Patricia Meyer Spacks, "Female Changelessness; or, What Do Women Want," *Studies in the Novel* 19 (1987): 273–283.

9. Spacks, 273.

10. Spacks, 278–80.

11. Spacks, 281.

12. See Margaret Lenta, "Comedy, Tragedy and Feminism: The Novels of Richardson and Fielding." *English Studies in Africa* 26:i (1983): 13–25, and Angela Smallwood, *Fielding and the Woman Question* (New York: St. Martin's Press, 1989).

13. See Katherine Rogers, "Sensitive Feminism vs. Conventional Sympathy: Richardson and Fielding on Women." *Novel: A Forum on Fiction* 9 (Spring 1976): 256–70 and Mary Anne Schofield, "Exploring the Woman Question: A Reading of Fielding's *Amelia*." *Ariel: A Review of International English Literature* 16:i (1985): 45–57.

14. John Richetti, "Representing an Under Class: Servants and Proletarians in Fielding and Smollett." in *The New Eighteenth Century: Theory, Politics, English Literature* (ed. Felicity Nussbaum and Laura Brown; New York: Methuen, 1987), 84–98.

15. Fielding, 2, 16, 840.

16. See Fredric Jameson, *The Political Unconscious: Narrative as a Socially Symbolic Act* (Ithaca: Cornell University Press, 1981). For Macherey, see Pierre Macherey, *A Theory of Literary Production.* (Translated by Geoffrey Wall; London: Routledge, 1978). For a Machereyan approach to the Gothic, see my essay, "The Unguarded Prison: Reception Theory, Structural Marxism and the History of the Gothic Novel," *The Eighteenth Century: Theory and Interpretation* 30:3 (Autumn 1989): 1–17.

David H. Richter is Professor of English at Queens College and the City University of New York Graduate Center. His most recent book is *The Progress of Romance: Literary Historiography and the Gothic Novel.* He is currently at work on two books, a cultural approach to true crime fiction and a study of difficulty in Biblical narrative.

Ideology and Form: Novels at Work

Patricia Meyer Spacks replies

If only "purely formal considerations" governed artistic choice! David H. Richter's wistful evocation of such a possibility hints at a desire for a literary situation less complicated than that delineated by most current critical practice, a longing for conditions in which the "aesthetic" and the "social" might constitute distinct categories. Once upon a time the literary-academic world widely hypothesized such distinctions, but no longer. The question is, should we deplore the present state of affairs? Would critics and novelists alike in the best of all possible worlds separate the formal from the ideological?

According to a writer's political/critical predisposition, ideology, rarely a neutral designation, readily adapts to praise or blame. Given the term's stretchy meaning, one can plausibly condemn anyone of opposing views as excessively or insufficiently ideological. Raymond Williams twenty years ago supplied an economical account of the word's divergent uses, concluding that "Historically, [the] sense of ideology as the set of ideas which arise from a given set of material interests has been at least as widely used as the sense of ideology as illusion."[1] I assume that Richter has in mind the first meaning, a meaning that to my mind usefully suggests certain large energies implicit in literary works.

Terry Eagleton elaborates the significance of ideology thus:

> The largely concealed structure of values which informs and underlies our factual statements is part of what is meant by "ideology." By "ideology" I mean, roughly, the ways in which what we say and believe connects with the power-structure and power-relations

> of the society we live in. . . . I do not mean by "ideology" simply the deeply entrenched, often unconscious beliefs which people hold; I mean more particularly those modes of feeling, valuing, perceiving and believing which have some kind of relation to the maintenance and reproduction of social power.[2]

In other words, ideology designates a system of ideas and feelings derived from assumptions associated with society's structural arrangements. Given such a broad definition, all literary criticism carries ideological implications, and I find it difficult to imagine the literary choice that would fail to carry ideological weight.

Formal and social considerations must intertwine in textual arrangements, given that form is a medium of meaning. The more conventional the form, the more likely it is to express social arrangements assumed as given. The point becomes particularly obvious in postmodern rejections of traditional structure, where refusal to indulge in shapely plot or coherent narrative manifestly declares the analogous disintegration of social as well as spiritual order. But even traditional literary scholars have long perceived connections also between the formal decisions of eighteenth-century novelists and their social and theological commitments. Aubrey Williams, Martin C. Battestin, and Leopold Damrosch, arguing for the Providential arrangements of Fielding's plots, implicitly or explicitly connect formal arrangements with social ones. Damrosch, writing most recently of the three, in full awareness of recent marxist criticism, points out at the beginning of his study that Puritanism may be considered "either as a faith or as a social ideology."[3] In either case, the fundamental point remains the same. Fielding's big formal decisions (like Defoe's and Richardson's and Pope's, to mention other authors treated by Battestin or Damrosch) reflect broader commitments. The novelist does not make them, to cite once more Richter's hopeful (or nostalgic) words, "on the basis of purely formal considerations."

The multiple energies at work in any novel guarantee that all "artistic decisions" will prove "overdetermined" (again, Richter's terms) if adequately examined. Like the rest of us, novelists can never fully understand every component of their own choices. Like the rest of us, they function in specific times and places, with unarticulated assumptions—including notions of form and concepts of beauty—derived from their cultural and historical situations. If committed to an art of representation, they must deal directly with social actuality. Formal arrangements involving the manipulation of "characters"—representations of human nature and experience—will reveal structures of belief and feeling reflecting cultural as well as personal facts. And critics who seek to elucidate those structures likewise possess belief structures founded in their own cultures. Precisely because Williams and Battestin and Damrosch, living two centuries later, cannot conceivably share precisely Fielding's assumptions, they possess a perspective useful for clarifying patterns that Fielding himself could assume rather than explicate.

Formal decisions in eighteenth-century novels entail arrangements of social happening. If, for instance, novelists decide, conventionally, to resolve their plots in marriage, they may be primarily concerned to create shapely structures of happening, yet the pressure of ideological assumption on their notions of shapeliness is obvious. Always, always, form contains ideology.

Nor do ideological presuppositions constitute a set of burdensome luggage the artist carries around by compulsion. They anchor artistic production in a sense of actuality. They allow teachers (and critics) to claim the connection between what one reads and how one lives—not because a writer deals with universals but because every writer writes out of direct experience of a world of psychic, social, and material particulars. The otherness as well as the sameness of the writer's world demands (and rewards) attention.

Richter's real concern, if I understand his essay, centers on the ideological predilections that might predispose a critic to find social causes for aesthetic choices: predispositions of the critic rather than the novelist. He believes that social causes only sometimes, perhaps only occasionally, account for textual arrangements and that seeking them tends to flatten the complicated texture of formally intricate novels. Fielding, he fears, will follow Smollett into critical disrepute if ideological critics have their way with him, making him less interesting than in fact he is.

Interest, of course, is in the mind of the beholder. I myself find Fielding more rather than less interesting when I think of him as motivated by ideological as well as purely formal considerations. And of course I am one of Richter's targets. It came as a shock to me to learn that I had deformed Henry Fielding into monstrosity by elaborating my perception that Amelia as a character is largely defined by her changelessness. According to Richter's reading of my essay, "Female Changelessness; Or, What Do Women Want?", I have used John Cleland and Henry Fielding (the piece pairs Fanny Hill with Amelia, both, in my view, male fantasies of the ideal woman) "to point to a universal truth about the construction of gender" that examination of "Austen and Scott and James and Woolf" readily refutes. My "inquiry about Amelia's constancy has been designed so as automatically to find the rationale within Fielding's sexual ideology."

I still like my essay on female changelessness (printed in expanded form in my *Desire and Truth*); I still believe what it says; readers can have a look for themselves.[4] Instead of reiterating my interpretation of Fielding, I want to ponder the larger problem Richter raises about the relation between ideology and form by looking once more at *Amelia*, along with Jane Austen's *Persuasion*, a book to which Richter alludes in pointing out that men write about female constancy and so do women and that men and women alike also describe male constancy, as well as both male and female inconstancy. I shall try to demonstrate how ideological alertness helps a critic discriminate among a novelist's formal choices. Richter sees *Amelia* and *Persuasion* as having something in common; I shall argue that what they have in common only emphasizes their differences. Both novels, however, perform serious ideological work.

Amelia seems a curious example of Fielding's claim to formal mastery, since, as many recent critics have observed, it manifests considerable incoherence in veering between a dark "social" plot concerning the corrupt ways of the world and an optimistic personal plot about how William Booth sees the light and lives happily ever after. Its contrasting patterns of action imply fierce criticism of social developments that the novel sometimes figures as gender disorders. The emphasis on the issue of female education in connection with Mrs. Atkinson, for instance, speaks of conscious ideological concerns. Mrs. Atkinson serves as an image of marital confusion; Amelia functions as emblem of stability. Description of either state necessarily involves perception of society's power relations, although Fielding does not invariably criticize such relations. Amelia's role as center of stability, changeless in the face of temptation, poverty, and marital neglect, organizes the personal plot, drawing Captain Booth back to her and guaranteeing her family's physical and spiritual survival. I take it Richter and I agree about that. Richter's implicit question, by nature unanswerable, is why Fielding chose to make her such a figure. A more useful critical inquiry, bearing on the same issues, might focus on the literary effects of Amelia's posited centrality.

How can one abstract those effects from gender issues? How discuss the rendered actions of men and women as though they represented individuals unconnected to generalizable social experience? The work that novels do illuminates the situation of imagined persons in an imagined world—but persons and world thrive on the page by virtue of their connection to the actual. The density of Fielding's richly populated fictions derives not alone from the sheer number of characters but also from the multiple levels of signification implicit in the imagining of those characters. The novels' continuing vitality depends partly on their implication with immediate social concerns. I must corroborate at least part of Richter's critique: I find it virtually impossible to imagine designing an inquiry into Fielding's literary effects that would not "automatically" find answers at least partly in gender concerns.

But gender issues are always historically inflected, by no means "universal." The matter of female constancy provides fertile ground for historical inquiry. Jane Austen's Anne, whom Richter sees as another model of such constancy, differs sharply from Amelia in her representation. The difference is worth investigating.

Austen's techniques and assumptions have little in common with Fielding's. *Amelia*, despite its title, concentrates on male experience. Its governing consciousness belongs to the obviously male narrator. Its cast of characters and its realm of allusion are large. In investigating intersections of the social and the personal, it emphasizes the heavy weight of social fact on individual possibility. *Persuasion*, in contrast, employs predominantly female consciousness (often, although by no means always, Anne's) to focus on female experience. The narrative confines itself to a relatively limited social realm (Anne's friend, Mrs. Smith, lives in poverty but belongs by origin to the gentry; the representatives of the Navy appear to be moving into, and changing, the same class) and a relatively small sphere of reference.

Female constancy indeed provides the moral center of *Persuasion* as of *Amelia*. Yet Anne Elliot changes in important ways between the beginning and the end of Austen's novel. (Fanny Price, in *Mansfield Park*, another of Richter's instances of constancy, likewise changes while still remaining absolutely steady.) The difference in this respect between her and Amelia, the difference between Fielding's imagining of a woman's emotional and moral stability and Austen's, measures a literary and social shift.

Inasmuch as this shift reflects cultural realities, it implicates more than gender concerns. Implicitly at stake in the question of change is the issue of personhood, sometimes understood as a purely "philosophic" question, but reflecting social perception as well as abstract principle. Fielding, writing in the era of Hume, asserted strongly the steadiness of human identity that Locke had earlier claimed. Locke defines personal identity as "the sameness of a rational Being" and makes it dependent on continued consciousness: "it is by the consciousness it has of its present Thoughts and Actions, that it is self to it self now, and so will be the same self as far as the same consciousness can extend to Actions past or to come."[5] Hume, however, in his *A Treatise of Human Nature* (published before *Amelia*: 1739–40), had used his famous metaphor of the mind as a theater of perceptions to insist that "there is properly no simplicity in [the mind] at one time, nor identity in different; whatever natural propension we may have to imagine that simplicity and identity.[6] Perhaps defending against the uncertainties of such contemporary views, Fielding in *Amelia* maintains the utter continuity of personhood. Defining Amelia's character, he adheres to the view of female possibility articulated by (among others) the Marquis of Halifax: "That which is to be recommended to you [his daughter and, by extension, women in general], is, an Emulation to raise your self to a Character, by which you may be distinguished, an Eagerness for precedence in Virtue."[7]

Amelia's stability in virtue, then, conforms to traditional expectations for her sex, exemplifying the highest possibilities for "character" in a woman, and that stability also affirms the permanence of identity that Hume had challenged. Indeed, one might make comparable points about her husband, despite his inconsistencies of behavior. Booth too remains stable in "consciousness." Although unfaithful to Amelia, he never deviates from his love and admiration for her; although foolish and extravagant in his expenditures of money, he remains devoted to his family and desirous of their good; although capable of blustering and posturing about his honor, he consistently understands his moral obligation as connected with his wife and children. As a man, he has freedom of action denied to Amelia. Although he uses that freedom unwisely, he remains good at heart. Hence his conversion experience, like Tom Jones's seeing of the light about his own sexual behavior, gives him a new rationale for controlling his conduct by principle, but it does not change his delineated psychic organization.

By the time Austen wrote *Persuasion*, not only had many thinkers questioned assumptions about the permanence of identity, but the inequities of women's experience had become a public subject. In saying so, I do not allude simply to the writings of such revolutionary spokespersons as Mary Wollstonecraft. Let me cite briefly instead a conservative conduct book by an anonymous woman published in 1782. Early in this work, the writer makes it clear that she takes for granted a social system that as she describes it virtually sketches the plot of *Amelia*: "Our sex is, and ever will be, exposed to suffer, because we are always in a state of dependence. Men are naturally tyrannical; they will themselves have pleasure and liberty, and yet always expect we should renounce both."[8] She does not conclude that women or men should make any effort to alter this state of affairs. On the contrary, she worries about the fact that girls too often are taught to think of themselves as "of vast consequence" and recommends therefore that "to obviate this evil, children cannot be too often, or too much instructed, in the doctrine of their utter insignificancy and nothingness."[9]

Anne Elliot, who even as an adult has been taught in just this fashion, perceives the social circumstance that supports such teaching. By no means an ideologue, as the novel nears its climax she nonetheless explicitly articulates her view of constancy as a gender issue.

> We [women] certainly do not forget you [men], so soon as you forget us. It is, perhaps, our fate rather than our merit. We cannot help ourselves. We live at home, quiet, confined, and our feelings prey upon us. You are forced on exertion. You have always a profession, pursuits, business of some sort or other, to take you back into the world immediately, and continual occupation and change soon weaken impressions.[10]

Captain Harville, her interlocutor, argues for men's strong feelings and describes the pain of a man forced to part from his family and the delight with which he rejoins them. Anne eagerly agrees to the proposition that men too feel "true attachment and constancy," but insists for her sex on the "privilege . . . of loving longest, when existence or when hope is gone."[11]

Anne's argument that social actualities help to determine the shapes of feeling for men and for women corresponds in some respects to my own "ideological" account of the meanings of Amelia's implausible and rather unnerving stability. Since I was concerned with literary representation rather than social fact, though, I also tried to consider the narrative function of this woman's unchanging nature. I concluded that Amelia, like Fanny Hill, satisfies a powerful male wish, for a woman defined by her unalterable commitment to gratifying the needs/desires of a man (or men). Like the goodness of Cinderella, although in quite another register, Amelia's virtue guarantees the happy ending. Its undeviating nature is the novel's central fantasy.

Anne Elliot, like Amelia, is represented as unfailingly good in action and unfailingly devoted in feeling. She too gratifies the wishes of others, men and women alike, serving her disagreeable sisters and yet more disagreeable father, making no claims for herself. In the perception of these relatives, "her word had no weight; her convenience was always to give way; —she was only Anne."[12] Unlike Amelia, then, she does not clearly fill an important place in anyone else's consciousness. Her sisters and her father see her as the old maid sister, with all the disagreeable connotations that such a phrase might imply: a subsidiary being, asexual, likely never to marry.

Unlike Amelia too, though, Anne is assigned a fully developed consciousness of her own, an interior life including resentment, envy, depression, regret, and boredom, as well as more appealing emotions. Amelia is an ideal woman, imagined specifically from a male point of view; Anne, merely good. She behaves with unfailing propriety, dignity, and thoughtfulness, responding sympathetically to her direct perceptions of others' needs. Action rather than feeling signifies her virtue. Her rendered capacity to act nobly even while entertaining ignoble feelings marks Austen's variety of realism. Frederick Keener, speaking of changes in literary modes of representing character from the seventeenth to the eighteenth century, comments that "the covert, disputed issue was the wisdom and propriety of studying man as he is rather than as he ought to be. It was empirical assessment of self and others that was being opposed and defended. While mankind and individuals could be studied psychologically, many thought they should not, for to do so was to accept them as they are."[13] (The "should not" argument Keener sketches of course lies behind Dr. Johnson's strictures in *Rambler* 4 about the impropriety of rendering "mixed" characters.) Shift the gender of Keener's dictum, and it elucidates the crucial contrast between Amelia and Anne as characters. Amelia exemplifies woman as she ought to be, woman as romance ideal; Anne, with her conflicted psyche, more recognizably resembles the good woman as she might exist in the world.

But Austen's "empirical assessment" of the character, despite its ironic awareness of weaknesses hidden from Anne herself, does not interfere with the romantic structuring of *Persuasion*. If *Amelia* conveys the pleasing notion that the good woman by her very existence insures that everything will turn out all right, *Persuasion* suggests, like many fictions before and after it, that true love triumphs over adversity. Like the schoolteacher in old Hollywood films who takes off her glasses and turns beautiful, Anne needs only a touch of sea breeze and a touch of nostalgic love to regain her lost beauty and youth. Her unfailing service to others—she even gave up her lover, Wentworth, the text tells us, thinking herself "prudent, and self-denying principally for his advantage"—ratifies her deserving status. Accident cooperates in her interest as in that of the Booth family, although Austen prefers relatively inconspicuous and relatively plausible events: at worst a misstep causing a young woman's fall, not the coincidence that the same corrupt lord sets out to seduce one virtuous wife by precisely the means he has used to ensnare another. Although no one Anne knows assigns her much importance through most of the novel, Austen organizes her fiction around Anne Elliot as center as certainly as Fielding organizes his around Amelia. In other words, Anne obviously has great structural (in Richter's terms, formal) importance in *Persuasion*. Why import ideology to explain her?

Because it's there. The change that occurs in Anne seems internal, private. She develops in the course of the novel from an altogether self-abnegating woman, her symbolic role that of playing music for others to dance by, to someone vividly aware of and responsive to her own desires. "It would be most right, and most wise, and, therefore, must involve least suffering, to go with the others," she reflects, early in the narrative,[14] deliberately subordinating her emotions to ethical and rational judgment. Again, a few pages later, in a parallel formulation, she comes to terms with her former lover's expressed opinion that she has changed physically so much that he would not have known her. The remark causes her pain, but she soon claims to "rejoice" that she has heard the words: "They were of sobering tendency; they allayed agitation; they composed, and consequently must make her happier."[15] Asserting what her emotions "must" be, she avoids confronting what they are. But as the novel approaches resolution, Anne's emotions increasingly control her perceptions. The narrator even allows herself a joke about the fact, commenting wryly that the heroine's pretty musings of love and constancy as she walks through the streets of Bath are "almost enough to spread purification and perfume all the way."[16]

Although personal history dictates Anne's emotional change, that history, as Anne's great speech on female constancy suggests, belongs to the larger history of women. And women's history, like men's, entails the operation of their culture's social organization, the workings of power in the larger community. Austen's consciousness of those workings, by definition "ideological," contributes vitally to the structure of *Persuasion*.

Anne in her constancy, like Amelia in hers, provides the fulcrum of a romance plot. But Austen interrogates the concept of female constancy as Fielding does not. Anne's explicit reminder of how the social situation of women implies their "fate" of fidelity provides a context for the entire novel. It also suggests a useful perspective on Anne's moral nature. In an obvious sense, Anne exemplifies the fate she describes. But she also transforms it. Dependent on her family for financial support and for occupation, dependent on Wentworth for happiness and suffering quiet misery in his withdrawal, she has had for most of her adult life little more than the option of refusal. She rejects Charles Musgrove's proposal; she internally refuses Walter Elliot; she repudiates various forms of emotional temptation. But she uses her confined experience as a medium for psychic growth. Mrs. Croft, the hearty wife of the admiral, embodies praiseworthy female force, insisting on her right to participate in sea life and in street corner conversation, guiding the carriage without calling attention to her interventions. Less conspicuous in her manifestations, Anne incorporates comparable force, clear in commitment, determined about her own course. She has, in other words, transformed social dependency into the moral equivalent of independence. Austen has a clear-eyed view of women's social situation and its costs.

Only by understanding the importance of this awareness can one grasp the significance of the heroine's moral achievement.

Despite its assertion of female power and possibility, Austen's message here is conservative, insisting that women's social fate does not restrict their real opportunity. To note this conservatism implies no condemnation of the novelist but a fuller delineation of her achievement. Another aspect of the social commentary in *Persuasion*, much noted in recent criticism, has more progressive implications. In its treatment of the Navy as representing a social class, the novel clearly endorses social change. As Anne comes to know Admiral Croft and his wife, who have rented Kellynch Hall from her father, she consciously realizes their moral superiority as guardians of the estate to those who hold the land by heredity. Revisiting the ancient association between aristocracy and virtue, Austen suggests that the virtues fostered by naval service define a new, improved governing class. Anne's capacity for flexibility and growth, as essential to her nature as her emotional constancy, fit her for life as a sailor's wife. *Persuasion* concludes with reference to the societal value of the Navy: "that profession which is, if possible, more distinguished in its domestic virtues than in its national importance."[17] It thus reminds the reader in its final sentence of its effort to juxtapose the "national" and the "domestic": the ideological and the personal.

The ideological differences between *Amelia* and *Persuasion* emerge implicitly in their opening chapters. Both novels begin by indirection. William Booth does not appear until the very end of Fielding's second chapter; Amelia makes her narrative entrance, in her husband's account of his past life, only in the first chapter of Book Two. The first chapter of *Persuasion* mentions Anne Elliot —her name appears in her father's Baronetage, and she is defined as "only Anne"—but the text provides little indication that she will be the central character.

Both novels open, in fact, by locating important ideological issues. *Persuasion* dwells on Sir Walter Elliot's obsession with his own rank and with his family's social position. The first chapter also calls attention to Elizabeth's marital concerns, which likewise concentrate on social position. The chapter ends by specifying the financial difficulties that will drive the Elliots from their estate, making room for the Navy. It thus foretells the novel's design of charting new movements of social as well as personal power.

Fielding follows more intricate procedures, appropriate to his complicated preoccupations. Although his first sentence announces his subject as "the various Accidents which befel a very worthy Couple, after their uniting in the State of Matrimony," the rest of the chapter generalizes the ethical issues involved in those "Accidents" and declares a moral/aesthetic program, defining the Booths' history and others like it as models of human life. The second chapter turns to the institution of law, offering general reflections on that institution as well as particular instances of its corruption. Booth makes his appearance at the end as one of the law's victims.

These chapters skillfully locate the novel's multiple subjects, suggesting the nature of the two plots. The romance plot, which will carry the "worthy Couple" through to happiness, will retain a moral orientation. The interventions of "Fortune" may appear to control its development, but the first chapter strongly hints the novel's providential commitment. The second chapter announces the "social plot," the darker plot. It even foretells the difficulty of integrating the two plots, since Justice Thrasher's determined administration of injustice will not be alleviated by anything that happens to the Booths. Injustice will continue although the Booths escape it. The novel's perception of social inequity cannot lead to remedy.

Both works in their openings intimate women's social subordination. Austen's skillful juxtaposition of references to Elizabeth and to Anne indicates a range of possibilities—but not a large range. Elizabeth, her father's favored daughter, possessed of apparent self-confidence, making the most of her social rank, must yet look to marriage to determine her fate. Although she expects more from life than Anne does, her opportunities are almost equally limited. If no eligible suitor presents himself, she must dwindle into insignificance. Even in her current state of arrogance and prestige, she endures, the text emphasizes, a monotonous and restricted existence. Anne, accepting her destiny of service to others, cultivating her internal life, expecting nothing, arguably feels more content, if only by virtue of denial. But neither young woman can exercise a great deal of significant choice about the external facts of her experience.

Amelia suggests women's subordination by ignoring women for the first two chapters. No female character appears, none is alluded to. Both the realm of moral generalization and that of public justice belong to men; women have no place in either, at least not as agents. When Booth reaches prison, he encounters women in three guises: fierce aggressor, weeping victim, and determined seductress. From the point of view of a late-twentieth-century critic, all three roles call attention to the costs for women of a social system that allows them few opportunities, but nothing in the immediate context suggests Fielding's awareness of this point.

One might surmise that this set of female figures exist as plot conveniences, the victim calling attention in a new way to the operations of judicial injustice, thus contributing to the plot of "public" concern; the violent woman establishing a set of responses polarly opposed to those of Amelia, who will soon enter at least the retrospective action; the seductress providing irresistible temptation to Booth, as well as a narrative that contrasts sharply with his own. Yet the women in the prison also contribute more profoundly to the dense implications of the Booths' story, which entail awareness of women's situation in society.

Miss Mathews exercises immediate sexual power, but her imprisoned situation emphasizes her restricted range of possibility. Amelia, in contrast, avoids using her sexual allure with men other than her husband, but she accretes remarkable force. She is, from the outset and increasingly as the narrative continues, a mythic figure whose imaginative power depends on her condensation of assumptions vital to the workings of a specific social system. As Booth tells his story to Miss Mathews, he reveals the psychic authority that the idea of Amelia holds for him. For him as for Fielding, the image of Amelia as the quintessence of unchangeable devotion, utter stability of commitment and of action, organizes the psychological and to some extent even the social universe.

The novel works out the implications of woman-as-myth with tact and subtlety. On the one hand, Booth's faith in Amelia's dependable goodness allows him to stray. His wife provides the fixed center for his divagations. He can permit himself every freedom because of her redemptive force. Booth in his imagination assigns Amelia too much power, conceiving her as virtually superhuman in her unfailing virtue. On the other hand, he gives her too little power in immediate experiential terms: he does not take seriously her Christian and her ethical commitment as providing a model relevant to him. Both of these attitudes reflect social facts about the position of women. Although the operations of Providence guarantee a happy resolution for the Booth plot, husband and wife recognizably inhabit the same social world that in its corruption governs the "public" plot.

The complexities of the narrative and ideological situations in *Amelia* mirror one another. One could hardly do justice to Fielding's novelistic achievement without recognizing the degree to which complicated social awareness governs narrative choices. Indeed, if the narrative lacked its Providential element, it might risk lapsing into social determinism. The myth of woman as unchanging, unfailingly consistent in action and in feeling, only intensifies the theme of characterological consistency implicit in male as well as female representations. "Moral growth" is not for Fielding the issue. Booth "grows" no more than does the Noble Lord who tries to seduce Amelia, having previously seduced her friend. From beginning to end, Amelia's husband remains virtuous in intention but fallible in action. When he happens to read the right book at the right time, he undergoes conversion: an instantaneous shift in moral perception, quite a different matter from growth. People are as they are in Fielding's world, products of the society they inhabit and of the kinds of upbringing that society entails. The difference between the good woman and the would-be good man derives from action, which in turn depends partly on gender-based possibilities for action, rather than from moral nature. The myth of the good woman involves the fantasy that action may utterly coincide with ethical imperative. Yet the notion of goodness itself rests on the assumption that moral nature is fixed.

Austen, in contrast, focuses attention on opposed possibilities of growth for morally responsible and irresponsible persons. Sir Walter Elliot, Elizabeth Elliot, Mary Musgrove: these characters never change. Anne Elliot, like Frederick Wentworth, develops in self-awareness, self-confidence, and emotional capacity, reflecting always on the relation between personal desire and social demand. In nature as well as in action, such characters change. The moral growth of the "good" appears to evade the stringencies of a society imagined, like Fielding's, as always urging individuals toward the least common denominator. This hopeful fantasy irradiates the narrative.

A critical consciousness informed by awareness of a novelist's cultural situation, concerned with questions about that situation's bearing on novels' shapes, can elucidate the import of what might be called formal achievements. The development from Fielding's representation of female constancy as male fantasy, its existence important for its effect on men, to Austen's vision of constancy as female fate, the sign of women's capacity for moral triumph over social restriction, is visible to the critic aware of gender concerns. That development participates in a larger movement, also ideologically informed, from the assumption of permanence as moral possibility and value to that of growth as a moral ideal—a movement related to philosophic inquiries into the nature of personal identity. Amelia's goodness inheres in her steady selfhood. So does her husband's, whose behavior often deviates from the ideal. Anne Elliot, in contrast, declares her goodness by her consistently benevolent behavior, which remains steady while her sense of self changes. Her interior life focuses the reader's attention precisely because of that possibility for change, whereas we interest ourselves in Amelia not because she will change but because of the obstacles she faces in remaining the same. For Booth, the obstacles involve discrepancies between the goodness of his nature and the meretriciousness of the world in which he must act. The reader anticipates the change of circumstance that will allow him more fully to display his essential virtue.

To see the bearing of culturally informed assumption on literary structure allows us to recognize the intricacy of formal decisions. I would not quarrel with Richter's apparent conviction that the best possible reading of a text issues from a consciousness "sensitized" by full awareness. Yet full awareness is not a property of mortal minds. In the world we actually inhabit, at the moment we inhabit it, "ideological" readings can reveal kinds of textual thickness that enrich rather than diminish the readings' objects. "Ideological" does not translate as "narrow" or "proselytizing." Ideological interpretations expose with special clarity the vital work that novels do, work that is itself always partly ideological. If Fielding falls into oblivion, it will not be because his readers have been thinking about the situation of women in society. A more damning way to discredit his achievement would be to claim that his preoccupations have no bearing on that crucial situation.

Notes

1. Raymond Williams, *Keywords: A Vocabulary of Culture and Society* (New York: Oxford University Press, 1976), 129.

2. Terry Eagleton, *Literary Theory: An Introduction*. (Minneapolis, Minn.: University of Minnesota Press, 1983), 14-15.

3. Leopold Damrosch, Jr., *God's Plot & Man's Stories: Studies in the Fictional Imagination from Milton to Fielding* (Chicago: University of Chicago Press, 1985), 1. See also Martin C. Battestin, *The Providence of Wit: Aspects of Form in Augustan Literature and the Arts* (Oxford: Clarendon Press, 1974) and Aubrey Williams, "Interpositions of Providence and the Design of Fielding's Novels." *SAQ* 70 (1971), 265–86.

4. See Patricia Meyer Spacks, *Desire and Truth: Functions of Plot in Eighteenth-Century English Novels* (Chicago: University of Chicago Press, 1990).

5. John Locke, *An Essay Concerning Human Understanding*, ed. Peter H. Nidditch, vol. 2 (Oxford: Clarendon Press, 1975), 2:335–36.

6. David Hume, *A Treatise of Human Nature*, ed. Peter H. Nidditch; 2d rev. ed., 1949, vol. 2 (Oxford: Clarendon Press, 1978), 253.

7. George Savile, Marquis of Halifax, *The Lady's New-years Gift: Or, Advice to a Daughter*, 3d ed. (London, 1688), 152.

8. *Letters Addressed to Two Young Married Ladies, on the Most Interesting Subjects* (London, 1782), 1:72.

9. Fielding, *Letters*, volume 2, 37–8.

10. Jane Austen, *Northanger Abbey* and *Persuasion* (1818; edited by R. W. Chapman; 3rd ed.; Oxford: Clarendon Press, 1933), 232.

11. Austen, 235

12. Austen, 5.

13. Frederick M. Keener, *The Chain of Becoming: The Philosophical Tale, The Novel, and A Neglected Realism of the Enlightenment: Swift, Montesquieu, Voltaire, Johnson, and Austen* (New York: Columbia University Press, 1983), 76.

14. Austen, 33.

15. Austen, 61.

16. Austen, 192.

17. Austen, 252.

Patricia Meyer Spacks, Edgar F. Shannon Professor of English at the University of Virginia, is working on a study of attitudes toward privacy in eighteenth-century England.

Ideology and Literary Form in Fielding's *Tom Jones*

John Richetti replies

After accepting David H. Richter's invitation to contribute to this group of essays about "ideology and form" in eighteenth-century English literature, I began to think again about just what ideology meant to me as a reader, and I almost hesitate to admit that the more I pondered the more it struck me as a nearly useless notion for literary understanding. The concept has a complicated and confusing history, modifying from its eighteenth-century beginnings as a neutral "scientific" term to its main nineteenth- and twentieth-century use as a polemical insult applied to one's enemies and oppressors. A good number of commentators have attempted to sort out the many, contradictory meanings that have accumulated over the two hundred years or so since the term was coined, but all their efforts have produced little clarity or unanimity. As far as I can tell, ideology has completely lost the positive and useful complexity it once possessed and degenerated into a term of abuse pure and simple. In literary critical discourse these days ideology is still surrounded by heavy scare quotes, and when applied to literary works it serves as a warning label like the ones on wine bottles and packs of cigarettes. Critics who use the term are generally out to expose its hidden presence in works that have been (lately) elevated by cultural conservatives to a realm of timeless truth specifically identified as beyond ideology. In the contemporary culture wars we are living through, ideology is for many leftish academics what literature and form are secretly and nefariously up to, and it is for such critics our moral duty to resist ideology's soothing and sanitized certainties and to expose the class or gender privileges it embodies. For the mostly non-academic conservatives alarmed by such radical palaver, literature partakes of a cultural and moral purity and qualifies as literature precisely because it excludes ideology and its dirty work of legitimation. For both right and left, it seems, ideology is a form of false consciousness, and I think most of us, of whatever political persuasion, have tended to use the term in just that way. "Ideologue" is a nasty word in any group.

And indeed in the latest attempt to make sense once and for all of ideology the irrepressible Terry Eagleton notes that the "most widely accepted definition" of the concept "has to do with *legitimating* the power of a dominant group or social class."[1] Eagleton usefully outlines six "strategies" by which such legitimation may be said to involve the following actions by a dominant social segment:

> *promoting* beliefs and values congenial to it; *naturalizing* and *universalizing* such beliefs so as to render them self-evident and apparently inevitable; *denigrating* ideas which might challenge it; *excluding* rival forms of thoughts, perhaps by some unspoken but systematic logic; and *obscuring* social reality in ways convenient to itself.[2]

But as Eagleton quickly and honestly notes, this definition restricts ideology and its distortions (of what is thereby presumably an available and stable truth of things which is "beyond ideology") to the power plays of dominant groups and exempts those in opposition to them, so that, for example, radicals of both right and left by this reckoning are not guilty of ideology. These days that claim is too much (even for Eagleton), so the rest of his book is a careful history of ideology that attempts to reformulate the notion and bring it up to date by making it less politically absolute, by giving up the essentially Enlightenment notion that in human or social affairs there is a simple truth available to unprejudiced inquiry and also by surrendering marxist certitudes about the opposition between bourgeois blindness (ideology) and radical insight (truth). Even for a late-twentieth-century marxist like Eagleton, then, ideology is no longer just the pernicious and conspiratorial legitimating strategies of the dominant class but rather indicates "a realm of contestation and negotiation, in which there is a constant busy traffic: meanings and values are stolen, transformed, appropriated across the frontiers of different classes and groups, surrendered, repossessed, reinflected."[3] Thus ideology is not simply "discursive partisanship, interested speech or rhetorical bias"; both dominant and oppositional ideologies seek to provide (in Eagleton's best formulation) "an organizing social force which actively constitutes human subjects at the roots of their lived experience and seeks to equip them with forms of value and belief relevant to their specific social tasks and to the general reproduction of the social order."[4] What this comes down to is that ideology needs to be understood not only as a legitimating imposition from above but also and much more usefully as an inevitable and necessarily complex negotiation (and sometimes a battle) within a culture for what social life and its organization are to mean for its participants. Or to put it more simply, we must always speak in an approving plural when we invoke this notion, since social life is constituted by nothing less than competing "ideologies," and there is no getting beyond them.

In human and moral or political discourse (as opposed to scientific or mathematical reasoning) ideology is nothing less than inevitable and pervasive, not simply a legitimating "false consciousness" (although it can operate that way) but part and parcel of consciousness in more or less modern societies. As Clifford Geertz argued some years ago, ideology needs to be understood precisely and historically as a specifically modern symbolic system that makes "an autonomous politics possible by providing the authoritative concepts that render it meaningful, the suasive images by means of which it can be sensibly grasped." With the decline, Geertz continues, of the "immediate governance of received tradition," as politics frees itself from the "direct and detailed guidance of religious and philosophical canons" and "from the unreflective precepts of conventional moralism," ideology emerges as a practical alternative to a "society's most general cultural orientations" and "its most down-to-earth pragmatic ones."[5]

Refinements of our understanding of ideology such as Eagleton and Geertz propose may just help to restore it as a meaningful notion for literary studies. Indeed, something like a rehabilitation of the concept might already be said to be established (if not always articulated) in the current intense reexamination of the origins and meanings of the British eighteenth-century novel, which in recent crucial reevaluations such as those of McKeon, Bender, Hunter, Davis, Mullan, Armstrong, and Warner is everywhere understood by these critics as an exploration of questions that are fundamentally sociocultural and thereby powerfully and essentially ideological.[6] What McKeon labels a "crisis of categorical instability" that provokes the eighteenth-century novel is, for example, specifically the recognition in narrative by writers that their prevailing generic confusion about how to write a narrative is directly related to social-institutional (i.e., ideological) uncertainty.[7] For all of these critics, the emerging novel stands in a relationship (as a response, side effect, promoter and promulgator, and even as part of a constellation of causes or contributions) to cultural changes in British society that can only be called ideological. Ian Watt's classic account of the "rise of the novel," which sees the new narrative methods and perspectives as the inevitable expression in literature of the shifts in social organization and moral values that mark an emerging secular modernity, is not so much discarded by all these revisionists as redefined in more specifically ideological terms so that the novel is understood as an instrument of social and cultural control rather than a means of insight or personal liberation for writers and readers. Rudely stripped of its singularity and its teleological fulfillment of the enlightened secular particularism of the rising urban bourgeoisie, the English Novel is now envisioned as an expression of the ideological ferment that accompanies these larger sociocultural changes; its emergence is now seen essentially in plural and multiple terms, as a constellation of competing narrative approaches and ideological positions rather than as the development of a new and superior genre of realistic or aesthetically pleasing or morally complex narrative.[8]

But of course for these critics (except Mullan and Hunter, I think) the various ideologies that eighteenth-century novels promote are operating in the bad old sense; authorial agency or meaningful self-consciousness for the writer and reader of fiction is not often an issue in these new accounts of the novel's emergence. The question that always remains after reading these critics is how individual novelists fit into this larger picture. How much awareness is manifested in particular novels of the cultural and therefore the ideological role of fiction? Operating as the eighteenth-century novelists were before the concept of ideology was formulated and disseminated, how can they be said to participate in the work of ideology, in whatever sense we choose to give it? Except for some of the racier fiction by Behn, Manley, and Haywood that Warner exalts, the novel in England is heavily didactic, and individual writers are open in their championing of moral truths which for them do not seem to be ideological in the negative sense.[9] And of course in the wake of the continuing debate between Namierian historians and recent revisionists of both right and left, we have to ask whether political ideology even in our modern and rehabilitated sense exists at all for the eighteenth-century? That is to say, for Namierians, ideology in the sense of a coherent and motivating system of legitimating beliefs is subordinate to the oppositions of competing material and selfish interests, whereas for more recent historians it is precisely a coherent body of beliefs, an ideology in Geertz's sense of the term, that sustains political life in the face of the deeply pragmatic and opportunistic nature of the modern administration of state power exemplified in the twenty-year rule of Robert Walpole but continued by his compromising successors.[10] I think that ideology in the novel partakes usefully of this revisionist historical understanding, since what narrative can deliver with special clarity is how ideology (in the sense of a coherent and more or less systematic set of beliefs given urgency by a prevailing administrative pragmatism) is sustained only with compromised but invigorating difficulty in social transactions such as those Eagleton evokes. The world of the eighteenth-century novel at its best and most revealing (for example in the novels of Defoe, Richardson, Fielding, and Burney) is that "realm of contestation and negotiation" in which characters' values are tested and transformed, personalized, and appropriated by particular and private action or speech, in which the dynamic interaction between moral values and social experience is dramatized for readers as "ideological" in our rehabilitated sense. Indeed, in one important sense the best novels of the period are precisely about tracing the possible ways of accommodating ideology to the painful experience of a secular world dominated by economic rapacity and unsentimental material interests.

Perhaps of all the major novelists (as I confess I continue to think of them) of the midcentury and later, Fielding is the most usefully self-conscious about what we can now see clearly as the ideological work of the emerging novel. And he is also in William Warner's terms the most open and explicit within the text of *Tom Jones* about his ideological contest with his novelistic competitors and scandalous female predecessors. Fielding's *Tom Jones* seems to me, in other words, especially relevant to the question of ideology and the novel form, since it has some salient features that locate it (in mid-eighteenth-century terms, of course) right in the middle of our current struggle to understand how literature is inseparable from a refined or re-complicated notion of ideology.

To be sure, in the final analysis Fielding's novel is a pretty good instance of most of the operations that define ideology in the bad old sense as legitimation by a dominant group; naturalizing, universalizing, denigrating, excluding, and obscuring as Eagleton describes them are clearly at work in *Tom Jones*. In Fielding's novel, as the majority of its commentators until recently have taught us, a comic artifice featuring a resolving uniformitarianism and universalism takes over to some extent and naturalizes everything and everyone. *Tom Jones* seems to be ideological in what might be called the classic and negative sense of the term.[11] But perhaps that is not quite the whole story, and in fact such a characterization is very much after the fact of reading and inattentive to many of the particulars and local effects of Fielding's text. In what follows I want to sketch out briefly how it might be possible to complicate what Fielding does in *Tom Jones* by considering how its classic shape is more complex in its (reconceived) ideological movements than it appears at first to be.

As he hits his stride as a novelist in *Tom Jones*, Fielding tells his readers on various occasions that he is out to establish and indeed to stabilize prose fiction (his "new province of writing"), and much of his commentary on the events he narrates is an urbane ridicule of vulgar or popular narrative practices such as romance and history.[12] Fielding claims to offer a mediated and tempered truthful representation in place of the complementary, ignorant distortions of actuality provided by the literal-minded particularity of popular history and by the extravagantly figurative mode of degraded romance. In so doing Fielding steadily represents what Eagleton calls the true work of ideology whereby it "aims to disclose something of the relation between an utterance and its material conditions of possibility, when those conditions are viewed in the light of certain power struggles central to the reproduction . . . of a whole form of social life."[13] It seems to me that *Tom Jones* displays the workings of ideology in this rehabilitated sense because, first of all, Fielding can be said to ground the entire conception and continuing production of his novel squarely within the material (that is to say, intensely commercial) conditions and contests for dominance in the literary marketplace of the late 1740s that his particular brand of revisionist narrative springs from, however reluctantly. And, second, at the level of those events the narrative itself represents, Fielding shows relentlessly (and comically) how identity and status are likewise negotiated within and derived from material conditions, from sociopolitical and economic circumstances that his novel not only never tries to ignore but makes the precise provocation of the special kind of satiric and comic narrative perspective he is after. As Jill Campbell has recently put it very sharply, "in the world of [Fielding's] novels, the individual formulates his identity through social conventions that are as transient, perhaps, as some of the literary conventions Fielding ridicules in his plays."[14] By virtue precisely of its comic classicizing and its satiric disdain for the self-seeking amorality of midcentury life, *Tom Jones* is a novelistic rendition of the inescapably ideological conditions of social life in England in the 1740s. All of those narrative gestures that are so obtrusively literary and traditionalist in *Tom Jones* are qualified by Fielding's ideological position and purpose, and he may be said to mark them for us as such pretty regularly.

Consider, for example, a remark the narrator offers as he describes Allworthy's revised understanding of Thwackum's character. As he comes to know the tutor, "upon longer Acquaintance" and "more intimate Conversation, this worthy Man saw Infirmities . . . which he could have wished him to have been without."[15] But Allworthy balances what he sees against Thwackum's good qualities as they manifest themselves to him. The narrator commends him for retaining the tutor, and he is careful to caution the reader:

> For the Reader is greatly mistaken, if he conceives that Thwackum appeared to Mr. Allworthy in the same Light as he doth to him in this History; and he is as much deceived, if he imagines, that the most intimate Acquaintance which he himself could have had with that Divine, would have informed him of those Things which we, from our Inspiration, are enabled to open and discover. Of Readers who from such Conceits as these, condemn the Wisdom or Penetration of Mr. Allworthy, I shall not scruple to say, that they make a very bad and ungrateful Use of that Knowledge which we have communicated to them. (3.5.135)

As readers of a structured comic artifact like *Tom Jones*, we have been encouraged to schematize and universalize. Within that frame, very obviously and effectively, Thwackum and his opposite number Square are defined, contained, and even neutralized by their comic balancing, but the narrator reminds us that the controlling knowledge of moral order he grants us has an ironic relation to another level of potential representation in which such transparent symmetry does not obtain, in which identity and virtue such as the Rev. Mr. Thwackum possesses are earned in the give and take of relationships within a larger social world that includes not simply his patron Mr. Allworthy but all those unnamed others within that arena Fielding invokes wherein Thwackum "had a great Reputation for Learning, Religion and Sobriety of Manners" (3.5.135). On the one hand, Fielding's comic panorama is reductive and satisfying in its simplicities and symmetries, but on the other hand, he reminds readers of the ironic distance between that pattern and an alternative realm far larger and more sprawling than his canvas where truth is negotiated, identity situational and provisional, and personality opaque and uncertain. That reminder and the complicated interplay between fact and fiction it invites in his reader marks *Tom Jones* at moments like this as ideological: dramatizing and encouraging a complex understanding of comic art and life and their relationship to one another.

This relationship between Allworthy and Thwackum, patron and client, is itself deeply ideological in its relevance to changing eighteenth-century institutions and values, and the success and failure of relationships like it are nothing less than the main subject matter of the novel. Fielding invites us in the opening books of *Tom Jones* to consider Paradise Hall and its inhabitants in the light of two kinds of context that the philosopher Alisdair MacIntyre reminds us accompany moral judgments: "We place the agent's intentions . . . in causal and temporal order with reference to their role in his or her history; and we also place them with reference to their role in the history of the setting or settings to which they belong."[16] Thwackum, Square, the odious Blifil brothers, and even the duplicitous Brigid Allworthy and Mr. Summer (Tom's father) are all being evaluated in this dual context in the early books of *Tom Jones*, and their various schemes take place not only in the pattern of their little lives but within the larger cultural and moral history of the decline or degeneration of the country house ideal and the possibility of mutual and honestly productive relationships between a patron and his client such as that between Fielding and Ralph Allen and George Lyttleton with which the novel begins. The entire plot of the novel rests not just on the personal histories of these characters but on their exploitation and negotiation within the ideology surrounding the country house and the patron-client system. One might find a similar ideological and historical resonance surrounding, say, the characters in *Clarissa* but one would be hard pressed indeed to find anything like that resonance in, say, Haywood's *Love in Excess*, where the characters have a deliberately self-enclosed emotional and sexual quality that cuts off any reader's interest in any history other than the personal.

Fielding's comic fiction presents its subjects within these historical and deeply ideological situations. The assumptions and artificialities of the narrative are subject to examination and ideological qualification by readers and in one remarkable instance by Tom Jones himself. Remember the philosophical dialogue between Tom and the Man of the Hill, whose career has allowed him to survey precisely those "mores hominum multorum" the book's title page promises readers. Although his experience of the social world has made him sour and deeply misanthropic, his rendition of universal depravity is related to the more genial universalism the novel articulates. To the Man of the Hill's disparagement of man as the only work in God's creation that does the deity any dishonor, Tom responds:

> 'You will pardon me,' cries Jones, 'but I have always imagined, that there is in this very Work you mention, as great Variety as in all the rest; for besides the Differences of Inclination, Customs and Climates have, I am told, introduced the utmost Diversity into Human Nature.' 'Very little indeed,' answered the other; those who travel in order to acquaint themselves with the different Manners of Men, might spare themselves much Pains, by going to a Carnival at Venice; for there they will see at once all which they can discover in the several Courts of Europe. The same Hypocrisy, the same Fraud; in short, the same Follies and Vices dressed in different Habits. In Spain, these are equipped with much Gravity; and in Italy, with vast Splendor. In France, a Knave is dressed like a Fop; and in the Northern Countries, like a Sloven. But Human Nature is everywhere the same, everywhere the Object of Detestation and Scorn. (7.15.482)

That Fielding shared the Man of the Hill's misanthropy is unlikely but irrelevant, since as Tom Jones arranges matters his attitudes are plausible if somewhat extreme within the book's entirely traditional satiric universalism. But the Man of the Hill's own story contextualizes and derives his attitudes and makes them to a large extent the result of his own unfortunate experiences, renders them primarily self-expressive rather than valid in some general sense. Tom himself realizes this weakness in the reasoning. In the give and take of their dialogue, Tom accuses his interlocutor of generalizing about mankind "from the worst and basest among them; whereas indeed, as an excellent Writer observes, nothing should be esteemed as characteristical of a Species, but what is to be found among the best and most perfect Individuals of that Species" (8.15.485). As Battestin's note hastens to inform us, the excellent writer Tom cites is Cicero in the *Tusculan Disputations* (presumably read under Thwackum's tutorship), and Tom's positive philosophy resembles the ethics of Shaftesbury (imbibed from Square?) and the latitudinarian divines. But the intellectual source of these ideas (if not their biographical basis for Tom) is less important in the context of the dialogue and the novel that contains it than their function: they are no less expressive of Tom's particular personality and history than the Man of the Hill's satire is for his.[17]

We have learned at least two separate lessons as readers of *Tom Jones*: within the comic fiction the narrator constructs order and symmetry prevail, and on that level this dialogue and others in the book address matters of fact or concern questions that possess a degree of cognitive stability; but the characters' discourse also points to that world (represented by implication and hypothetically, the antiworld of the comic narrative, the potential actuality known only by its differences from the structured and artificial order) in which Thwackum has earned his reputation for piety and learning and in which Tom would have probably been hanged or pressed into the navy. That is a public world in which subjects compete for status and power and in which personal worth and even virtue exist only in an ideological context, as individuals are shown being socially and rhetorically constructed out of the available materials for making a self. Although Tom and the Man of the Hill are responsible and well-informed individuals, their dialogue cannot be totally separated in its implications for self-expression and ideological negotiation from other more obviously self-expressive and comically noncognitive interchanges and verbal exchanges such as those between Thwackum and Square, Squire Western and his sister, Di Western, or Lady Bellaston and

Lord Fellamar, nor for that matter from the implicit dialogue between the narrator and his readers. Long recognized by critics as the distinctive essence of Fielding's narrative manner, this exchange (I submit) takes place in the ideological arena and is subject to the conditions of ideological give and take I have been evoking, and right from its opening gambit combines the two activities of literary production and self-expression or self-realization that *Tom Jones* marks as ideological in our special sense.

From the outset, of course, Fielding is a curiously evasive rhetorical entity in his capacity as narrator, where he is clearly working against what he will often evoke as the lamentable generic drift and degraded cultural functions of the new mode of narrative in which he finds himself writing and which he proposes to reform. So in the very first chapter he offers an extended and facetiously self-deprecating comparison between his book and a "public Ordinary" or restaurant. Each book, he tells us, will feature a bill of fare or menu describing the dishes to follow, which the reader may peruse and decide whether he wants to buy and eat. An author hopes to please a hungry but fickle public, and what matters is not the food itself so much as its effective preparation. Writing is like cookery, a matter of dressing or preparing the food stuffs of human nature:

> the Excellence of the mental Entertainment consists less in the Subject, than in the Author's Skill in well dressing it up. How pleased therefore will the Reader be to find, that we have, in the following Work, adhered closely to one of the highest Principles of the best Cook which the present age, or perhaps that of *Heliogabalus*, hath produced. This great Man, as is well known to all Lovers of polite eating, begins at first by setting plain Things before his hungry Guests, rising afterwards by Degrees, as their Stomachs may be supposed to decrease, to the very Quintessence of Sauce and Spices. In like manner, we shall represent Human Nature at first to the keen Appetite of our Reader, in that more plain and simple Manner in which it is found in the Country, and shall hereafter hash and ragoo it with all the high *French* and *Italian* Seasoning of Affectation and Vice which Courts and Cities afford. By these Means, we doubt not but our Reader may be rendered desirous to read on for ever, as the great Person, just above-mentioned, is supposed to have made some Persons eat. (1.1.33–34)

But of course good reading is not quite like such eating, and moral discrimination of the sort Fielding's novel will encourage in his readers has exactly the opposite trajectory from the decadent gormandizing catered to by the best cook of this age. In offering his customer-readers a preliminary bill of fare and promising to please them so that they will pay for the privilege, Fielding is to some extent parodying or echoing the language of consumer culture, imagining vulgar readers/consumers who long for the voyeuristic excitements of represented vice and whose insatiable curiosity will keep them reading past all moderation as they seek to satisfy an artificially extended appetite for narrative, such as that catered to by his implicit rivals in the novel market, the purveyors of amatory and sensational fiction.

Fielding is invoking a tradition going back to Plato's *Gorgias* (which attacks rhetoric for resembling cookery in its transformatory deceitfulness; making bad food taste good or changing the taste of food is like the sophistical trick of making the worse appear the better cause). But his attack on gormandizing is more immediately accessible in classical satiric (as well as John Bullish) suspicion of the art of cookery as a disguise of essence and as a sign of moral unsoundness. Fielding's ideal reader knows who Heliogabalus was and about the gluttony he had come to stand for, and that reader may well wonder at first if this book is really going to model itself on the deeply suspect practice of haute cuisine. The exact resolution of the joke is not obvious in this opening, and Fielding's ironies initiate a double-voicing such as Bakhtin has described, as he both echoes and refuses the hucksterish idiom of the new consumerism that partially impels readers to buy long and expensive novels like *Tom Jones*. In moments like these, we may say, Fielding takes a chance with his own authority as narrator and surrenders by virtue of the force of the novelistic moment something of the stability and finality of the essayistic mode of his introductory chapters; and we find his discourse in Bakhtin's sense "subject to the same temporally valorized measurements, for the 'depicting' authorial language now lies on the same plane as the 'depicted' language of the hero, and may enter into dialogic relations and hybrid combinations with it (indeed, it cannot help but enter into such relations)."[18] What Bakhtin dramatizes in this passage as the novelist's voice becoming like the discourses in the temporal world he represents, I am calling ideological in the rehabilitated sense I have been pursuing. Fielding is working out or negotiating his relationship to this contemporary institution of narrative in the literary marketplace; his speech is positional and self-expressive in its disingenuous ironies.

Fielding may be said in this crucial opening chapter to convey to his ideal reader the following implicit irony: as the purveyor of human nature "dressed," he is pretending to cater to a depraved modern taste for scandal, lubricity, gossip, and vice. This description of his work is transparently false, of course, and Fielding's opening statement that what matters is not the subject but the author/cook's skill in dressing is shown in the events that follow as not true. Fielding's effort moves in the other direction: as a satirist his aim is in part to undress, to present underneath the fancy sauces or clothing or speech the raw and the naked, the self-seeking "design" as he calls it of many of the characters. But faithful, overall, to ideological complexity, as we have seen, the novel will offer readers a far less absolute state of things in which individuals (and the narrator himself) are situated in those two divergent realms I have been evoking: the patterns and symmetries of comic romance and universalized moralism, and the ongoing history of a large variety of changing institutions like the new novel and the literary marketplace, the country house ideal, patron-client relationships, the game laws, the justice system, and the marriage market, to name the most obvious areas the novel explores. To be sure, Fielding in *Tom Jones* also resists this process of dialogic erosion or ideological self-definition of his authorial persona. He encounters Bakhtin's "inconclusive present" in order to reduce it by his brand of representation to those recurrences and that universalizing comedy that are usually taken as his stock in trade. But it is exactly the persistence of the ideological next to and indeed squarely within the comedy that makes *Tom Jones* the masterpiece it is.

Notes

1. Terry Eagleton, *Ideology: An Introduction* (London and New York: Verso, 1991), 5.
2. Eagleton, 5–6.
3. Eagleton, 101.
4. Eagleton, 222–23.
5. Clifford Geertz, "Ideology as a Cultural System, " in *The Interpretation of Cultures* (New York: Basic Books, 1973), pp. 218–19.

6. Michael McKeon, *The Origins of the English Novel: 1600–1740* (Baltimore and London: Johns Hopkins University Press, 1987); John Bender, *Imagining the Penitentiary: Fiction and the Architecture of Mind in Eighteenth-Century England* (Chicago: University of Chicago Press, 1987); J. Paul Hunter, *Before Novels: The Cultural Contexts of Eighteenth-Century English Fiction* (New York: Norton, 1990); Lennard Davis, *Factual Fictions: The Origins of the English Novel* (New York: Columbia University Press, 1983); Nancy Armstrong, *Desire and Domestic Fiction: A Political History of the Novel* (New York: Oxford University Press, 1987); John Mullan, *Sentiment and Sociability: The Language of Feeling in the Eighteenth Century* (Oxford: Clarendon Press, 1988) ; William B. Warner, "The Elevation of the Novel in England: Hegemony and Literary History, *ELH* 59 (1992): 577–96.

7. McKeon, *Origins of the English Novel*, 20. The novel, according to McKeon, "attains its modern, institutional stability and coherence at this time because of its unrivaled power both to formulate, and to explain, a set of problems of categorical instability, which the novel, originating to resolve, also inevitably reflects. The first sort of instability with which the novel is concerned has to do with generic categories; the second with social categories."

8. Warner's essay, "The Elevation of the Novel in England: Hegemony and Literary History," treats the literary history of the "rise of the novel" as itself an ideological construction, a moment in which twentieth-century critics fail to question the effacement by the moral novel of Richardson and Fielding of the earlier narrative tradition represented by the romantic and scandalous fiction of popular women writers such as Aphra Behn, Delarivier Manley, and Eliza Haywood. Warner also develops this scenario in his "Licensing Pleasure: Literary History and the Novel in Early Modern Britain," in *The Columbia History of the British Novel*, ed. John Richetti (New York: Columbia University Press, 1994).

9. One of the flaws or potential weaknesses in revisionist work like Warner's (and in feminist recuperations of Behn, Manley, and Haywood) is such critics' clear preference for these "racy novels of love" (in Warner's phrase) to the sober didacticism of the ethical novel tradition that overwhelms them. In that preference, Warner inevitably and perhaps unreflectively reveals his own ideology, taking pleasure in a subversive and oppositional sexuality articulated by writers who represent an oppressed or marginalized group and implicitly finding an authenticity in such writing lacking in the canonical novels.

10. See especially J. C. D. Clark, *English Society 1688–1832: Ideology, Social Structure and Political Practice During the* Ancien Regime (Cambridge: Cambridge University Press, 1985), and J. G. A. Pocock, *Virtue, Commerce, and History* (Cambridge: Cambridge University Press, 1985).

11. I have in several essays in recent years explored just this aspect of Fielding's work. See "Representing an Under Class: Servants and

Proletarians in Fielding and Smollett," in *The New Eighteenth Century: Theory, Politics, English Literature*, ed. Felicity Nussbaum and Laura Brown (New York and London: Methuen, 1987); "The Old Order and the New Novel of the Mid-Eighteenth Century: Narrative Authority in Fielding and Smollett," *Eighteenth-Century Fiction* 2 (April 1990): 183–96; and "Class Struggle Without Class: Novelists and Magistrates," *The Eighteenth Century: Theory and Interpretation* 32 (autumn 1991): 203–18.

12. No one has put this better than Leo Braudy: "The process of Fielding's fiction attempts to free the reader from the false forms imposed by other literary structurings of actuality. . . . Both the excessive subjectivity of romance and the excessive objectivity of public history are sham orders that can pervert and distort human values." *Narrative Form in History and Fiction: Hume, Fielding, and Gibbon* (Princeton: Princeton University Press, 1970), 211–12.

13. Eagleton, 223.

14. Jill Campbell, "Fielding and the Novel at Mid-Century," in *The Columbia History of the British Novel*, ed. John Richetti (New York: Columbia University Press, 1994), 105. In his *Occasional Form: Henry Fielding and the Chains of Circumstance* (Baltimore: Johns Hopkins University Press, 1975), J. Paul Hunter drew attention to the anticipations in Fielding's plays of the formal and by extension the ideological qualities of his novels: "Probably no other playwright before Pirandello and Brecht was so intrigued by the theoretical issues the form suggested. . . . Fielding emphasizes the radical factitiousness of the form, its tendency to isolate, and compare, the fictional and the real worlds." (50)

15. Henry Fielding, *The History of Tom Jones*, ed. Fredson Bowers, with an introduction and commentary by Martin C. Battestin (Middletown, Conn.: Wesleyan University Press, 1975), 3.5.135. All further page references in the text are to this edition.

16. Alisdair MacIntyre, *After Virtue: A Study in Moral Theory*, 2d ed. (Notre Dame, Ind.: University of Notre Dame Press, 1984), 208.

17. In *Philosophical Dialogues in the English Enlightenment: Theology, Aesthetics, and the Novel* (Cambridge: Cambridge University Press, 1996), Michael Prince relates in very powerful terms the rise of the realistic novel to the failure of the philosophical dialogue and sees in novelistic appropriations of ethicoreligious inquiry a shift from a discredited transcendental dialectic to the expressivity of aesthetic and narrative embodiment for the articulation of ideas.

18. M. M. Bakhtin, *The Dialogic Imagination: Four Essays*, trans. and ed. Caryl Emerson and Michael Holquist (Austin: University of Texas Press, 1981), 28.

John Richetti is the Rosenthal Professor of English at the University of Pennsylvania. His most recent book is *The English Novel and History 1700–1780*. He is currently writing a critical biography of Defoe.

Tom Jones: The Form in History

Ralph W. Rader

In his reply to David H. Richter's "Ideology and Literary Form in Fielding's *Tom Jones*," John Richetti follows Terry Eagleton (and Clifford Geertz) in offering a "rehabilitated" concept of ideology as "no longer just the pernicious and conspiratorial legitimating strategies of the dominant class but rather . . . 'a realm of contestation and negotiation,'" "not only as a legitimating opposition from above but also and more usefully as an inevitable and necessarily complex negotiation . . . within a culture for what social life and its organization are to mean for its participants."[1] Richetti goes on to examine *Tom Jones* as a work "especially relevant to the question of ideology and form in the novel, since it has some salient features that locate it (in mid-eighteenth-century terms, of course) right in the middle of our current struggle to understand how literature is inseparable from a refined or recomplicated notion of ideology" (35). But Richetti begins by reiterating something close to the negative view of ideology in *Tom Jones* for which he had been criticized by Richter:

> To be sure, in the final analysis Fielding's novel is a pretty good instance of most of the operations that define ideology in the bad old sense as legitimation by a dominant group. Naturalizing, universalizing, denigrating, excluding, and obscuring as Eagleton describes them are clearly at work in *Tom Jones*. As the majority of its commentators until recently have taught us, in Fielding's novel a comic artifice featuring a resolving uniformitarianism and universalism takes over to some extent and naturalizes everything and everyone. *Tom Jones* seems to be ideological in what might be called the classic and negative sense of the term. (35–36)

But Richetti also sees a "rehabilitated" ideology as present, in *Tom Jones* and other novels, in a more positive (and contradictory?) sense, not as an imposition from above, but as involving "the dynamic interaction between moral values and social experience" of characters (and authors) as individual agents. Indeed "the best novels of the period are precisely about tracing the possible ways of accommodating ideology to the painful experience of a secular world dominated by economic rapacity and unsentimental material interests." Here ideology is understood, in the Geertzian sense Richetti also develops, as a validating conception (faith, belief) deployed not only against competing conceptions but in the face of and in response to external socioeconomic circumstances. In one formulation, the comic form of *Tom Jones* is now said to have a positive role: "By virtue precisely of its comic classicizing and satiric disdain for the self-seeking amorality of mid-century life, *Tom Jones* is a novelistic rendition of the inescapable ideological conditions of social life in England in the 1740s" (36), while in another "Fielding's comic panorama" is still held to be "reductive" (though satisfying) "in its simplicities and symmetries" (38). In keeping with his earlier claim that "literature is inseparable from a refined or re-complicated notion of ideology," Richetti concludes finally that "it is exactly the persistence of the ideological next to and indeed squarely within the comedy that makes *Tom Jones* the masterpiece it is" (31). "Masterpiece" is a suspect term these days, and Richetti early on disdains the idea that there is any "realm of timeless truth" (43) beyond ideology in which masterpieces are situated, but he nonetheless seems to think of masterpieces as being at least relatively timeless just because their forms display an admixture of the ideological. But how is a timebound "rendition of the conditions of social life in 1740s England" actually dynamically melded into the unified reading experience of a "structured comic artifact" like *Tom Jones*?

My own answer to this question will be developed here as a critique and revision of R. S. Crane's classic description of the comic form of *Tom Jones*, a description which, for all its power, I see as nonetheless neglecting the historico-ideational dimensions of that form. The resulting synthetic conception is intended as a more complete and integrated formulation than Richetti's of the ways in which the formal and ideological in *Tom Jones* are functionally interrelated.

I may begin with some intellectual autobiography, starting with an account of my meeting Crane at Indiana University long ago when he was a visiting professor and I a graduate student. I had then been working on a dissertation study of Fielding's novels as functions of his latitudinarian faith (following the lead of my director, James A. Work) and was of course eager and awed to think of meeting Crane, who seemed to know more about the latitudinarians and eighteenth-century thought in general than anyone else. But it was just because of Crane's mastery of the historical background that I was troubled and puzzled by the essay on *Tom Jones*. As I told Crane when I bounced into his office for a talk about it all, I could not make out why someone who knew as much about the historical setting of the novel as he did should deliberately choose to write a totally ahistorical analysis of it, and I went on to detail my view of the shape and intelligibility of *Tom Jones* and Fielding's other novels as constituting an imaginative rehearsal of faith in his latitudinarian version of the world. Crane listened at first with amusement but finally (I am glad to say) with some respect, without as I recall saying a great deal in explicit answer to my question, so that I did not then gain much further understanding of his views. That came later, at Berkeley, as I argued about Fielding with Sheldon Sacks, whose views had been much shaped by Crane's. Sacks would point out insistently that the life and reality of a novel, of *Tom Jones*, lay in its power to move a reader in the act of reading, to induce him to accept its illusion and feel its effect, so that a twentieth-century reader, taking *Tom Jones* from a drugstore rack, could find himself in immediate contact with its moving aesthetic force, that is to say, with the essential meaning and value of the novel. Despite my own quite passionate sense of the fact that the value of literature, however described, was indeed inseparable from its immediate power to move (it was this sense, in truth, which had brought me into the profession), I nevertheless saw Crane and Sacks as too narrowly preoccupied with what I thought of as the mere "affective mechanics" of literature as opposed to its significant connection with the world. But my analysis of Fielding's novels as functions of his ideas was tending to an inevitable conclusion quite at odds with my appreciation of the primacy of the fact of their twentieth-century vitality: the conclusion that the meaning and significance of the novels was limited by their eighteenth-century context. Listen to me, I was ready to say after my studies, and I will take you back from the twentieth century and show you the wonderful meaning the novels could and did have for Fielding and his like-minded contemporaries; but that put their meaning and value back from the twentieth century into the eighteenth, and my statement of the value of the novels in terms of embodied ideas (I had to admit to myself) tended to thin out and dilute my actual sense of their concrete imaginative qualities, particularly their comedy. More and more I had to recognize that the historico-functional explanation was to some degree at odds with the facts of reading experience and with the experienced fact of the trans-temporal nature of literary value. In consequence I began to concentrate my critical interests on the problem of understanding the formal power of the concrete work to move the reader in the act of reading and so became a postgraduate pupil of Crane and Sacks and a fellow traveler in the neo-Aristotelian fraternity. From the first, however, and increasingly, I have been something of a dissident and schismatic because of my continued dissatisfaction with the neo-Aristotelian emphasis on the aesthetic autonomy of the literary work, which cut its lifelines off from their sources in the writer's individual purposes and agency, describing it in terms solely of a formal blueprint of an effect which might have been realized by any artist of sufficient capacity at any place, in any time. My own impulse was to preserve something of my original historical emphasis by following out even more radically the revisionist tendencies of Sacks and Wayne Booth and conceiving the literary work and its effect as immanently shaped and conditioned by extra-aesthetic dimensions of the author's creative intention which in fact are *experienced* if only tacitly as part of the work's concrete significance and value.

Now the correctness of something like this view of literary effect is in fact conceded by Crane at the end of his *Tom Jones* essay, where he specifies that his method

> is one which depends on the analytical isolation of works of art, as finished products, from the circumstances and processes of their origin. It is better fitted to explain those effects which would be specifically the same in any other work, of whatever date, that was constructed in accordance with the same combination of artistic principles, than those effects which must be attributed to the fact that the work was produced by a given artist, in a given period, at a given stage in the evolution of the species or tradition to which it belongs.

Just below he reemphasizes the power he claims his method does have to analyze the literary work as "a self-contained whole endowed with a power of affecting us in a particular way by virtue of the manner in which its internal parts are conceived and fitted together."[2] But this assertion is in some tension, not to say contradiction, with the larger passage quoted, where he speaks of "effects" which must be attributed to the influences of external circumstances. But such extrinsically derived effects must be just as much a part of our experience of the work as "a self-contained whole" as those which are intrinsically derived.[3]

This conclusion would seem clearly to require that any full analysis of a work's effect take extrinsic influences into account to the degree that they modify and organically enter into the work as intrinsically experienced, since no account in terms of timeless artistic principles can render the work fully intelligible in its actual concrete construction as created by the timebound author and registered by the reader. But apparently Crane never completely followed out this line of thought, and certainly never offered an example of practical criticism based upon it, partly I think because the pluralism to which he was so deeply committed encouraged him in actual analysis to separate the intrinsic from the extrinsic, partly because he thought of external influences as sufficiently subsumed, for practical critical purposes, in the purely affective intention of the work. Whatever the reason, I think that his conception of the structure of *Tom Jones* as the cause of its effect, though accurate in its location of the innermost moving principle of the work, is significantly incomplete, in ways that I shall indicate in the balance of this essay.

Crane develops his analysis of *Tom Jones* as an imitation of a comic action. The neo-Aristotelian emphasis on literature as imitation or representation in my view offers, if adequately adapted, a more potent basis for explaining the imaginative properties and effects of literary works than contrasting conceptions of literature as some kind of mediated propositional or ideological discourse. It is important to note that the neo-Aristotelian idea of imitation has no reference, as do other contemporary notions of mimesis, to any notion of literature as reflecting, in the sense of having some truth relation to, the external world or the human beings in it. (This is an important point to which I shall be returning later.) The neo-Aristotelian conception refers rather to the fact that matter that is not a thing can be so disposed that we see that thing in it: in the presence of a piece of stone worked by Michelangelo we see Moses starting in anger; reading what is merely language we seem to be with Tom Jones striding down the highway to London. Imitations offer us an integral *object* of imitation, realized in a specific *medium* (which in literature is always of course language), by an artist working in a certain *manner* of representation, to achieve a distinctive working or *power*, which is the effect realized in and by the whole, and for the sake of which the whole *as* a whole is presumed to exist.

In the *Tom Jones* essay Crane sketches a number of general formal possibilities for extended mimetic forms as realizable in the dramatic or narrative manner. He thought of any extended action as involving the representation of a protagonist undergoing a complete change in fortune (or character or thought) for the sake of a spectrum of effects ranging from the tragic to the comic. *Tom Jones* achieves its affective vitality through those artistic choices of Fielding which give it a pervasively comic working or power. Generally speaking, we can think of any successfully realized action as raising concern for a protagonist by developing a dynamic tension between what we think ought to happen to him—his desert—and what we think will in fact happen to him—his fate—in the short and long run, and then resolving that tension by an extension of the means used to raise it so as to give us the greatest satisfaction in the whole. In a comic action there is developed in us from the first and throughout a sense of reassurance that the adverse long-run fate which threatens and causes our concern for the protagonist we are led to favor will somehow not eventuate, though we see not how; and meanwhile our response to the painful short-run predicaments in which the protagonist is involved as a condition of his apparently adverse fate is sharply attenuated, so that what would otherwise be painful is experienced by the reader as a kind of pleasure. (One can think here of that movie cartoon rabbit suddenly handed a bomb which, before he can react, blows him in pieces; we laugh at what in actual life would be horrifying because we have no doubt that the pieces will reassemble into our familiar animal friend and because we are meanwhile not shown the bodily dismemberment as involving any bloody tearing of fur and flesh.)

In comic, as in all actions, Crane notes, our view of the protagonist's desert and fate is conditioned among other things by "the opinions we are made to entertain concerning the degree and kind of his responsibility for what happens to him, as being either little or great and, if the latter, the result either of his acting in full knowledge of what he is doing or of some sort of mistake" (632). The special quality of *Tom Jones*, Crane goes on to say, derives from our general feeling of comic security about Tom's ultimate fate together with "our perception of the decisive role which Tom's own blunders are made to play, consistently, in the genesis of all the major difficulties into which he is successively brought—always of course with the eager assistance of Fortune and of the malice or misunderstanding of others" (635–36). Viewing his final fate against the dark background of the potentially serious developed in the novel, "we are not disposed to feel, when we are done laughing at Tom, that all is right with the world or that we can count on Fortune always intervening, in the same gratifying way, on behalf of the good" (638).[4]

By this entire formula Crane means to locate in an explicit conception the basis of our dynamic emotional response, our feelingful interest, in reading *Tom Jones*, a response the causes of which normally lie below the threshold of the reader's awareness, giving life to his experience of the novel; just because it *is* the form of our immediate experience of the novel, the principle of its intelligibility and force, it can be neglected by critics who nonetheless stand on its solid if unacknowledged ground in erecting their own interpretations. We can understand the analytic bearing of the formula, and eventually something of the incompleteness I have mentioned, if we take an extended look at the episode in which Jones, in prison, has reached the nadir of his fortune. Believing himself given up by Sophia and subject to hanging as the seeming murderer of Fitzpatrick, he hears even worse news from Partridge who comes into his prison room in the wake of Mrs. Waters's departure: Fielding describes Partridge as "stumbling into the room with his face paler than ashes, his eyes fixed in his head, his hair standing on end, and every limb trembling," looking as he would have done had "he seen a spectre, or had he indeed, been a spectre himself." Daunted by his appearance, Jones asks him what is the matter.

> "The matter, sir? good heaven!" answered Partridge, "was that woman who is just gone out the woman who was with you at Upton?"—"She was, Partridge," cried Jones.—"And did you, sir, go to bed with that woman?" said he, trembling. "I am afraid what passed between us is no secret," said Jones. "Nay, but pray, sir, for

> Heaven's sake, sir, answer me," cries Partridge. "You know I did," cries Jones. "Why, then, the Lord have mercy on your soul, and forgive you," cries Partridge; "but as sure as I stand here alive, you have been abed with your own mother."

"Upon these words," Fielding continues,

> Jones became in a moment a greater picture of horror than Partridge himself. He was, indeed, for some time struck dumb with amazement, and both stood staring wildly at each other. At last his words found way, and in an interrupted voice he said, "How! how! what's this you tell me?" "Nay, sir," cries Partridge, "I have not breath enough left to tell you now, but what I have said is most certainly true. That woman who now went out is your own mother. How unlucky it was for you, sir, that I did not happen to see her at the time, to have prevented it! Sure the devil himself must have contrived to bring about this wickedness."

Jones replies:

> "What thou has told me, Partridge, hath almost deprived me of my senses! And was Mrs. Waters, then but why do I ask? for thou must certainly know her. . . . Oh, good heavens! incest with a mother! To what am I reserved!" He then fell into the most violent and frantic agonies of grief and despair.

The narrator then comments:

> If the reader will please to refresh his memory, by turning to the scene at Upton, in the ninth book, he will be apt to admire the many strange accidents which unfortunately prevented any interview between Partridge and Mrs. Waters, when she spent a whole day there with Mr. Jones. Instances of this kind we may frequently observe in life, where the greatest events are produced by a nice train of little circumstances; and more than one example of this may be discovered by the accurate eye, in this our history.[5]

After Partridge returns from a fruitless search for Mrs. Waters, Jones, in "a state of desperation," becomes "almost raving mad" at Partridge's report, and in this condition receives and reads the following letter from Mrs. Waters:

> "Sir—Since I left you I have seen a gentleman, from whom I have learned something concerning you that greatly surprises and affects

> me; but as I have not at present leisure to communicate a matter of such high importance, you must suspend your curiosity till our next meeting, which shall be the first moment I am able to see you. Oh, Mr. Jones, little did I think, when I passed that happy day at Upton, the reflection upon which is likely to embitter all my future life, who it was to whom I owed such perfect happiness. Believe me to be ever sincerely your unfortunate
>
> J. Waters
>
> P. S. I would have you comfort yourself as much as possible, for Mr. Fitzpatrick is in no manner of danger; so that whatever other grievous crimes you may have to repent of, the guilt of blood is not among the number."

Jones

> having read the letter, let it drop (for he was unable to hold it, and indeed had scarce the use of one of his faculties). Partridge took it up, and having received consent by silence, read it likewise; nor had it upon him a less sensible effect. The pencil, and not the pen, should describe the horrors which appeared in both their countenances.

Our feelingful response to this episode is predicated, as elsewhere in the book, on our sense of Jones's immediate and ultimate fate in relation to his immediate and ultimate desert. At this darkest point in the decline of his fortunes, our view of Tom's fate is not the one taken by him and Partridge. We do not feel the horror they feel because we do not believe in the impending Oedipal doom as they do. Partridge's often demonstrated fallibility and gullibility do not encourage us to place the reliance on his testimony and conviction that Tom does, and we see Tom's belief—"for thou must certainly know her"—as characteristically precipitous, exemplifying the impulsiveness which has brought him into so much needless trouble before. Mrs. Waters's letter seems to confirm Tom's conclusions, but the reader sees that it does not actually do so and, in implication and tone, contains a good deal of evidence to the contrary, so that the reader actually views it as sufficient to sustain Tom's horrified belief while offering further support to the reader's sense that such response is premature, especially in the postscript about Fitzgerald which shows a silver lining at the edge of the dark cloud of Tom's fate. This judgment is strongly reinforced by the narrator's marked unconcern as implied in his digressive dissertation on causality in the story. Thus, despite the illusion of disaster, the reader maintains his long-term reassurance as to Tom's eventual good fate, but since he has no material knowledge to the contrary of what lies beneath the appearances, he has the intensest interest in how—not whether—Tom's happiness is to be brought about.

Meanwhile the reader's sense of Jones's immediate fate—his painful predicament of even believing that he has committed incest—is here as elsewhere sharply attenuated by the emotional distance produced by Fielding's generalized description, rather than close transcription, of Tom's "most violent and frantic agonies of grief and despair" and his use of conventional phrasing for the extremes of dark emotion—"picture of horror," "struck dumb with amazement," etc. Such tired description is a distinct narrative virtue here, softening and comically stylizing Tom's suffering. Concomitantly, we are not displeased to see Tom punished by his too-eager belief because we feel that he has been reckless and deserves such punishment as warning and instruction; attenuated as it is, we in a certain sense enjoy his pain, and are pleased at the amendment in him promised by his recognition of his own responsibility as, in a passage I have not quoted, he cries:

> "Sure . . . Fortune will never have done with me till she hath driven me to distraction. But why do I blame Fortune? I am myself the cause of all misery. All the dreadful mischiefs which have befallen me are the consequences only of my own folly and vice."

Jones had earlier told Mrs. Miller that he had already "'resolved to quit a Life of which I was become sensible of the Wickedness as well as Folly'" (17.5.894) and had told Mrs. Waters of "his resolution to sin no more, lest a worst thing should happen to him" (17.9.911), a resolution which has been validated by his refusal to respond to the several renewed advances of Mrs. Fitzpatrick, Lady Bellaston, and Mrs. Waters herself. This amendment, joined to the reader's larger sense of his merits (considered below), is such as to give him at last a desert to match the great final shift in his fortune, from despair to happiness, which developments reflected in this episode conceal while actually advancing.

If the episode thus manifests the general dynamic character of a comic action as described by Crane, it also displays to our notice those qualities which Crane posits as distinctive to the novel:

both in Tom's reference to Fortune and the narrator's disquisition on concatenating chains of little circumstances (as well as in Partridge's references to ill luck and the devil) we see the presence of that coincidentality in the book which, in Crane's view, makes Tom's final good fate seem, in the face of his many indiscretions, a matter of good luck. Now Crane's emphasis on the fact that we are made aware, against the background of serious evil in the world of the novel, that things do not always work out as well for others as for Tom is very well taken as a description of a primary quality of the overall effect; but the attribution of Tom's personal good fate to luck does some injustice to our actual sense of Tom's special qualities of goodness as portrayed and communicated in the novel. Crane sees our desires for Tom's good fortune as deriving from the fact that he is better than anyone else in the novel and at least the equal of ourselves in moral quality, but this is not fully adequate to the imaginative sympathy Fielding develops in us for that inborn, deeply instinctive goodness in Tom which reaches spontaneously out to the help and relief of others without any calculation of his own advantage. This peculiar goodness in Tom is everywhere portrayed and emphatically instanced in the book, standing out with special clarity because it is in such sharp contrast with the conduct of the majority calculatedly and hypocritically devoted to what Fielding calls the "art of thriving." Tom is, as critics have perceived, Fielding's version of the latitudinarian "good-natured man," one of those characterized by an innate "glorious lust of doing good."[6] But why did not Crane, author of a classic and originating article about the genealogy of the man of feeling in the eighteenth century, fail to note the special historical quality of Tom's goodness? Because, I think, of his assumption that characters in mimetic literary works are both presented and responded to as if they were real people in the natural world; to draw attention to the fact that the imitation of a character was mediated by an idea would violate the neo-Aristotelian doctrine that there is a great gulf fixed between the mimetic and didactic, the representational and ideational. Crane was right, of course, that Tom Jones is presented by Fielding and registered by readers not as an idea but as an imaginatively believable man, a point that those scholars who see Tom as the embodiment of doctrine go reductively astray in not bearing in mind; but this does not mean that his qualities as presented are in actual fact like those of a real human being or that we judge those qualities in the same terms that we would bring to bear in judging a real human being. (This is actually implicit in the neo-Aristotelian doctrine that imitation is not referentially mimetic.) The natural grounds of our sympathy and judgment are draw upon and marshaled by Fielding in a very special way as he invests Tom's character and career with values and circumstances, deeply colored by his own personal ideas and feelings as charged by his own character and experience, which ignite and sustain our caring for Tom and make us wish him well in a feelingful empathy more precious and special than Crane's analysis allows.

But if Crane's account of Tom's moral nature is inadequate to define the full dimensions of his desert, so also is his account of Tom's good nature as it causally conditions his fate. In assessing "the degree and kind of [Tom's] responsibility for what happens to him," Crane, as we have seen, puts great emphasis on the causal role of chance and Fortune and Tom's impulsive indiscretions, without paying sufficient attention to the reader's registration of the ways in which Tom's spontaneously benevolent nature influences his fate. If we recognize that passional indiscretions which are the defects of his benevolent virtues consistently condition Tom's short-run bad luck, we need also to recognize that his acts of goodness in conjunction with fortuity create his ultimate good fate. Each of the several agents who in the denouement contribute directly to Tom's exculpation and the revelation of his identity—Mrs. Waters, most crucially, but also Mrs. Miller, Nightingale, and Square—is motivated by a signal act of spontaneous generosity on Tom's part which binds that person to his cause and leaves him disposed to contribute in Jones's final need. As Fielding implies in his comment quoted above, the causal connections are intricate and striking, and involve the interplay of Jones's active goodness with the responses of a number of persons casually encountered, including for instance the beggarman who finds Sophia's pocketbook and the highwayman Enderson who turns out to be Mrs. Miller's son-in-law. The most central and prominent of these occurrences, however, involve the chain of events which brings Jones in touch with Mrs. Waters. The first of these is Jones's stalwart rescue of the Man of the Hill, an event which causes him to tarry with the old man long enough to be the agent as well of the rescue of Mrs. Waters, and so leads directly to his involvement with her and finally to her crucial role in the revelations of the denouement. The precise circumstances of the rescue require attention. Hearing the screams of Mrs. Waters, Jones "ran, or rather slid, down the Hill, and, without the least Apprehension or Concern for his own Safety, made directly to the Thicket whence the Sound had issued" (9.2.495). After the rescue, we are shown the Man of the Hill sitting still on the crest of the hill, "where, though he had a gun in hand, he with great patience and unconcern attended the issue" (9.2.497). Thus Fielding indicates that it is Jones's spontaneous propensity to help others, so emphatically in contrast with the contemplative hermit's indifference, which is the necessary if not sufficient causal condition of the chain of events which leads him to his destiny.

Now Crane speaks not at all of Jones's acts as causally conditioning his destiny because, thinking of the action in terms of a universal sense of life appropriate to a timeless work, there was no way to conceive of fortuities as other than a morally indifferent, causally unconnected aspect of universal human experience, an aspect which could be accepted to the degree that it was figured by Fielding as Fortune. If fortuity is so conceived, then Tom's isolated acts of goodness obviously have no causal moral significance for the overall shape of the action. But this is not the way the action feels to the reader. As Dorothy Van Ghent pointed out long ago, "Fortune, capricious as it is, has some occult, deeply hidden association with Nature (in Fielding); therefore, in the long run, good nature does infallibly lead to good fortune, bad nature to bad fortune."[7] I shall consider more fully later why that "occult relationship" is actually felt by the reader as immanent in the action, but here we may note that its conceptual source, as has been indicated by several scholars, is clearly that latitudinarian doctrine which held that whenever the operations of what men call accident, luck, chance, or fortune took on retrospective shape and significant purpose, such operations were to be seen as those of Divine Providence.[8] Consider Fielding's remark about the nice trains of little circumstance in his novel in the light of this comment by his favorite divine Isaac Barrow on similar circumstantial trains in actual life:

> If that one thing should hit advantageously to the production of some considerable event, it may with some plausibility be attributed to fortune, or common providence: yet that divers things having no dependence or coherence one with the other, in divers places, through several times, should all join their forces to compass it, cannot well otherwise than be ascribed to God's special care

> wisely directing, to his own hand powerfully wielding, those concurrent instruments to one good purpose. For it is beside the nature, it is beyond the reach of fortune, to range various causes in such order. Blind fortune cannot apprehend or catch the seasons and junctures of things, which arise from the motions of causes indifferent and arbitrary: to it therefore no such event can reasonably be imputed.[9]

In *Tom Jones* the narrator himself only indirectly (though clearly) refers to the providential nature of fortuity in the novel, since to do otherwise would violate the notion of Providence as hidden beneath the operation of second causes. But Fielding's labeling is nonetheless unmistakable. Tom tells the Man of the Hill, for instance, that "Providence alone" has sent him to his assistance. "'Providence, indeed,' cries the old Gentleman, 'if it be so.'—'So it is, I assure you,' cries Jones, ... 'Be thankful then to that Providence to which you owe your deliverance'" (8.10.448). And to Mrs. Waters Jones says that "Heaven seemed to have designed him as the happy Instrument of her Protection" (9.2.496), and the narrator himself, some pages on, speaks of Jones's "providential Appearance" on that occasion (9.8.521). This kind of underlining appears at other points to reanimate the providential implication, most notably when Jones in prison declares his reliance on "a Throne still greatly superior" (17.10.908) and climactically later when, as the inner secrets of the action miraculously unfold, Allworthy declares that "'The Lord disposeth all Things'" (18.7.942).

Now why did Crane, who had read as many latitudinarian sermons as any scholar who has since been concerned with Fielding, choose to term as Fortune and luck what Fielding finally labels providential? Because to recognize the presence of providentiality in the book would have been to admit into his timeless, mimetic conception of form an element that was clearly historical and didactic. But, as I have been and will be suggesting, this element of extrinsic origin can best be thought of as incorporated, not directly as doctrine, but as part of the represented action as incompletely described by Crane. My point, here as elsewhere, is that Crane's rigorous attempt to conceive *Tom Jones* as an autonomous artistic construct directed toward an intrinsic effect caused him to miss the full dimensions of the effect as actually intended and felt.

The dimensions of the book I have just spoken of fit fairly well as indicated into an enlarged if impure version of Crane's notion of an organic comic action, but there are manifestly a number of other structural features of *Tom Jones* which can by no means be explained as resulting from the simple intention of constructing a comic action of the kind Crane describes. Why, we may ask, should a comic action centered on a single protagonist have in it such a wealth of characters from all levels of society? Why in purely artistic terms should it include glimpses of and encounters with the Jacobite rebellion of 1745? Why in a novel imitating concrete human action, we may ask further, should some characters—Tom Jones, Allworthy, Sophia, Western, Thwackum, Square—have quasi-universal, allegorical names? Why should a unified action include such digressive stories as those of the Man of the Hill and Mrs. Fitzpatrick? Finally, we may ask why, in a mimetic action of the kind Crane describes, free of didactic intent, Fielding should so emphatically declare that his work has a moral? We may ask these questions of Crane's model, but we will get no answers, and we will get no answers because (once more) Crane's model is not a complete model of Fielding's intention in the work.

But Crane can help us to understand what that complete intention was. In a long note to the *Tom Jones* essay Crane is at pains to show how Aristotle's conception of mimetic works as realized for the sake of purely affective ends was corrupted by the neoclassical emphasis on the merely rhetorical and didactic ends of literary art (617–19), so that it no longer offers an adequate account of the principles upon which mimetic works like *Tom Jones* (or *Hamlet* or *Tess of the D'Urbervilles*) are actually constructed. But this does not mean that inaccurate neoclassical description could not become a prescriptive influence on writers like Fielding seeking to construct a work in a particular genre, namely for him a comic epic in prose. I do not at all suggest that conscious ideas of what an epic ought to be constituted for Fielding the actual intrinsic working principle of his novel, but that in intuitively constructing an affectively vital work whose inner principle I would hold must be something like that described by Crane, Fielding accepted and attempted to accommodate certain extrinsic formal conceptions which he understood as part of epic decorum, and that this attempt to accommodate the concrete affective work to external doctrine presented him with problems of artistic construction the solutions of which left their distinct marks upon the work.

If we do in fact assume that Fielding's intention was to construct a comic action *as a comic epic*, we get quite good explanation of the problematic features listed above and of others also. I do not want to claim that Fielding's book answers to the example of any previous work or to any one set of rules for the epic (as if it wholly could), but only to point out that these distinct but puzzling features can be seen to reflect common background doctrine about the epic as synthetically described for instance by H. T. Swedenberg in his well-known book on the theory of the epic in England. If we consult that volume, we can see that even such a seemingly aformal part of Fielding's work as his suggestion that Allworthy's character reflects that of Lord Lyttleton and Ralph Allen may not be merely flattery but a response to the notion, articulated by Dryden, that an epic writer might follow the precedent of Virgil and Spenser and represent his friends and patrons in his work.[10]

Turning from this small but illustrative point to the larger features noticed above, we can see that the wide social scope of *Tom Jones*, embracing many real life figures and places, including the background of the '45, reflects the generally held doctrine that national history should be the basis of the epic, though the epic should properly be a mixture of history and fiction, or as Joseph Trapp had it, "partly real, and partly feign'd."[11] But such a commitment to social inclusiveness and amplitude threatened disintegration to the action as an action; and we can understand Sheldon Sacks's post-Cranean analysis of *Tom Jones* as a combined episodic and continuous action—in which some characters and lines of causation carry through the story, while some merely cross those lines with a local contribution to the action and disappear into a larger world[12]—as an empirical discovery of a structural feature, not logically envisioned by Crane's conception, which is responsive to the problem posed by this aspect of Fielding's intention. The problematic digressions in the novel can be somewhat similarly understood. Crane and Sacks argue (I think successfully) that the digressions are in fact made to function organically in the action as an action, but this does not explain why Fielding chose to introduce such shape-distorting elements in the first place. Acquaintance with neoclassical doctrine suggests, however, that they are deliberately introduced as "episodes"—like those of the *Odyssey* or *Paradise Lost*—suitable to, indeed demanded by, the tradition of the epic.

In analogous fashion, we can understand the universalizing names of the novel to result from the pressure of the specification, as in Fielding's favorite Le Bossu, that the epic action be allegorical and universal. To make the story generally allegorical would have destroyed its effect as literal comic action, but by assigning some of his characters different kinds of generalizing names, Fielding could honor the doctrinal requirement and give his epic an appropriate breadth of reference and implication. This is a very different thing from making the characters stand for ideas or from attempting to fit the meanings suggested by the names into a pattern or relation of ideational significance. Again, one can see that Sacks's extension of Crane's analysis to show how such characters as Square and Thwackum function in the action both as concrete characters and as types is in fact a description of Fielding's operational response to the disparate pressures of the intrinsic and extrinsic dimensions of his artistic intention.

Fielding's flat statement that he means his novel to have a specific moral, of which Crane takes no notice, is in direct general conflict with Crane's notion that literary works divide into watertight compartments of mimetic and didactic and is in specific conflict with his idea that any moral elements in a mimetic work are subordinated to its nondidactic effect. But Fielding's statement is of course in complete accord with the fact noted by Swedenberg that almost every critic of the period taught that "the epic is a great organ for the inculcation of virtue" (194), and the specific view of Le Bossu that a moral ought to be the underlying foundation of an epic action.[13] It is interesting then to note once more that Sacks's revision and extension of Crane's account of the action structure of *Tom Jones* should discover the presence of Fielding's moral intention in it. But Sacks's conclusion about the relation of moral belief to the action form and *Tom Jones* in particular seems not quite adequate either, partly because he fails to distinguish sharply enough between his minimum general thesis—that the artistic end of writing an action "exerts no pressure on a writer to make insincere [moral] judgments" of the characters—and his specific conclusion that *Tom Jones* embodies Fielding's particular moral intention, in principle separable from the action, which is "to recommend goodness and innocence" (249–50). Since Sacks like Crane thinks of the action form as a fixed, timeless structure, he infers that the moral intentions he finds embodied in Fielding's action novels are a normal feature of the form. But my claim here is that his first, minimum conclusion alone is true of any realization of the general principle of the action form, while the fact that *Tom Jones* and other eighteenth-century novels reflect the embodiment of specific moral intentions is an historically introduced modification of the action form which generates, as I have tried to show in another essay, the distinctive shapes of the Richardson-Fielding-Burney-Austen line of action novels.[14]

I would note furthermore that Sacks's assessment of the influence of Fielding's moral intention on his action is incomplete. Examining the possibility that the whole shape of an action (implicitly the action of *Tom Jones*) can express a moral implication by displaying a causal connection and equation between the protagonist's merit and fate, Sacks concludes that it cannot, essentially because the comic action form in itself ensures an equation between fate and desert, which therefore cannot be read as carrying extrinsic implications (252–62). Now this is certainly true, I would say, of such comic actions as Jane Austen's, whose happy endings seem to have no doctrinal overtones, but it is not true of *Tom Jones*, in which as my account of providentiality has already suggested, there *is* such a causal equation and moral parity, as Le Bossu's notion of the realization of the moral in the whole structure of the action would require. But this formal situation is in distinct contrast with that envisaged in Crane's conception, where any moral element is introduced entirely subordinately, in the service of comic catharsis. This is the clearest and most relevant illustration of my central point about the inescapable modification of the intrinsic by the extrinsic, since it involves the articulation of the inner action principle itself. And it illustrates as well a matter of very general literary theoretical interest, of particular relevance in our own time, namely that an incorrect and incomplete critical conception of previously achieved forms—here the idea that epics had been and therefore ought to be didactic—can act as a preconception and prescription leading to the production of works which actually do fit the formula. Writers can be so hampered by such prescriptive burdens that their works are deadened, as many eighteenth-century novels are by didactic intentions that fail of organic aesthetic realization, and as are many works in our own time in seeking semantic complexity or political relevance at the price of incoherence or affective inertness.

But the point here is just that prescriptive influences are successfully embodied in the working form of *Tom Jones*, and this can bring us to a fuller consideration of the providential dimension of the book, which answers not merely to a moral didactic intention but to an aesthetic one also in that it involves the actual concrete achievement of an effect prescribed for epics, namely, the effect of the marvelous. Again, my point can rest on an independent empirical analysis of the quality of the form of *Tom Jones* conceived apart from any specific notion of providentiality, this time not by Sacks but by another critic working in the revision and extension of Crane's conception, Robert Wess, whose powerful essay on the probable and marvelous in *Tom Jones* is insufficiently known and appreciated.[15] In too short summary, Wess's attempt is to show that Crane's analysis of the causality of the action of *Tom Jones* as merely probable does not account for the so often praised effect of its "wonderful" plot, the effect of "the marvelous." Wess locates the basis of the felt effect in the absolute polarity of merit developed between Jones and the thriving characters of the book, in particular Blifil, as contrasted with their apparent fates which, at the low point of Tom's fortune earlier examined, are so completely opposite to those merits. Without this sharply defined polarity of merit, the reader would not feel the complete reversal produced by the denouement as the startling and wonderfully satisfying transition he does in fact feel it to be. The effect depends further on the reader's perception of the causation of the reversal, which Wess notes is probable in that no action of any character is inconsistent with his represented capacity—a principle specifically announced by Fielding—but that the joint result of such actions is surprising and improbable when considered in their interconnections, which depend so heavily, as Fielding emphasizes, on coincidence. Though he stops short of the specific inference, what Wess's analysis does is to extend Crane's conception of the structure of effect in the book to display the formal sources of that sense of "occult connection" mentioned by Van Ghent and to indicate thereby how Fielding's representation of providential agency working not by divine intervention but through second causes actually becomes aesthetically effective as "the marvelous" in the comic action of a modern epic.

I turn now from consideration of the form of *Tom Jones* in terms of Fielding's conception of it as an epic to consideration of it, again in relation to Crane's analysis, in terms of our modern perception of it as a novel. It is a striking fact that, quite apart from any agreement on an explicit definition, our preanalytic application of the intuitive notion "novel" should be as uniform as regular as it is, implying, it would seem, that the notion has a strongly fixed cognitive content.[16] But it is nonetheless clearly a concept of a historically delimited form and agrees quite well with the standard handbook notion that Richardson's *Pamela* is the first novel; for it can be successfully asserted that before *Pamela* there are no prose fictions which all readers and critics respond to as unambiguous novels, whereas after *Pamela* there are many. Now it is remarkable, I think, that Crane in describing the form of *Tom Jones* standing near the origin of the novel form should, though he calls it a novel—notice how awkward it would be to refer to it as anything else, including an epic—attribute to it no affective properties that would account for our registration of it *as* a novel. Since Crane's conception is of a timeless form, one could expect it a priori not to account for a historically delimited form, but the reason for this shortcoming of Crane's conception—which I take to be a signal explanatory deficiency—lies not with his conception of the action form so much as with his more general concept of imitation, as we can see if we try to give our intuitive conception of the novel some explicit content. If that concept is basically invariant from reader to reader, it must have a content compatible with our most common formulations that the novel is "realistic"—by which I think we mean that our experience of it seems to be like our experience of the real world—and that it is "dramatic" and "shows" rather than "tells"—by which we mean that in a novel the presented characters seem to exist and act from within themselves, with the hidden shape of the story emerging from their actions as if independent of the author's purpose. Let me put a little more tightly what I am claiming is the content of everybody's intuitive notion of the novel form, by saying that a novel is a story which offers a focal illusion (to use Michael Polanyi's convenient terms) of characters acting autonomously for their own ends, as if in the world of real experience, within a subsidiary awareness of an authorial purpose which gives their story, virtually real, a shape of implicit significance and affective force. Now Crane's view of imitation—of literary illusion—as indicated earlier, turns on the fact of its imaginative autonomy—on the fact that it is constituted by the artist's disposition of his material, not by any reflective relation to the real world. But this conception, valid enough as an attempt to define the inherent force of a representational text as a text, cannot in itself express the fact, pointed to by my definition, that the specifically novelistic illusion involves a sense of imaginative immersion in the real world. This does not at all mean that Crane's conception is to be judged in error in contrast with notions of realism as reflective of the actualities of the real world, for such conceptions in their turn have no way to speak of the internal affective structure of the novel, while they miss emphatic expression of the fact that the inner formedness of the novel, which energizes it aesthetically and affectively, is in actual conflict with any claim it might offer to be at bottom really like the unformed world.

A view more nearly adequate to the facts would be to say that the novel imitates in two distinct but intervolved senses, in terms of its intrinsic or inherent power to secure illusion, as its own world, and then, in its characteristic quality, to maintain that illusion as if it were of the uninvented external world known to the reader. But the logic of Crane's conception of imitation as well as his belief in the aesthetic autonomy of the text prevented him from taking direct conceptual notice of a dimension which in *Tom Jones* and all novels is a chief source of their affective power: the sense given to the reader that his experience of the novel is in significant connection with his experience of his own life-world. But as I have already noted, the realistic illusion of the novel *is* an illusion and not a truly verisimilar image because of its formal artistic understructure, and I believe that Crane's conception of the action form does locate the principle of the understructure of the standard novel of plotted suspense, though as with *Tom Jones* that structure must be conceived as varying in response to extraformal pressures. In fact the conception of the action structure, with its implication that from the outset the reader at some level realizes that both his expectations and desires are being developed to meet one another, offers a clear-cut way to describe the standard novel's means to both pleasure and significance: the action novel is thus seen as a controlled objective fantasy in which the reader's satisfaction in the discovered significance and order in the novel's image of the world is realized through and experienced against his implicit sense of the opacity and incoherence of the real world as it actually is.[17]

Thinking of *Tom Jones* as a novel, we can see in the terms set forth that Fielding's decision to place his epic story in a virtual real world—a world based directly on and imaginatively conflated with his own life-world—is what gives it the status as a novel it would not have had he followed the precedent of other epic writers of the period who centered their works on a Leonidas or Prince Arthur. Epic doctrine indeed gave his innovating genius some impetus in this direction, as we have seen, in suggesting that the action be part real, part fictional; and his need to realize the marvelous in terms of "self-moving agents, working with knowledge and choice," as in Barrow's account of a nonmiraculous providence of second causes, moved him toward the construction of a world peopled with autonomous characters, with a hidden causal dimension to be informed by the plan of an unseen author-god. It is important to notice in this connection, I think, in view of all the commentary on Fielding's intrusiveness into the story, that in fact we are not really able to think of the characters as manipulated by Fielding as narrator, despite his assertion of his control, and it is this experienced autonomy of the characters as their joint action eventuates in the shape of the story which gives it in our imaginations its unequivocal identity as a novel.

Nonetheless we can see that Fielding's inherited notions of epic structure and his neoclassical assumptions in general were to some degree in conflict with his emergent intuition of the demands of the new kind of "history" he was trying to bring into being and that his concrete resolution of the conflict left the book with characteristics that can, as they often have been, interpreted as formal deficiencies when viewed in terms of the long-term logic of the novel form, committed as our definition suggests to the absorption of representation into the substance of the represented, but which are at the same time clearly the marks of its success as the achieved particular form it is. Thus Fielding's narrative prominence just mentioned obviously results from the fact that he conceives his function as in the choral tradition of the epic narrator, a role explicitly urged by Trapp and other contemporary critics in the requirement that an epic be a "Narration that comes immediately from the Poet."[18] But it is his vital presence in this role which permits him—"he most handsomely possessed of a mind," in James's famous phrase[19]—to surround and infuse with his own vitality characters who as noted needed to be kept comically distanced and rendered in terms of relatively simple and clear moral contrasts. Collaterally, the epic breadth of the story enables Fielding to offset and qualify the potentially anti-novelistic archetypal schematism of the central action by introducing many peripheral characters of mixed morality and uncertain destiny, as in the world, giving the sense as Crane says that things don't turn out so well for everyone as for Tom and thus pleasingly shading off the clarities of design into the obscurities of the real.

So in general does the pervasive stylization of the book deriving from Fielding's neoclassical assumption that art should be explicitly artful, manifestly *made*, work together with the very unstylized life represented to give the novel its distinctive texture. Several recent critics have countered criticism of the novel as insufficiently realistic by properly emphasizing the positive value of its calculated artificiality, yet we probably have some way to go in appreciating how the distinctive polarity of earthiness and artifice functions organically in the action. Thus Allworthy's articulation of a consistently stiff and programmatic morality makes Fielding's paragon seem rather a dead stick to many readers, but through Allworthy as thus presented Fielding is able to establish the firm reference point of an apparently objective, explicitly rational, principled, and public scheme of values to which Tom's more subjective fluid and intuitive morality can be ultimately attached in implicit validation, all in the service of maintaining that firmly structured sense of moral perspective and judgment upon which, as we have seen, the overall effect of the action depends.

Similarly, from the opposite direction, Squire Western is used to introduce elements of feeling which neoclassical decorum could not allow direct expression. In the denouement, for instance, Fielding needs to suggest a sensual fullness in Tom and Sophia's union appropriate to Tom's often demonstrated and Sophia's implicit natural feeling but he cannot dramatize this explicitly without rendering the sexual Tom even more opprobrious than he has been to many readers and compromising in Sophia that complete freedom from sexual feeling conventionally required in pre-twentieth-century heroines. Fielding's solution is to have Tom declare his impetuous love in the innocuous terms of high romantic rhetoric ("'O! my *Sophia* . . . do not doubt the Sincerity of the purest Passion that ever inflamed a human Breast.

Think, most adorable Creature, of my unhappy Situation, of my Despair,'" etc.), while Sophia remains firm in her insistence that Tom redeem his earlier inconstancy by a period of faithful waiting: "'Time alone, Mr. *Jones*, can convince me that you are a true Penitent'" (18.12. 972), and fixes her term, "'a Twelvemonth perhaps.'" This is accepted without protest, by Jones, who is indeed beside himself with joy: "'O! transporting Thought! am I not assured the blessed Day will come, when I shall call you mine; when Fears shall be no more, when I shall have that dear, that vast, that exquisite, ecstatic Delight of making my *Sophia* happy?'" And he kisses her "with an Ardour he had never ventured before" (18.12.974). Had Fielding left it at this, with decorum and delicacy satisfied, his novel would have lacked a great deal of the satisfaction of its actual ending, as it would have also if he had shown Tom and Sophia eager to satisfy their love without punctilio. His solution is a remarkable piece of art. Before the interview between Tom and Sophia, Allworthy remarks to Western that Sophia was "'the finest Creature in the World.'" "'So much the better for *Tom*,'" says Western; "'for d—n me if he shan't ha the tousling her,'" at which remark Sophia is reported "all over Scarlet" (18.12.970). Then just at the point where Tom ventures on his kiss, Western bursts in and exclaims with the crudity long established as inseparable from his hunting squire's character, "'To her Boy, to her, go to her.——That's it, little Honeys, O that's it. Well, what is it all over? Hath she appointed the day, Boy? What, shall it be to-morrow or next Day?'" Western then breaks out over Jones's protesting "'Let me beseech you, Sir,'"

> "Beseech mine A— . . . I thought thou had'st been a Lad of higher Mettle, than to give way to a Parcel of maidenish Tricks.—I tell thee 'tis all Flimflam. Zoodikers! she'd have the Wedding to-Night with all her Heart. Would'st not, *Sophy*? Come confess, and be an honest Girl for once. What, art dumb? Why do'st not speak?" "Why should I confess, Sir," says Sophia, "since it seems you are so well acquainted with my Thoughts."—"That's a good Girl," cries he, "and do'st consent then?" "No, indeed, Sir," says *Sophia*, "I have given no such Consent."—"And wunt nut ha un then to-Morrow, nor next Day?" says *Western*.—"Indeed, Sir," says *Sophia*, "I have no such Intention." "But I can tell thee," replied he, "why hast nut, only because thou dost love to be disobedient, and to plague and vex thy Father."—"Pray, Sir," said *Jones*, interfering.—"I tell thee thou art a Puppy," cries he. "When I forbid her, then it was all nothing but sighing and whining, and languishing and writing; now I

> am vor thee, she is against thee. All the Spirit of contrary, that's all. She is above being guided and governed by her father, that is the whole Truth on't. It is only to disoblige and contradict me." "What would my Papa have me do?" cries *Sophia*.—"What would I ha' thee do?" says he, "why, gi un thy Hand this moment."—"Well, Sir," says *Sophia*, "I will obey you.—There is my Hand, Mr. *Jones*." (18.12.974–75)

Every reader must feel Fielding's effect here but perhaps not always with full awareness of his artistic strategy. By her comically quick but entirely delightful act of obedience, Sophia in effect incorporates in her assent and accepts, without having to take responsibility for, the bawdy view of the union which Western has taken, and the reader (also without responsibility) can feel the pleasure of including Western's sentiments in his own. The subtle process of expression through displacement is climaxed when, after Allworthy assures Sophia that Tom will "'use his best Endeavors to deserve'" her merit, Western exclaims: "'His best Endeavors! . . . that he will, I warrant un.——Harkee, *Allworthy*, I'll bet thee five Pound to a Crown we have a Boy to-morrow nine Months'" (18.12.976).

Our understanding and perhaps full appreciation of the art of such an episode, as I believe of the whole of *Tom Jones*, depends on our sense of the way in which an artist in a particular historical situation has shaped and aesthetically energized his materials as historically given in a structure which, remaining intelligible and moving beyond its time, yet in its timelessness speaks to us of its time and makes it live in us and us in it. This is the power of great literature and the mark of both its success and limitation as a specifically human product. Perhaps more adequately than any other single critical theorist, R. S. Crane offered a coherent and consistent conception, at once comprehensive and detailed, of the complex of internal and external causes which bear on the work of literature as the concrete product of individual human beings acting in time. My endeavor here has been to suggest (however incompletely) that Crane's pluralistic attempt to define the effect of a work in terms only of a timeless aesthetic structure results in an inadequate analysis because, as at times Crane himself directly recognized, the actual structure of effect in a work inevitably reflects timebound influences. In correction of Crane's view, I think that it is only as the intrinsic artistic structure of a work is seen in relation to extrinsic influences that it can be understood in its full power to move. By the same token, however, the aformalist historical critic needs to be reminded, from Crane's enduring point of view, that it is only as the extrinsic is absorbed into felt significance in the living shape of the work that it can be said to have any literary meaning at all.

Specifically in relation to Professor Richetti's analysis, the argument here suggests a number of points. First, that the formal, affective dimension of *Tom Jones* is not at all an instrument of ideological domination, but the necessary condition of its being the specific kind of masterpiece that it indeed is. The book is not merely "reductive *and* satisfying" (Richetti 211; my italics) but satisfying (that is, affectively successful) inherently *because* it is comically reductive and simplifying. At the same time, it achieves realistic complexity, as Richetti like Crane realizes, because Fielding consistently manages to suggest the fact of a ruder, darker, more threatening world within and beyond the comic world of the novel. Furthermore, the form of the book clearly displays an ideological dimension in its dynamic incorporation of Fielding's conceptions of good nature and Providence, but it is clearly of the Geertzian kind, a personal ideology employed defensively against a threatening world, so that the book stands as an aesthetically dynamic, time-transcendent rehearsal of Fielding's personal faith.

Notes

1. Page references are to the original version of Professor Richetti's article in *The Eighteenth Century: Theory and Interpretation*, 37:3 (fall 1996). 33.

2. "The Concept of Plot and the Plot of *Tom Jones*," in *Critics and Criticism: Ancient and Modern*, ed. R. S. Crane (Chicago, *1952)*, 646-47. Subsequent references to this work are given parenthetically in the text.

3. Crane later moves more broadly to this same conclusion in his great monograph *Critical and Historical Principles of Literary History*, ed. Sheldon Sacks (Chicago, 1967), where his insistence that an adequate literary history must be predicated on a conception of literary form as intrinsic leads him to see external influences as bearing on this intrinsicality in ways that clearly condition the total quality and effect of the work in our indivisible experience of it.

4. In *Fiction and and the Shape of Belief* Sheldon Sacks brilliantly elaborates and illustrates Crane's assertion in his assessment of the contributions of Tom's episodic encounters with various characters, for instance of the Quaker Broadbrim who disowns his daughter for marrying against his will: ". . . Broadbrim appears, tells his tale of self-induced

misery, and departs from the novel: he himself, his shadowy daughter and his son-in-law—the last two shadowy enough to be Tom and Sophia or any other couple—remain in a limbo of permanent unhappiness in no way lightened by the facts that Tom becomes prosperous, marries his Sophia, and lives happily ever after. . . . Not only Tom but the reader sees that 'there are madmen, and fools, and villains in the world' and the latter knows precisely what the important relevant forms are that comprise madness, villainy, and foolishness in the worlds of the novels: though particular forms of the three are defeated by or for the protagonists at the end, we have clear evidence they need not have been defeated and are threats still" (198).

5. *The History of Tom Jones, A Foundling*, ed. Martin C. Battestin and Fredson Bowers (Middletown, Ct., 1975), 18.2.915-17. Subsequent references in the text are to this edition.

6. "Of Good Nature," *Miscellanies by Henry Fielding, Esq.*, ed. Henry Knight Miller (Oxford, 1972), 1:31.

7. Dorothy Van Ghent, *The English Novel: Form and Function* (New York, 1953), 79.

8. The topic of Providence in *Tom Jones* has been extensively treated by Martin Battestin in *The Providence of Wit: Aspects of Form in Augustan Literature and the Arts* (Oxford, 1974); by Aubrey Williams in "Interpositions of Providence and the Design of Fielding's Novels, *SAQ* (1971):265-86, and by Leopold Damrosch, Jr. in *God's Plot & Man's Stories: Studies in the Fictional Imagination from Milton to Fielding*, 281ff.; but my own account is based on independent research and follows a different analytic line.

9. *The Works of Isaac Barrow, D. D.* (New York, 1845), 1:118.

10. See H. T. Swedenberg, Jr., *The Theory of the Epic in England: 1650-1800* (Berkeley, 1944), 53.

11. *Lectures on English Poetry* (1742), 330, quoted by Swedenberg, 160.

12. Sheldon Sacks, *Fiction and the Shape of Belief: A Study of Henry Fielding, with Glances at Swift, Johnson, and Richardson* (Berkeley, 1964), 193-229. Hereinafter cited parenthetically in the text.

13. See [René] Le Bossu, *Treatise of the Epic Poem*, tr. W. J. (2nd ed.; London, 1719), I. vii. 28ff.

14. "From Richardson to Austen: 'Johnson's Rule' and the Development of the Eighteenth-Century Novel of Moral Action," in *Johnson and His Age*, ed. James Engell (Cambridge, Mass., 1984), 461-83.

15. Robert V. Wess, "The Probable and the Marvelous in *Tom Jones*," *Modern Philology* (1970), 32-45.

16. The following account of the novel form is absorbed and greatly expanded in my "The Emergence of the Novel in England," cited above. My argument there is made in explicit contrast with that of Michael McKeon in *The Origins of the English Novel, 1600-1740* (Baltimore, 1987). Professor Richetti sees McKeon's and other recent re-evaluations of the

novel form as exploring "questions that are fundamentally socio-cultural and thereby powerfully and essentially ideological" understood in the "bad old sense" of "social and cultural control rather than a means of insight or personal liberation for writers and readers"; "authorial agency," he notes, "is not often an issue in these new accounts of the novel's emergence. The question that always remains after reading these critics is how individual novelists fit into this larger picture" (207-08). My attempt in the article cited is to show that individual agency was in fact the crucial element in the contingent emergence and development of the novel form.

17. On this point see my "Defoe, Richardson, Joyce and the Concept of Form in the Novel," in William Mathews and Ralph W. Rader *Autobiography, Biography, and the Novel* (Los Angeles, 1973), 29-72; rptd. in David Richter ed., *The Critical Tradition: Classic Texts and Contemporary Trends* (Boston, 1989) and (partially) in Harold Bloom, ed., *Eighteenth-Century British Fiction* (New York, 1988). Cf. Richetti's view that the novel gains its ideological resonance by in various ways implicating and indirectly representing an "anti-world," the world of real experience, present in the novel only as a "potential actuality known only by its differences from the structured and artificial order" (213).

18. The quoted phrase occurs in a passage from *The Art of Poetry on a New Plan* (London, 1762),2:181, given by Swedenberg, 162. The work is apparently hackwork by Goldsmith and John Newberry, and Swedenberg *(105)* emphasizes the commonplace nature of the views it advances.

19. Preface to *The Princess Casamassima*, reprinted in *The Art of the Novel: Critical Prefaces in Henry James*, with introduction by R. P. Blackmur (London, 1934), 68.

Ralph Rader is Professor Emeritus of English at the University of California, Berkeley. He is currently working on two books, one on the emergence and development of the novel form in English and a second on the structure of Joyce's *Ulysses*.

Making Fielding's Novels Speak for Law and Order

Gerald J. Butler

As David H. Richter points out in "The Closing of Masterpiece Theater: Henry Fielding and the Valorization of Incoherence," feminist, neomarxist, and deconstructionist critics can now dismiss Fielding's novels altogether. The *image* of Fielding's work that has evolved in our century, but especially over the last three decades, has been of a well-structured, "coherent" expression of a Christian humanism that no longer seems very interesting. But over thirty years ago, Ronald Paulson expressed some misgivings about this image that was evolving. "Instead of looking to the escapades of Tom Jones or Billy Booth," he told us, "we turn today to the periodicals, the essays, the legal tracts and reports, and the discursive parts of the novels for Fielding's attitudes and ideas. In these we see the public mask.... But... [s]ubmerged in the public image is the Fielding who creates Lady Booby and Slipslop, Trulliber and Blifil, Adams and Jones." But although Paulson questioned the "Christianizing" of Fielding, he still insisted that if "the subject matter of Fielding's best work is not the medicine of Christian morality," it is "the disease for which it may be prescribed."[1] And so Paulson in his own way Christianized and moralized Fielding.

Critics and scholars in our century generally equate the meaning of Fielding's novels with the ideals Fielding professes.[2] We can begin an examination of this process of cleaning up his novels with Cross's 1918 biography. When Cross endeavors to rescue the writer's reputation, he endows Fielding with a character more serious, and moral in the conventional sense, than hitherto was believed. "Dr. Bland was so skilled a hand at the birch that the culprit always felt a recurrence of the old tingling sensations along his posteriors whenever he thought of Eton," Cross tells us, and stresses the classical education received at the "birchen altar" as a credential of Fielding's merit.[3] "Three or four of the ancients whose acquaintance he made at Eton," he goes on to say, "he never turned against in any mood. Aristotle, whom he was fond of quoting, may have been a later discovery; but Plato, a book of his youth, he took with him on his last voyage. His quotations from Cicero were never ending. . . . Finally there was Lucian—'the incomparable Lucian'—whose dialogues had been in the Eton collections for a century. Lucian he joined with Cervantes and Swift, as 'the great triumvirate'—'the great masters' who 'sent their satire . . . laughing into the world.' Lucian, first read in extracts at school, he studied above all writers."[4]

Interestingly, in all the discussion of the meaning and purpose of Fielding's novels that follows from Cross down to the present time, we hear a good deal about Plato, Aristotle, and Cicero, but little about Lucian. Lucian, of course, does not present us with any clear-cut moral position such as we can more comfortably derive from the really classical classics. In 1927, Cross's follower, Frederick T. Blanchard, extends the vision of a serious and conventionally moral Fielding into a reading of his novels themselves and evokes a piece that is written in direct imitation of Lucian to do so, but it is not the Menippean satirist whom tradition up to Fielding's time had called "Anti-Christ" that Blanchard envisions. The philosophy that

> Fielding expanded and clothed in flesh and blood in his novels appears . . . pithily in that scene in the *Journey from this World to the Next* in which Minos sits in judgment upon the souls who throng the entrance to Elysium. . . . Here we have the gist of Fielding's philosophy, which was also that of the Saint Paul whom he so much admired. Only through works, he thinks, can faith be adequately expressed . . . [only through] Charity—Brotherly Love. No novelist has ever surpassed Fielding in illustrating this noble rule of life; yet to many of the aristocracy of the day he was only a "low fellow"; by the pompous clergy, he was often regarded as a buffoon; and in the minds of many otherwise worthy persons he was merely the "facetious" author of the dissolute *Tom Jones*.[5]

In Blanchard's reading we already have much of what will come in twentieth-century academic notions of Fielding's vision—the role of judge, the emphasis on charity, and the conviction that the alternative to seeing in Fielding's novels this affirmation of Christian moral ideals is only seeing the novel as essentially meaningless. And we can see already that the elements of Fielding's "philosophy"—the classicism and the Christianity—go together only in a somewhat fuzzy way.

In 1949, James A. Work, who will give a start to the Christian-humanizing efforts of Martin C. Battestin, recognized the conflict between Christianity and certain classical ideals. Arguing against Digeon's assertions that Fielding was a deist, and Maria Joesten's that he was essentially a Stoic, he asserts that from

> a careful reading of his works it is clear by the time of *The Champion*, when he first spoke out in his own voice, Fielding was in all significant points an orthodox believer in the rational supernaturalism of such low-church divines as Tillotson, Clarke, and Barrow, and that he experienced no important changes in belief throughout the remainder of his life.

Indeed, for Work Fielding becomes "the most important Christian moralist of his generation."[6] So, by 1951, Fielding and Dr. Johnson seem to have so much in common after all, according to Robert E. Moore, that we have to wonder why Johnson ever made such damning remarks.[7] In the following year, F. Homes Dudden attempts to describe this "philosophy" which seems to contain so many different strains and further reveals what a muddle it is. After conceding the lack of coherence, Dudden then insists that what he takes to be the quality "on which he laid the most stress," namely, "Good Nature," "needs to be accurately defined"; it "must not be identified with the foolish, sentimental softness, which shrinks from inflicting on the vicious or criminal the punishments which they deserve."[8] In other words, Dudden wants to prevent what to many readers "Good Nature" indeed could be identified with—a softness that isn't much inclined to punishing anyone—just as Tom Jones himself, supposedly the epitome of "Good Nature," never inflicts any punishments on anyone, not even Blifil.

Later, Dudden implies that Fielding did not aim "to elaborate a system for the learned, but to formulate principles for the vulgar." In this endeavor, Dudden sees him putting together in one idealistic bolus ingredients "derived from the Bible, the writings of Cicero, and Lord Shaftesbury's *Inquiry Concerning Virtue*." He even asserts that "Sir John Hawkins was not far out when he described Fielding's morality as 'that of Shaftesbury vulgarized'" (2:672). Yet Hawkins was, in this description, denying Fielding's Christianity and even morality. Even the Christianity Dudden presents us with is a muddle. "Of 'enthusiasm', or religious emotionalism," Dudden tells us, "Fielding was always profoundly distrustful," but then he gives us an example from *Amelia* of Dr. Harrison's being "fervid" and points out that these "sentiments remind us of those expressed in *The Champion* and by the Man of the Hill in *Tom Jones*" (2:868).

In 1956, Lyall H. Powers reinforces the notion that Fielding's classicism, rather than his Christianity, expresses his meaning by taking seriously Virgil's *Aeneid* as the model for *Amelia*. Miss Matthews is supposed to be Dido. Booth, a military man on half-pay, is supposed to be Aeneas. The prison where they have sexual intercourse is supposed to be the cave in which Dido and Aeneas consummate their love, and going to a masquerade at Ranelagh is supposed to be an epic visit to the underworld.[9] These allusions to the *Aeneid* seem like material for one of Fielding's burlesques—as if Lucian were operating, irrepressibly, even in this somber novel—but, for Powers, the intended classicism is *successfully* achieved: one is not supposed to laugh at it (though of course people did).

"But what, precisely, is the moral basis of Fielding's art?" Martin C. Battestin asks in 1959 in *The Moral Basis of Fielding's Art*—even though he confesses at the start that what is "most memorable about Fielding is not his morality or his religion, but his comedy."[10] "The job of defining the moral basis," he nevertheless insists, "inevitably involves a shift of focus away from comedy" (6). And he is quick to tell us that we must distinguish, as Fielding himself informs us in the preface to *Joseph Andrews*, between the *comic* and the burlesque. Thus Battestin, following Fielding's own intentions as spelled out for us, sharply distinguishes *Joseph Andrews* from *Tom Thumb*, *The Covent-Garden Tragedy*, the *Vernoniad*, *Juvenal's Sixth Satire Modernized in Burlesque Verse*, and, of course *Shamela*,—especially from the early part of his career to which the government put an end. Battestin then tells us that, "largely inspired by James A. Work's essay, 'Henry Fielding, Christian Censor,' recent scholarship has achieved some success in clearing away the old clouded notions" (7–11); we are now supposed to know that it is "the liberal moralism of the Low Church divines—not the principles of Cicero or

Shaftesbury—that underlies the ethos, and much of the art, of *Joseph Andrews*" (13). Battestin goes on to summarize the position of these latitudinarian divines as a reaction against

> the cynical moral relativism of Hobbes, the strict rationalism of the neo-Stoics, and the Antinominian tendencies of Calvinism. Developing an optimistic (though unorthodox) interpretation of human nature, they formulated, in effect, a religion of practical morality by which a sincere man might earn his salvation through the exercise of benevolence. Against the author of the *Leviathan*, for example, Tillotson defended the naturalness of the benevolent social affections. . . . And because they placed so much emphasis upon the tender passions that motivate charitable actions, the divines criticized the Stoic ideal of insensitive detachment as both reprehensible . . . and unrealistic. (14–15)

Nonetheless, we later learn that *Joseph Andrews* recommends, along with charity and chastity, "the classical ideal of life" (88). Indeed, Wilson's interpolated history provides us with "the apparent lesson" of "*vanitas vanitatum* and its solution in a 'retired life' of love and simplicity"(127)—hardly a latitudinarian or even a Christian ideal but rather a classical one of "detachment" that is at least a bit "insensitive."

So the clouds are not dispelled after all. Leroy W. Smith in 1961 argues that studies of Fielding "which amply develop his ties with the Latitudinarian divines and the benevolists . . . link him only indirectly with those writers who believed that the selfish passions control man's actions. But the latter group—variously called skeptics, antirationalists, or self-love psychologists and headed by Hobbes, Bayle, and Mandeville—strongly and directly influenced Fielding's thought."[11] Indeed, into the reasserted muddle comes the suspicion that Fielding's novels may have "failed" after all—the only alternative possible to the critic who needs any kind of "moral basis" for art. Thus, in 1964 Homer Goldberg finds the critical commentary on the theory asserted in Fielding's Preface to *Joseph Andrews* marred with "critical confusion and misunderstanding" of Fielding's own causing.[12] David Goldkopf in 1969 finds Fielding's attempt to justify his novels in terms of classics as "wishful" and asserts that in *Joseph Andrews* "he slid into the mock-epic mode to reconcile his appetite for vulgarity with his respect for the neoclassical concept of decorum." Goldknopf is just as hard on *Tom Jones*, in which he sees Fielding trying to submit to a "discipline fundamentally unsympathetic . . . to the neoclassical canon."13 But in talk of Fielding's "failure," which recalls the critical attitude towards his work of his own time, we have at least a recognition of something in Fielding's writing that always opposes the ideal—that never quite submits to the birch.

In 1974, Battestin generalized his moralistic view of Fielding's novels in his *The Providence of Wit: Aspects of Form in Augustan Literature and the Arts*. Here he asserts that "On one level, the design of *Tom Jones is* the argument of the novel; and this argument is, in sum, the affirmation of Providence—a just and benign, all-knowing and all-powerful Intelligence which orders and directs the affairs of men towards a last, just close."[14] But, no matter in what detail Battestin supports this argument, it must always remain only a probable statement of Fielding's idealistic *intentions*. And the intentions can only constitute the *meaning* of the novel if they are *realized* in the novel. "The happy ending of *Pamela* is unacceptable," Battestin tells us, "because the novel asks to be taken as a faithful (even in a pious sense) representation of actuality. Fielding's fiction makes no such claim. Ultimately he asks us to consider not Tom Jones, but 'Human Nature.'"[15] Battestin slides over here much too effortlessly from the "no such claim" that he says "Fielding's fiction makes" to "he asks"—as if there were no difference between meaning achieved and meaning intended. But if in fact the novel shows us "Human Nature," it does so through Tom and not in spite of him: Tom would illustrate it. And, in so far as he provides this illustration, Tom's characterization would have to ask "to be taken as a faithful (even in a pious sense) representation of actuality." Battestin's argument serves to ignore Tom's behavior in order to make him illustrate the philosophy, the ideals, the Christian humanism; but if we do not render Tom into such an abstraction, and if we persist in seeing his characterization as representing actuality as much as Pamela ever did, we will see instance after instance when Tom—and all the other characters—in fact subvert and undercut whatever idealism or "philosophy" is intended.

Nevertheless, in 1975 Bernard Harrison argues that we should take Fielding's work seriously as moral philosophy—deserving to be considered along with the work of Immanuel Kant: "The task is thus not to conquer desire but to direct and govern it by prudence. This Tom learns and this fits him to be Sophia's husband and Allworthy's heir. . . . Tom does not merely become a rich and happy man; he enters worthily into power and magistracy."[16] But closer to the Fielding that his own contemporaries saw are those who estimate Fielding as "failing" to express any such idealistic intention. Thus Gene S. Koppel argues in 1980 that

> the sexual education of Tom and through him of Fielding's reader . . . never achieves coherence, and . . . one important reason for this failure is that the basic sexual values built into the world are themselves hopelessly muddled. . . . Tom shows himself perfectly capable of continuing his affair with Lady Bellaston . . . even *after* Sophia has clearly let him know that she loves him and would like to marry him. . . . Thus by the time the reader reaches Tom's statements about overcoming the "grossness" of the male sex, he is thoroughly convinced of the opposite—that, other than not hurting anyone, Tom has *no* real sense of any dimension of man's sexual nature other than the most basic physical one.[17]

Why can't the meaning of the novel insofar as it concerns sex be that there *is* no real "dimension of man's sexual nature other than the most basic physical one"? Such a meaning—though it would certainly be opposed today (contemporary insistence that sex is essentially created by culture resembles the old notion that it is essentially controllable by moral constraints)—would have far-reaching implications in the novel and in life. It is really the need to deny any such "failure"—and such meaning—that perpetrates the muddle. And the muddle persists: the classical ideal—if it is to be a classical one—against which to measure Tom and the other characters is still not decided on in 1981: Fredrich G. Ribble notices that Stoicism is creeping into Battestin's later formulations of Fielding's philosophy and, moreover, maintains that Fielding anyway is more Aristotelian than he is Stoic.[18]

And what about Aristotle in all this? "An analysis of the presence of and importance of Aristotelian ethics in this novel," Laura F. Hodges says in 1984 about *Tom Jones*, "reveals that Fielding conflates Aristotelian and Christian ethics." She doubts whether Cicero is so much the basis of Fielding's classicism as is the *Nicomachean Ethics*, and she asserts that it is misleading to relegate "classical influence to a minimum role" as does Battestin.[19] And Shaftesbury, Lance St. John Butler notes, in "Fielding and Shaftesbury Reconsidered: The Case of *Tom Jones*," that "Fielding was less of a Christian than the Battestin school allows for (witness the triumphant conclusion of *Tom Jones* in which religion makes no appearance whatsoever), and Shaftesbury was more of a Christian than is generally admitted."[20] More muddle: in 1987 Aaron Schneider sees a "conflict between an ethics of reason and an ethics of passion" in *Joseph Andrews*. He sees Fielding expressing "a tangible skepticism concerning the efficacy of the sort of pure good nature Battestin describes" when Battestin "lumps Clarke with the other latitudinarian divines . . . [and] implies that Clarke partakes of the whole benevolist ethic. . . . Clarke's emphasis was entirely in the other, rationalist direction." Schneider sees the influence of Hutcheson and Shaftesbury on Parson Adams's character and argues that the latitudinarians themselves "should be seen in broader contexts of ironic undercutting and intellectual duality."[21]

Nevertheless, in spite of these perennial arguments, in his massive 1989 biography Battestin still speaks as if there were no difficulties. He sees resolved *in the novels* all Fielding's own struggles of a passionate, unruly nature against the ideals he believed in or wanted to believe in: a resolution that, while Battestin does not see it occurring in his *life*, we are supposed to believe occurred in his *art*, and the subsequent reading of the novels Battestin gives banishes all subversion from them more surely than the Licensing Act of 1737 was able to banish it from the English stage.

Interestingly, there is an anticlassical strain to Fielding's idealism, a sentimentalism that actually allies him to Richardson. No doubt Hobbes's conception of the power of the passions is itself a source of the sentimental tradition. And Locke's psychological theory, telling us that all our knowledge is ultimately derived from sensations, opens the way for the devaluing of the "innate faculties" of understanding and judgment upon which classical thinking is supposed to depend. This enables the passions, which are all that are then left as the foundation of morality and rule, to be exalted as able to be good in themselves, in contradistinction to the classical disregard for all of them. These "good" passions are, of course, situated in the "heart." "Much can be forgiven if the heart is right," Janet Todd tells us about the sentimental tradition, and that this is "the premise also of Fielding's *Tom Jones*";[22] Tom affirms in the end to Sophia that his "Heart" was always hers. On the other hand, much can be blamed on the passions because they overwhelm the understanding, as Hume blames them for "superstition" and "enthusiasm," but whether blamed or revered, the heart becomes a "basis" for rhetoric rationalizing rule in Fielding's century. Indeed, Sir Robert Chambers said in his Oxford lectures of 1767–73 that "the end of *criminal* law is to prevent those mischiefs which the depravity of the human heart unawed and unrestrained would frequently occasion."[23] And behind the expressions of Fielding's ideals in *A Charge delivered to the Grand Jury* (1749), *An Enquiry into the Causes of the late Increase in Robbers, &c.* (1751), and *A Proposal for Making an Effectual Provision for the Poor* (1753) is the judge who must hang and flog the common people. Battestin admits, too, that Fielding realizes this—and also that the rich cannot really be touched by justice. This virtue is for the poor, and Fielding even comes—just like Mandeville and Hume—to be "convinced that reason and the will, the agents of morality in classical moral philosophy, were powerless to regulate men's emotional nature" and that one can "govern society" only by appealing to the passions, "the strongest of them, hope and fear": one must *terrify* the multitude into obedience.[24] Thus Cicero and sentimentalism ultimately join hands.

Here is the unity in the muddle of ideals: contradictory to each other though they may be, all Fielding's ideals have one thing in common, as Thwackum and Square had one thing in common in their enmity against Tom: they all seek, even if they compete with each other, to impose rule on the unruly, to whip them into line.[25] Battestin describes the flogging that was traditional at Eton, but then goes on to say—reassuringly—that the "goal" of this flogging was "something better—to initiate young men into . . . the great Christian humanist tradition."[26] But Battestin omits what Dudden includes early in his biography—that "At Eton, as in all the great public schools of the period, the boys fared badly. . . . Pitt . . . told Lord Shelburne that 'he scarcely observed a boy who was not cowed for life at Eton.'"27 What—as long as it is an ideal—cannot be found expressed in Fielding's novels? As Work puts it in 1949, there is "God's plenty" (140) in Fielding's writings. But what unifies them all is that each one provides a "basis" for *judgment* and, ultimately, for *punishment* and for "cowing." After Fielding was called to the Bar in 1740, his "Rage" for justice—as one of his contemporaries put it—that provided the occasion for even the "irregular" farces and burlesques could henceforth go into his practice of law.[28] Presumably, this "rage" for justice would also pass into his novels, which he begins to publish in 1742, shaping their plots and building up their muddled "coherence" and what Battestin calls their "architecture."

However, to see that Fielding's plots and "architecture" are only things *imposed* on his novels, and that his idealistic intentions are not really illustrated by his characters, is to see a meaning emerging that is not this "rage." It is also to see an irrepressible continuation of burlesque and farce into the novels. The influence of his "beloved" Lucian and the tradition of laughter that runs through him from Aristophanes, whose *Plutus* Fielding translated with Young, has been admitted, but as merely a source of "technique" by which to deploy a "philosophy."[29] But the Aristophanic-Menippian-Lucianic line in Fielding cannot be reduced to a "technique" conveying a positive "philosophy"; the Menippus of Lucian's dialogue finds *all* the schools ridiculous. "The intellectual preferences of Lucian are not easy to establish," reflects Barry Baldwin in his *Studies in Lucian*, just as, we have seen, such preferences are not easy to establish in Fielding: "Isidore of Pelusium thought Lucian a cynic; set aside the *Cynicus* as spurious, and the idea is left with little support. Epicurean sentiments can be inferred from the *Alexander*, but that sect profits in his pages from its hostility to the prophet, and the tastes of Celsus may be catered to beyond the point of sincerity. It is palpable that he was not a Platonist, Peripatetic, or Stoic; skeptic might seem an obvious label, but it would be rash to detect any special reverence for Pyrrho."[30] In his introduction to his translation of Lucian, Bryan P. Reardon says that "it is fair to . . . describe Lucian as practicing rhetoric under the guise of philosophy."[31] We can say something like that about Fielding: as if in spite of himself he turns whatever philosophy he is espousing into rhetoric, and actually reveals it as no more than rhetoric. True, Nancy Ada Mace has recently argued that Fielding's library "shows that Horace, not Lucian, significantly influenced Fielding's satirical theories and practices . . . . He refers so rarely to Lucian and to other ancient satirists that ancient satire cannot be a source for his novels."[32] But "A Dialogue between Alexander the Great and Diogenes the Cynic," "An Interlude between Jupiter, Juno, Apollo, and Mercury," and "A Journey from this World to the Next," published in his *Miscellanies* in 1743, are themselves takeoffs of Lucian. And the "authorities" he refers to more than to Lucian often do not necessarily actually constitute the most important influence on his writing. Besides, Booth says in *Amelia* that

> ". . . tho' I should agree that the Doctor [Swift] hath sometimes condescended to imitate *Rabelais*, I do not remember to have seen in his Works the least Attempt in the Manner of *Cervantes*. But there is one in his own Way, and whom I am convinced he studied

> above all others—You guess, I believe, I am going to name *Lucian*. This Author, I say, I am convinced he followed; but I think he followed him at a Distance; as, to say the Truth, every other Writer of this Kind hath done in my Opinion: For none, I think, hath yet equaled him. I agree, indeed, entirely with Mr. *Moyle* in his Discourse on the Age of the Philopatris, when he gives him the Epithet of the incomparable Lucian; and incomparable I believe he will remain as long as the Language in which he wrote shall endure. What an inimitable Piece of Humour is his Cock."[33]

But I do not wish to argue for a Lucianic as opposed to a Ciceronian or Aristotelian or Stoic or sentimental or latitudinarian "basis" for Fielding's art. Rather, I mean to argue that if all the Christian humanism and "structure" turns out to be as superficial as Johnson, Richardson, Hawkins, and even people in our own century, from Ford Madox Ford to scholars who really do seem to know their Cicero or Aristotle, are telling us, then Fielding was still preserving in his novels the uproarious, anarchic, bawdy and "low" comedy of his plays—as if no amount of "flogging" could ever really change him. And we do not need to see his novels as therefore meaningless or "incoherent" but, indeed, as taking their meaning and their coherence from the undermining of all morals and all ideals that end in flogging and in death. It is time to start reading Fielding's novels for such meaning, and we can do that by envisioning the characters, Lady Booby and Slipslop, Trulliber and Blifil, as well as Tom and Sophia and Booth and Amelia, as Paulson reminded us thirty years ago, seeing what they actually do and feel in their fictional worlds, and not merely reading them as if they were simple, unproblematic illustrations of the legal tracts and reports and of the novels' discursive parts. If criticism, scholarship, and now "theory"[34] have tried to remove Fielding's novels from us, ensuring better than outright censorship that no one need be "corrupted" by them, we can still come into contact with them in a "crude" reading that sees them as about people—people of flesh and blood for whom no ideal is satisfactory or even worthy.[35] We need very little, if any, of Plato, Aristotle, Cicero, Hobbes, Shaftesbury, the latitudinarians, Roland Barthes or Jesus Christ himself—or even Lucian—to read Fielding's novels; these names around which to arrange our pedantry mainly just get in the way. The old "scholarship" that killed Fielding's novels by equating them to his idealistic intentions, and now the new "theory" that carries off the corpses, both serve to make his novels into nothing that can disrupt the law and order built into contemporary readers.

Notes

1. Ronald Paulson, ed., *Fielding: A Collection of Critical Essays* (Englewood Cliffs, N.J., Prentice-Hall, 1962), 1–2.

2. It is true that in his *Studies in the Eighteenth-Century English Novel* (East Lansing: Michigan State University Press, 1969) Arthur Sherbo has questioned Battestin's use of scholarship concerning the latitudinarian divines in his reading of *Joseph Andrews*; but Sherbo's view of the novel then is that it is just "sheer entertainment" (115), a view which Andrew Wright in his *Henry Fielding: Mask and Feast* (Berkeley: University of California Press, 1965) is really not far from admitting himself when he makes so much of the "playful" and "festive" quality of Fielding's novels. Mark Kinkead-Weekes, who points out in a footnote to his "Out of the Thicket in *Tom Jones*," that he and C. J. Rawson are "lonely figures" (quoted in K. G. Simpson, ed., *Henry Fielding: Justice Observed* [London: Vision, 1985], 56) in their opposition to Battestin's reading of Tom as in need of the virtue of prudence, nevertheless asserts that the novel is showing Tom as needing to learn to love "more and better" (Simpson, 148). In his *Henry Fielding and the Augustan Ideal Under Stress* (London and Boston: Routledge and Kegan, 1972), Claude Rawson reads *Jonathan Wild* in other than traditional moralistic or Christian terms. But, aside from Rawson's courageous reading, exceptions to the statement that criticism has generally seen Fielding's novels as realization of their professed idealistic intentions are almost invariably either only apparent or seem to make the novels shallow and even meaningless.

3. Wilbur R. Cross, *The History of Henry Fielding*. 3 vols. (New Haven: Yale University Press, 1918), 1:48.

4. Cross, 1:46–47.

5. Frederic T. Blanchard, *Fielding the Novelist: A Study in Historical Criticism* (1926; New York: Russell and Russell, 1966), 138–39.

6. James A. Work, "Henry Fielding, Christian Censor," in *The Age of Johnson: Essays Presented to Chauncy Brewster Tinker* (New Haven: Yale University Press, 1949), 140–48.

7. Robert E. Moore, "Dr. Johnson on Fielding and Richardson," *PMLA* 66 (1951): 162–81.

8. F. Homes Dudden, *Henry Fielding: His Life, Works and Times*, 2 vols. (Oxford: Clarendon Press, 1952), 1:272.

9. Lyall H. Powers, "The Influence of the *Aeneid* on *Amelia*," *Modern Language Notes* 71 (May 1956): 330–36.

10. Martin Battestin, *The Moral Basis of Fielding's Art* (Middletown, Conn.: Wesleyan University Press, 1959), x.

11. Leroy W. Smith, "Fielding and Mandeville: The 'War Against Virtue,'" *Criticism* 3 (winter 1961): 7.
12. Homer Goldberg, "Comic Prose Epic or Comic Romance: The Argument of the Preface to *Joseph Andrews*," *Philological Quarterly* 43 (April 1964): 196.
13. David Goldknopf, "The Failure of Plot in *Tom Jones*," *Criticism* 11 (September 1969): 262–63.
14. Martin C. Battestin, *The Providence of Wit* (Oxford: Clarendon Press, 1974), 145.
15. Ibid., 161.
16. Bernard Harrison, *Henry Fielding's* Tom Jones: *The Novelist as Moral Philosopher* (London: Chatto and Windus, 1975), 111–12.
17. Gene S. Koppel, "Sexual Education and Sexual Values in *Tom Jones*: Confusion at the Core?" *Studies in the Novel* 12 (spring 1980): 1–11.
18. Fredrich G. Ribble, "Aristotle and the 'Prudence' Theme of *Tom Jones*," *Eighteenth Century Studies* 15 (fall 1981): 28.
19. Laura F. Hodges, "Aristotle's *Nicomachean Ethics* and *Tom Jones*," *Philological Quarterly* 63 (spring 1984): 224–34.
20. Butler, Lance St. John, "Fielding and Shaftesbury Reconsidered: The Case of *Tom Jones*," quoted in K. G. Simpson, ed., *Justice Observed* (London: Vision, 1985), 73.
21. Aaron Schneider, "Hearts and Minds in *Joseph Andrews*: Parson Adams and a War of Ideas," *Philological Quarterly* 66 (summer 1987): 384–88n.
22. Janet Todd, *Sensibility: An Introduction* (London: Methuen, 1986), 72.
23. Sir Robert Chambers, *A Course of Lectures on the English Law (1767-73)*, 2 vols., ed. Thomas M. Curley (Madison: University of Wisconsin Press, 1986), 1:90.
24. Battestin, *Fielding*, 517–18.
25. Of course, Fielding had ideals to impose specifically on women. Battestin tells us that Fielding's first wife Charlotte was for him "the flesh-and-blood reality behind the ideal" embodied in Sophia Western (Battestin, *Fielding*, 187). In his "To a Friend on the Choice of a Wife," Fielding writes: "Superior Judgment may she own thy Lot; / Humbly advise, but contradict thee not." But how far does Sophia actually embody or illustrate this ideal?
26. Battestin, *Fielding*, 41.
27. Dudden, 1:11.
28. Quoted in Battestin, *Fielding*, 239.
29. Thus, the study of Lucian's relation to Fielding in Chapter Six of Henry Knight Miller's "Lucianic Sketches" (in *Essays on Fielding's* Miscellanies: *A Commentary on Volume One* [Princeton: Princeton University Press, 1961], 365–419) notices mainly stylistic parallels. Christopher Robinson, acknowledging his debt to Miller (in *Lucian and His*

Influence in Europe [Chapel Hill, 1979], 198), reminds us of Fielding's "panegyric" to Lucian in the *Covent Garden Journal* and notes the many obvious parallels to Lucian in articles for *The Champion* for Saturday, 17 and 24 May 1740; *Eurydice* and *The Author's Farce*; the auction scene of *The Historical Register for the Year 1736*; *An Interlude between Jupiter, Juno, Apollo and Mercury*; *A Dialogue between Alexander the Great and Diogenes the Cynic*; and articles for *The Covent-Garden Journal* (nos. 7 and 8); and, of course, *Journey from This World to the Next*. But Robinson thinks there is in Fielding, as opposed to Lucian, "a positive vision of goodness which is entirely alien to anything in Lucian. . . . If one can, in fact, meaningfully talk of *influence*, it is, as Fielding himself indicates, a stylistic influence" (222–23); it is just this positive "message" that I am questioning as establishing the meaning of Fielding's works.

30. Barry Baldwin, *Studies in Lucian* (Toronto: Hakkert, 1973), 116.

31. Bryan P. Reardon, "Introduction" to *Lucian: Selected Works* (Indianapolis: Bobbs-Merrill, 1965), xviii.

32. Nancy Ada Mace, "Henry Fielding's Novels and the Classical Tradition" Ph.D. diss., Pennsylvania State University, 1990, abstract in Dissertation Abstracts International 51 (1990): 573A.

33. Henry Fielding, *Amelia*, ed. Martin C. Battestin (Oxford: Clarendon Press, 1983), 325.

34. Much academic literary theory—notably Roland Barthes's denial that characters in fiction have any life of their own—would prevent us from reading this way. In spite of this, at least one critic sympathetic to Barthes and to deconstruction has seen that "the study of character—especially that of 'psychological' character—is not a critical *cul-de-sac*. . . . The semic surplus which signifies a character's 'reality' both asserts and subverts the authority of the discourse in which it is embedded." See Andrew J. Scheiber, "Sign, Seme, and the Psychological Character: Some Thoughts on Roland Barthes' *S/Z* and the Realistic Novel," *The Journal of Narrative Technique* 23 (fall 1991): 270.

35. My *Fielding's Unruly Novels* (Lewiston, N.Y.: Edwin Mellen, 1995) attempts this kind of reading.

Gerald Butler is Professor of English at San Diego State University and writes about ways literature is rendered innocuous or dismissed by practices common in academic institutions. Readings of Lawrence, Fielding, Defoe, Radcliffe and others have provided him with examples. He is at present working on a book on how such *de facto* censorship affects the way we see the eighteenth-century British novel.

Closing Down the Theater, and Other Critical Abuses

Carol Houlihan Flynn

In his provocative essay, "The Closing of Masterpiece Theater," David H. Richter seems to be looking back with a certain nostalgia to a more innocent time when "critical interest in Fielding was stronger than any other eighteenth-century novelist." In trying to explain Fielding's "relative eclipse," Richter finds "Fielding's Georgian valorization of tight economy of plot, coherence of tone, and elegance of expression" out of favor in "an age whose aesthetic ideology valorizes incoherence, disjunction, and *différance*." Richter admits that Fielding "profited from the prevailing formalism of the 1950s and sixties," when *Tom Jones* engaged the energies of critics fascinated by Fielding's erection of formal plot structures famous for their brilliant, dazzling visibility. Critics like R. S. Crane, Dorothy Van Ghent, John Preston, and Eleanor Hutchens taught us that to recognize the architectonic formal properties of the text was to master its underlying ironies, to recognize a transparently apparent truth waiting behind the structure itself.

What Richter finds particularly offensive about recent theoretical readings of Fielding is the distortion, the degradation of the text that accompanies a critical search for a "truth" outside the text itself. "The problem," he argues, "with ideological readings . . . is that they . . . substitute a raw, crude vision of sexual, social, political life for the subtle and complex vision that Henry Fielding represented" (11). When he argues against "crude" ideological readings that molest the text, he suggests that while formalism was true, innocent, unbiased, theory is corrupt, self-interested, false. As William Epstein made clear in his study of "Cold War

Criticism," we need to remember that in the golden age of formalism, critics were not so innocently rewriting the "meaning" of texts to suit their own—and their culture's—desire.[1] In a time of political conformity, the most irregular literary figures were being revised to fit a cultural taste for coherence and regularity. Thus Maynard Mack's "persona" theory sanitized and moderated the most cantankerous and venomous outbursts of Swift and Pope. Even more elaborately, Mack produced *The Garden and the City*, which recreated Pope's art and life in the serenely methodized model that Pope himself aspired to, but frequently failed to attain.[2] The Pope hurling abuse at his enemies, those Westphalian hogs, was not Mack's Pope, carefully cultivating his garden when he wasn't polishing his grotto stones.

The golden age of Fielding studies also produced biographically driven studies that promised historically neutral truth. Empowered as the invisible, "neutral" editor of Fielding's texts, a sort of "historical" formalist, Martin C. Battestin frequently makes critical arguments in footnotes which often refer back to his own articles.[3] These articles attempt to "reform" his subject, imbuing him with a spiritual and moral purpose which gives shape to the sloppiest actions of occasionally irregular characters. His *Tom Jones* and *Amelia* become latitudinarian tracts promoting the pursuit of prudence, while his Fielding, immersed in the pure ether of the sermons of Barrow and Hoadley, finds providential patterning in God's perfect plot. This is not to take away from the compendious supply of valuable annotation that Battestin supplies his reader, but he exacts a high price along the way, by controlling his reader's responses with footnotes that shape the critical meaning of his texts. Mack and Battestin speak for their culture in their attempts to recuperate their subjects, to find in their work and their lives a learned, uplifting consistency and coherence. Their subjects' natures become deliberately methodized, while their own critical methods become naturalized. We are not supposed to find their critical constructions "crude" or raw, but rather elegant, responsible, transparently "true." But then, formalist critics could find patterns in the most inchoate texts. The wrinkled and unruly Defoe, who seldom divided up his novels into paragraphs, let alone chapters, was carefully ironed out by George Starr and Paul Hunter into the most tidy of writers, one who found providential patterns in every page of God's novel, while Dorothy Van Ghent created archetypal and mythical patterns to structure *Clarissa*.[4]

Indeed, without imposing mythic "form" upon the novel, Van Ghent finds the work "perverse." Her mythic interpretation saves the work from its historical implications.

The Critic as Clerk

When Richter complains that formalism is disappearing, he really seems to be saying that critics, particularly theoretically engaged critics, have become more critical of their subjects and more obvious in their intentions. These critics no longer pretend an innocent neutrality, nor do they demonstrate their allegiance to their subject. He seems most uneasy about Patricia Meyer Spacks's dissatisfaction with the constancy of Amelia's character. Even while he concedes that Spacks "doesn't think Fielding is a bad guy" (8), he hints here that the lady critic is not as admiring as she should be. Like Fielding, putting uppity critics in their proper places, Richter seems to relegate the critical role to the clerical, transcribing function. It's no good for them to rear up and try to be "Masters."[5] He looks for a critical role that should be familiar to many of us who learned to serve as the translator and mediator of another culture, an older culture, a more English culture. We American critics of a certain age were trained to turn ourselves into little eighteenth-century men, possessed by the spirit of the greats which we would then infuse into our students. This practice may have been easier for men to follow, but we women worked at it nonetheless, doggedly learning how to be "like" the eighteenth-century men we were expected to admire. Of course we separated ourselves from the conservative politics of our period (who would want to be Whig or Tory?), for most academics then, as now, were liberals, but nonetheless we were taught that it was tasteless and naive to harp too much about the economic and sexual oppressiveness of the time.

We can find this attitude alive and well in Battestin's biography of Fielding.[6] Battestin is introducing Fielding's *Enquiry*, with instructions for his reader: when Fielding scorns the mob, he speaks for his culture as a proponent of the happy theory of subordination. Battestin cites, with seeming approval, Fielding's statement of order, "the analogy between the functional organicism of the microcosm, man, and that of the body politic":

> The Gentleman ought to labour in the Service of his Country; the Serving-man ought to wait diligently on his Master; the Artificer ought to labour in his work; the Husbandman in tilling the Ground; the Merchant in passing the Tempests; but the Vagabonds ought clearly to be banished, as is the superfluous Humour of the body, that is to say, the Spittle and Filth; which because it is for no Use, is put out by the Strength of Human Nature.

It is essential, Battestin argues, to "grasp the significance of this analogy" which determines his attempts to heal the "Constitution," and the "body politic," and energizes him as he sat in "his study in Bow Street, at the heart of the depraved capital of Georgian England" dreaming of "an orderly and honorable past" which had faded into "a wilderness of vice and roguery." Critics like Battestin, entering so dramatically into his subject's dilemma, lead us to understand how Fielding could not have thought differently, and we become in such critical moments perilously close to adopting his culture's conservatism, or at least not asking how it could have been altered. Such critical appreciation and identification cancels the arguments that Peter Linebaugh makes against what he labels "Tyburnocracy," in *The London Hanged*, a revisionary history of the mob of "scourges and parasites" Fielding loathed.[7] Once Linebaugh tells the tales of the lives taken at Tyburn to preserve "peace and order," he makes us read Fielding differently. This does not mean that we must burn Fielding, but rather that we need not sympathize so enthusiastically with his desire for the beauty and regularity of law and order.

Late in the seventies, many critics, particularly female critics, stopped appreciating the beauties and forswore laughing at the symmetry of Moll Seagrim's sexual scrapes. We became in the process a tendentious, quarrelsome lot quick to take offence at the excesses that we were expected to find clever. Some of us lost our sense of humor altogether. Lovelace's rakish fantasies sounded less witty, while Tom Jones, learning about sexual maturity through the good offices of Moll Seagrim, Mrs. Waters, and Lady Bellaston, one lady for each architectonic tripodal part, began to get on our nerves. And some critics got nervous. What worries Richter, I suspect, is that critics today are less concerned with admiring the beauties of a work than they are with addressing the ideological concerns of their own times. In the good old days, when we were being little eighteenth-century men, we particularly guarded ourselves from the grave error of applying our own political positions to the privileged world of eighteenth-century letters. Instead, in learned innocence, we carefully transcribed the master narrative, like good clerks, Now, when we interrogate the sexual politics or the class assumptions of Richardson or Fielding, Burney or Goldsmith, we do so not to "degrade" them or their works, but to ask how, in the last decade of the twentieth century, we have become what we are. Conducting a discourse that challenges historical constructions of sexuality, of public space, of private life is no longer an innocent or neutral act, but deliberate and necessarily self-conscious.

In their essay, "Author and Authority: Writing the New Cultural Geography," Denis Cosgrove and Mona Domosh charge theorists across disciplines to recognize their cultural agendas and disavow their critical innocence:

> When we write our geographies, we are creating artefacts that impose meaning on the world . . . as a series of cultural constructions, each representing a particular view of the world, to be consulted together to help us make sense of ourselves and our relation to the landscapes and places we inhabit and think about. These stories are to be read not as approximations to a reality, but as tales of how we have understood the world, to be judged not according to a theory of correspondence, but in terms of their internal consistency and their value as moral and political discourse.[8]

By calling their productions "stories," Cosgrove and Domosh emphasize the provisional, tentative quality of their work. Not only are they not creating masterpieces, but even more, they are not endorsing masterpieces, preferring to disclose the intentional, personal aspects of their writing. This is what separates theory from earlier critical attempts to fix meaning and to translate cultural differences for readers, who in understanding them, would then admire their creators. When Maynard Mack created a gentler, nobler Pope, he did so presuming that his readers could not, indeed should not, embrace a waspish, domineering, nasty Pope. The poet had to be reformed for his own good, and for the benefit of readers trying to comprehend his meaning. Parts of him had to be left out. When Richter worries that Fielding is being read as a playwright and a political journalist, rather than the author of comic masterpieces, he must also leave a lot of Fielding out.[9] A Fielding who only writes masterpieces loses the multivarious properties of a complete Fielding, always in transition, the young, brash playwright who worked closely with Charlotte Charke, the author (disputed) of *The Golden Rump*, the gout-ridden magistrate who worked so hard to understand the plight of the urban poor, and listened with sympathy to Elizabeth Canning's story of abduction. If we stick to the masterpieces, we lose the Fielding writing about the Penlez case, the Fielding setting up the Universal Register-Office, and advertising the miraculous properties of Glastonbury water, and the Fielding collaborating with Hogarth in his schemes to correct social abuses (*An Enquiry into the Causes of the late Increase in Robbers* was published one month earlier than Hogarth's *Gin Lane*). All of these parts of one "unified," contradictory Fielding open up possibilities of critical understanding (and admiration) of a most creative, responsive writer, a thinker driven to expose and embarrass, as delighted to "degrade" as to elevate structures of Palladian intricacy. What particularly interests me is this late Fielding, the magistrate "detecting" in the streets themselves the cultural history of the city that both liberates and contains him.

Something in the Critical Vein: or How I Would Write about Fielding

I want to think about Fielding's relationship to the cultural and spatial topography of London, particularly the late Fielding, who served as Magistrate and established the Universal Register while writing *Amelia* and *An Enquiry into the Causes of the late Increase in Robbers*. Central to my understanding of Fielding's project in *Amelia* is the John Rocque map, published in 1746. Its size is important: thirteen feet wide and six-and-a-half feet deep. The awkwardness created by the large scale of the Rocque map—one inch represents two hundred feet—was understood from the outset. In his *Proposal* (1740), Rocque suggests that "by rolling it up on a Roller, to the Cornish of the Wainscot, it will not interfere with any other Furniture; and yet by the Means of a Pully, it may be let down for Examination at Pleasure. And a small Plan will be given to such who bind up the Sheets in a Volume, for the Sake of presenting a View of the Whole at once." Such a solution—another was to apply all twenty four sheets to a "beautiful and useful" folding screen—cannot remove the original problem of "so large a Size." Even cranked down on a pulley, the map remains too big to be viewed without considerable difficulty. The scale still gets in the way. Rocque's final solution, to bind the twenty four sheets into one volume, an early *A to Z*, pretends that the sheets themselves constitute a manageable mass, when in reality, they are outsized and cumbersome.[10] As the cartographer attempts to provide a large enough surface on a large enough scale to represent reality "correctly," the map itself becomes a symbol of a realism strained and stretched. It testifies to a cultural faith in empiricism which promises a knowledge which remains, for material reasons, out of reach.

The Rocque map also speaks to a cultural faith in the accumulation of facts, collected to reveal an unambiguous truth. Rocque's map was the first survey of London conducted since 1682, tracing the progress of a city that had grown in population from approximately 450,000 to 675,000 and that had expanded considerably, particularly westward. As a representation of civic pride, as well as an instrument of order and control, the proposed map immediately received support from the Corporation of London. The Foucaldian implications of such a project, enthusiastically endorsed by ward beadles, are almost too obvious.[11] In its attention to "all the Squares, Streets, Courts and Alleys . . . Ground Plots . . . Roads and Foot paths," the Rocque map promises comprehensive understanding of the networks of a city, which no doubt particularly interested the author not only of *Amelia* and the *Enquiry*, but of the Bow Street runners, the prototypes of the police force. What both the map and the novel attempt to do is fix, comprehend, "know" its subjects, placing them on grids topographical and cultural.

Rocque and his assistants took nine years, from 1737 to 1746, to walk every one of London's streets and roads. They covered over 10,000 acres of ground, measuring each thoroughfare either with a chain or an instrument called a waysider, a cyclometer pushed like a wheelbarrow, carrying a wheel eight feet three inches in diameter which measured 640 revolutions to a mile. Rocque also used a theodolite to note the exact angles at street corners (the instrument took its trigonometrical bearings from church steeples), making his ultimate survey by comparing the measurements and trigonometrical findings.

Unfortunately for Rocque, the distances that he took with his waysider did not tally with distances calculated trigonometrically, and had to be remeasured. The project was too big for its time table. Over 5,000 place names had to be verified and established and revised, distances needed to be corrected, and it took five more years before the map was ready for publication. When the

London map was finally published, Rocque's name had disappeared entirely from the proposal, presumably for financial reasons. Cartographers, like authors, were often an insolvent, bankrupted lot.

When the map was advertised in 1746, the publishers, Pine and Tinney, sounding remarkably like Richardson canvassing friends and readers for advice on his revisions of *Clarissa*, appealed to the public for their careful "corrections," promising that "nothing shall be wanting to make the work Correct as possible."[12] The advertised emphasis on correctness and on the scientific method of the project places the Rocque map squarely in the Enlightenment, alongside fellow projectors like Richardson and Fielding. Rocque's map promises verisimilitude while it expresses a faith in the quantifiable nature of spatial relationships that informs the sort of realism expressed by other textual productions like the novel. Not that Rocque's map could ever be "correct" in spite of the number of curious spectators he employs to make corrections. Like Johnson's *Dictionary*, his encyclopedic project is subject to the vicissitudes of inevitable mutability. Rocque attempted to anticipate some of the changes in the territory he was mapping, including the Westminster Bridge, which would not be built until 1750, and completing on paper those parts of the Foundling Hospital yet to be erected. An interesting omission in a map promising completeness is the location of his print shop, Hyde Park Road. Like Mrs. Sinclair's "real" address in *Clarissa*, that street which is not Dover Street, and like Amelia's "watchman of a certain Parish (I know not particular which) in the Liberty of Westminster, " (17) Rocque's uncharted street teases the reader looking for a truth he pretends to guarantee, while it allows the map's author to recede, achieving in his disappearance neutrality, objectivity, and unauthorized "truth."

When Rocque made his survey of London, he carried out a cultural action, one that would be repeated throughout his century. The eighteenth century was a time for surveying, from China to Peru, from Chelsea to Deptford. Rocque belongs to a tradition of measuring, spectating, reporting. He resembles Addison and Steele, Defoe and Richardson, Gay and Pope (the *Dunciad's* Pope), Hogarth, Johnson, Boswell, and Burney in their own rambling, spectating attempts to measure the monster city and comprehend its networks. As one of the authors of the "modern" personality being measured and projected onto grids both geographical and cultural, Fielding can offer us a place to investigate the cultural desire for accountability and comprehension. His centrality in the modern project of surveillance becomes curiously apparent in an odd work written in 1752, the year after *Amelia, A Plan of the Universal Register-Office*, and the *Enquiry*, the same year he wrote *The Covent-Garden Journal*. *Examples of the Interposition of Providence in the Detection and Punishment of Murder* illustrates the strange workings of criminal detection and God's surveillance in thirty cases of murder. Looking back to the "providence" tradition, but forward to what will become a cultural fascination with criminal "detection," Fielding uncannily intimates nineteenth-century projects of surveillance overseen by projectors like Dickens's Bucket and Pancks and Doyle's Sherlock Holmes, detectives looking to impose order upon the uneven urban terrain.

The map is of course crucial for projects of surveillance and detection. Rocque's map seems to certify its accuracy in its attention both to tedious detail and to "vacant spaces." The empiricist map excludes the "unmeaning" ornamentation and bias found in earlier maps, replacing the florid allegorical decoration so characteristic of the Renaissance map with the seemingly factual neutrality of white space. The map itself ceases being the artistic product of an individual and becomes a scientific instrument, the mechanistic product of an objective survey.[13] The individual mapmaker, consumed by the project, becomes as invisible as Mr. Spectator, as anonymous as the Richardsonian editor, or for that matter, as Fielding's decidedly recessed reporter of the trials of Amelia and Billy Booth. We are left with the map "itself," a seemingly transparently abstract and functional system designed for the factual ordering of spatial relations reflecting a faith in the universality of knowledge and in the methods of scientific observation.

At first, the Rocque map looks naked in its gridlike assumption of a reality that can be accurately charted. Its frame, however, emphasizes places of power. Rocque extends his map towards Ranelagh and Vauxhall in the southwest, paying homage to the two significant spaces of luxury and entertainment, and carries his map eastward into Deptford to include the London Docks, site of empire and international trade. Its grid structure, seeming so flat and fair, differs markedly from earlier bird's eye maps that seem to privilege the compacted spaces of the city, celebrating in their aggregated masses of buildings the world of commerce. The Rocque grid, however, charting out the estates of the West End and comparing them to the crowded mazes of East London, celebrates the expansive spaces pushing westward towards Chelsea and Knightsbridge. Rocque's white spaces—he calls them "vacant"—are beautifully naturalized to produce for the map reader an empty territory that invites gentlemanly expansion and investigation. The top of Tottenham Court Road is improved by garden patches. Even the trees, each one represented with its individual shadow—the sun is shining from the West, source of empire and expansion—replace the "unmeaning" ornament of earlier maps with a naturalized topography that extols cultivation and growth. Like Conrad's "white spaces" in *Heart of Darkness*, these vacant lots capture the imagination and ask to be filled. Such detail, each tree shadowed, each hillock crosshatched, on such a large scale, takes time and space. It is in the tedious collection of detail that the mapmaker, like the novelist, establishes a claim to truth telling. Rocque's map is so large and cumbersome that it must be true. By begging the verisimilitude of its own baggy, awkward representation, it reminds me of the novel.

On the Verge of the "Real"

The sheer size and bulk of the early English novel, that "dilated" representation of life also makes it formally impossible to ignore. Richardson's *Clarissa* takes up so much room, physically and imaginatively, that it represents on some irresistible level reality. Partly this is because Richardson informs his readers of the efforts he is making on their behalf to provide a corrected, amplified version of his story. It is an effort that Fielding seems to reproduce in *Amelia*, a novel much more concerned with "circumstantial detail." Attending to particular streets, Monmouth for buying and selling old clothes, Gray's Inn Lane for sponging houses, shops like White's for chocolate, Brown's for coffee, Madame Chenevix's for toys, and public gardens like Ranelagh and Vauxhall for entertainment, Fielding commits himself in his final novel to chart the actual streets in a narrative that depends upon his own characters' awareness of the limitations of the space they are allowed to fill.

By mapping specific locations in London, both Richardson and Fielding make their readers imaginary Londoners busy accumulating knowledge of the networks of urban life. Richardson produces for his readers a Vade Mecum of urban life, the places open to his spectating gaze that can be approached or avoided.[14] Fielding shares this pragmatic optimism, constructing in *Amelia* a grid that creates within his readers a sophistication, as well as an awareness of the services that London provides. When Fielding wrote his last novel, he was also pursuing an ambitious social project directly tied to London life, an enterprise called The Universal Register-Office, managed by his half-brother John, located "opposite *Cecil-street* in the *Strand*." (*Amelia*, 572) The agency was designed to serve as a London clearing-house: servants and apprentices could link up with their masters and mistresses, soldiers with their commissions, house sellers with buyers and teachers with students. In the first edition of *Amelia*, he refers quite shamelessly to its benefits, advising his reader that his own literary production has depended upon the "Materials of a private Nature" which were communicated to him "by one of the Clerks of the Universal Register-Office; who by having a general Acquaintance with Servants, is Master of all the Secrets of every Family in the Kingdom." (571) Even when Amelia is faced with the sad prospect of having to pawn her "little All" to provide food for her family, she cheers up considerably when she remembers that her "Husband had told her there was no kind of Information whatsoever, which was not to be had at the Universal Register-Office" where she "immediately drove, and was there recommended to a Person, who not only advanced her the money she desired, but at a much less Interest than the Pawnbroker would have insisted on" (575). Critics taking issue with Fielding's puffery forced him to remove his six references to the agency in later editions. His original impulse, however, reveals much about the author's belief in the value of information and networks of exchange.

If information is power, its lessons can also be monitory. Fielding, ideologically in collaboration with Hogarth (and Richardson), reinforces in his novel the cautionary (and gendered) warnings about public spaces waiting to swallow up the unprotected female. Amelia at Vauxhall, made the center of unwanted attention, teaches her unattended female readers to avoid the perils of such marginal areas. Fielding teaches a lesson that Frances

Burney, Maria Edgeworth, and Jane Austen learned well, inspiring lady authors to represent London as a dangerous wilderness that demands an expensive sophistication and creates hard hearts.

Fielding's faith in networks does not entirely survive the confining structures of *Amelia*. No matter how adaptable and knowledgeable they prove to be, the Booth family remains on the margins of the information network, reduced in circumstances to exist in an increasingly confined space which is geographically and socially determined. Fielding's novel demands that we question such a debilitating condition of containment. But it becomes impossible to resist the structures of surveillance and oppression, which Fielding himself keeps in play as magistrate, part of a system which sends debtors to sponging houses and unpaid servants to Monmouth Street where they pawn stolen dresses. Can "universal" schemes of intelligence allow for reformation and expansion?

While the novel virtually begins in Newgate, that generic place of confinement and incarceration, its plot revolves around a less well-known area of confinement, the Verge of the Court, where Billy Booth, because of his debts, is forced to live. The Verge was an area around St. James's Palace and Whitehall under the jurisdiction of the Lord Steward of the Royal Household. As such, it was a protected space in which the civil authorities, the bailiffs and Sheriff's men, had no power. Within the Verge, Billy Booth and his fellow debtors can roam freely, but once they leave its boundaries, they can be legally apprehended for their debts. The Verge becomes central to an understanding of Billy Booth's actions, rendering him essentially inactive six days of the week. The novel's plot, like Booth, revives every Sunday, "that happy Day" (176), "that one Day in seven" when he is able "to taste the fresh Air" (194), "that Day of the Week in which all Parts of Town are indifferent" (229), when the hero is allowed to act outside his circumscribed space. By calling attention to the Verge rhetorically, employing periphrastic tags to remind the reader of Booth's constant spatial and temporal predicament, Fielding emphasizes the significance of Booth's London map. While his own movements are reduced, the unhallowed grounds, places like Vauxhall and Ranelagh Gardens, become particularly threatening as locations outside of his power, places where Amelia is subject to seduction and insult. It takes the divine intervention of the unsatisfying Dr. Harrison to release the Booths from a life of dreary containment as Billy moves almost mechanically from one carcereal space to another, substituting his rooms at Newgate for his rooms in Spring Garden for his accommodations at the sponging house in Gray's Inn Road.

Amelia ends happily, with a little help from her friends, Dr. Harrison and the "Waves of the Mob," five thousand strong— "for no less Number were assembled in a very few Minutes" (520). This final scene of liberation unexpectedly resolves a plot which has depended until this moment upon inexorable limitations. It takes divine intervention and the mobile, vulgar power of Londoners demanding justice in the streets, a mob soberly attended to by a "Magistrate just sitting down to his Dinner" (521). It is particularly noteworthy that Fielding, a Magistrate famous for reading the riot act,[15] allows in this scene a certain legitimacy to the rough justice he is sworn to resist. His resolution tempers the overwhelming pessimism of *Amelia* while it complicates our own understanding of the limits of the topography he is surveying.

Both Richardson and Fielding provide their readers with maps of a city that remains almost too large and complicated to be comprehended. Rocque's map, Richardson's *Clarissa*, and Fielding's *Amelia* are all projects motivated by a faith in the efficacy of social and empirical structures. If you apply a large enough scale, if you provide a large enough grid, if you accumulate enough realistic detail, perhaps you will be able to approach a version of truth. *Amelia*, like *Clarissa*, leaves us with bleak reminders of the city's power. We are also left with John Rocque, whose own street cannot be found anywhere on the map. He seems to disappear entirely from his own project for the most mundane and critical of reasons, the sort of financial strain that put Billy Booth into the Verge and Clarissa into the sponging house. It may be argued that what is ultimately charted in these cultural productions is the power of financial institutions and the cost of the bourgeois project. But then we are left with Fielding's almost breathless invocation of the mob interrupting the justice's dinner: Pope's "wretches hang, that jurymen may dine." Fielding offers a more open system of justice, as long as he is dispensing it, and we may take heart in his vision, as long as we forget his opening chapters illustrating so harshly "the Excellency of the English Constitution" administered by the likes of Justice Thrasher. It all depends where we choose to do our hardest, most critical reading; we critics are more interested in the baggy inconsistencies of Fielding's last "masterpiece" than in the architectonic delights of the more symmetrically pleasing *Tom Jones*. And it matters which story we choose to tell.

Notes

1. William Epstein, in "Counter-Intelligence: Cold War Criticism and Eighteenth-Century Studies," *ELH*, 57 (Spring 1990): 63–99, argues that in the "cryptographic" criticism practiced by the academy in the fifties and sixties, the historical was often suppressed in arguments that depended upon critical reconstructions of social and literary acts. Thus Maynard Mack's "persona" theory allowed the critic to ascribe an assumed identity to the nominal speaker of a literary work, virtually guaranteeing that the historical implications of the "speaker/maker" of the work could be revised, disregarded or recuperated.

2. Maynard Mack, "The Muse of Satire," *Yale Review* 41 (1951): 80–92; and *The Garden and the City: Retirement and Politics in the Later Poetry of Pope* (Toronto: University of Toronto Press, 1969).

3. Henry Fielding, *Amelia*, ed. Martin C. Battestin (Middletown, Conn.: Wesleyan University Press, 1983). See pages 15–16, 31, 37, 70, and 87 for some examples of Battestin's self-referential footnotes. All citations for *Amelia* come from this edition.

4. George A. Starr, *Defoe and Spiritual Autobiography* (Princeton: Princeton University Press, 1965), and J. Paul Hunter, *The Reluctant Pilgrim: Defoe's Emblematic Method and Quest for Form in Robinson Crusoe* (Baltimore: John Hopkins University Press, 1966). Dorothy Van Ghent, *The English Novel: Form and Function* (New York: Rinehart Press, 1953).

5. Henry Fielding, *The History of Tom Jones, A Foundling*, ed. Fredson Bowers, with an introduction and commentary by Martin C. Battestin (Middletown, Conn.: Wesleyan University Press, 1975): "Of THE SERIOUS in writing; and for what Purpose it is introduced," 5:1, 209–215.

6. Martin C. Battestin with Ruthe R. Battestin, *Henry Fielding: A Life* (London and New York: Routledge Press, 1989), 515.

7. Peter Linebaugh, *The London Hanged: Crime and Civil Society in the Eighteenth Century* (London: Penguin, 1991).

8. *Place/Culture/Representation*, ed. James Duncan and David Ley (London and New York, Routledge Press, 1993), 37–38.

9. David H. Richter reports as a sign of a "devastating trend," that "the 421 books and articles [written between 1981–90] contain a high and growing proportion of items on Fielding's work as a playwright and as a political journalist." (1)

10. *The A to Z of Georgian London*, ed. Ralph Hyde (London: London Topographical Society, 1982), iv, vii.

11. See Edward W. Soja, *Postmodern Geographies: the Reassertion of Space in Critical Social Theory* (London and New York: Verso Press,

1994), and Derek Gregory, *Geographical Imaginations* (Cambridge and Oxford: Blackwell Press, 1994), for recent applications of the theory of Michel Foucault and Henri Lefebvre on the social implications of spatial relations in the early modern city.

12. *A to Z*, pp. vi–vii.

13. See Matthew H. Edney's discussion of the Enlightenment cartographical project in "Cartography without Progress: Reinterpreting the Nature and Historical Development of Mapmaking," *Cartographica* 30:2–3 (Summer/Autumn 1993): 54–68.

14. See Edward Copeland, "Remapping London: Clarissa and the Woman in the Window," *Samuel Richardson: Tercentenary Essays*, ed. Margaret Doody and Peter Sabor (Cambridge: Cambridge University Press, 1989), 51–69, for his demonstration of the ways that "the map of London, its public landmarks, its churches, inns, and parks, the business of its streets" seem to give the option of freedom to Clarissa, p. 68.

15. Fielding defends himself against critics of his actions against the mob in *A True State of the Case of Bosavern Penlez*, 1749.

Carol Houlihan Flynn is Professor of English and Director of American Studies at Tufts University. She is currently working on a book that will look at the ways that people became urban in eighteenth-century London. Its working title is *Walking the Urban Walk: Learning Urbanity in Eighteenth-Century London*.

Jonathan Wild and True Crime Fiction

David H. Richter

One of the persistent and most interesting intertextual relationships between history and literature occurs in the borderland occupied by true crime fiction. This subgenre of narrative about crime and punishment falls in between historical narratives of actual crimes (such as we find in the *Notable British Trials* series) and entirely fictional narratives of invented crimes. In true crime fiction, the names, the precise circumstances, and the motivations may have been altered, but not out of recognition, and can easily be traced back to real and recognizable versions of events that have appeared in pamphlets, broadsides or the newspapers. But the author's interest clearly lies elsewhere than in reconstructing as closely as possible the crime as an historical event. This feature serves to differentiate crime fiction from the "faction" narrative which seems to have begun with Truman Capote's *In Cold Blood* and continued with Norman Mailer's *Executioner's Song.* Murder here is not a fine art in itself, as De Quincey once taught us, but the stimulus to a different sort of fine art.

This borderland is inhabited by nineteenth-century novels like Wilkie Collins's *The Woman in White* or Fyodor Dostoevsky's *The Idiot*; in the twentieth century examples are legion, from Alain Robbe-Grillet's *Le voyeur* to Peter Ackroyd's *Hawksmoor.* The authors' motives for writing such texts can vary enormously. Very occasionally a true crime writer will "novelize" a case to cope with the inadequacy of the available factual record, as when F. Tennyson Jesse tried to understand an otherwise incomprehensible murder by recreating the principals with the psychological density of fictional characters, as she did with the Thompson-Bywater case in *A Pin to See the Peep-Show.* As with Fielding's

Jonathan Wild, the primary motivation may be political satire; or as in the case of Aldous Huxley, a homicide that had been given an unsatisfying "shape" by real life (the Harold Greenwood trial of 1920, in which a solicitor accused of poisoning his wife was acquitted) could be awarded a richer pathos and depth under depth of irony as "The Gioconda Smile." Most often the texts are generated by a vector sum of two forms of ideology: the ideology of crime—the social awareness at a given time of how people come to break the law and bring themselves within range of its penalties—and the aesthetic ideology of fiction, the social construction of what at a given time makes a good story.

One reason *Jonathan Wild* is such a challenge to this project is that, with the modern and contemporary fiction on which I have already written, the landscape is crowded with available models of crime fiction and true crime narrative to which the borderland text is forced to assimilate itself. In the period in which Wild's crimes were committed and Fielding's novel is set, however, the relationship between history and fiction is itself deeply unsettled, and the novel itself, the canonical form that will rise by the mid-nineteenth century to the pinnacle in the ordering of the arts, is hardly under way. Martin Battestin posits that *Jonathan Wild*, first published in 1743 with the *Miscellanies*, a year after *Joseph Andrews*, was actually written no later than the spring of 1740; if so, it was Fielding's first extended attempt at prose fiction. Most important, it was shaped before Richardson's *Pamela* had taught Fielding what he needed to know about constructing within a fiction a seemingly autonomous narrative world.[1] By comparison with the novel, the factual literature of crime was well developed.[2] As recent researchers from Richetti to Faller have shown, criminal biography was one of the major popular genres of Augustan England, which had developed rich and complex literary conventions of its own,[3] and which was one of the popular forms that led directly, according to Lennard Davis, to the development of the novel itself.[4]

Famous criminals generated catchpenny pamphlets and Wild, the most reviled criminal Augustan England produced, was no exception.[5] Within a few months of the execution of Jonathan Wild on 24 May 1725, literally dozens of journalistic accounts of his life and death had been published. While I cannot claim to have seen all of them, one is struck by the way the peculiar career of

Jonathan Wild created difficulties for the journalist in reconciling the facts of that career to the Augustan ideology of crime.[6]

The usual "famous criminal" memorialized by Tyburn journalism was a thief or highwayman born in poverty, shaping a brief career as an adventurous spirit, run down by the law, perhaps escaping several times from prison like the legendary Jack Sheppard, until he was finally strung up on the gallows, still in his youth, with a sympathetic crowd in attendance. As John Richetti says in his study of early eighteenth-century narrative patterns, "highwaymen . . . are heroes in that their stories are gratifying fantasies of freedom—moral, economic and erotic. . . . The criminal's end provides further gratification and completes the myth as he suffers for the guilty power and independence which he and his readers have desired and enjoyed."[7] The ultimate moral too was very clear: irresponsibility or idleness leads to a life of crime;[8] crime does not pay; honesty is the best policy. The problem is that Wild's career was so very different that it wasn't clear at all what its moral was. It was therefore more disturbing and more disruptive to those who would turn it into a standard narrative pattern.

As Gerald Howson has described it, Wild's system involved making money in two different ways. On the one hand, merchandise that was stolen by a thief, or a gang of thieves, could be melted down, otherwise altered, and turned into specie abroad by his factor, Roger Johnson, or alternatively, particularly in the case of securities and articles of sentimental value, it could be returned to its rightful owner for a consideration through the "lost property" office Wild ran out of his house in the Little Old Bailey. On the other hand Wild shared in the government rewards of £40 for each thief that he captured, for whom he could provide courtroom evidence resulting in condemnation.[9] By the first sources of income, Wild was in effect a crook; by the last, he was in effect a combination of policeman and district attorney.

Yet the two sides of the system were not separable: they were inextricably linked. It was Wild's encyclopedic knowledge of London crime, his ability to know who had probably taken an article based on what sort of article it was and where it was taken, which came from the way he had organized the gangs of thieves and footpads into districts and venues, and his understanding of the criminals and their women, their friends, their associations, that made him so incredibly dangerous a thieftaker. But it was precisely Wild's dangerousness as a thieftaker—including his corruption of tame judges of sessions—that made the London gangs willing to allow him to organize them and prescribe the venues of their operations, to return some bits of booty for the reward and export other bits to Holland. Those gangs who insisted on independence, who refused to work for the portion of the take Wild allowed them, were quickly destroyed and the members taken, tried, and hanged or transported. It was a totalized system in which the more Wild knew, the more power he had, and the more power Wild acquired, the more money he made, and the more money he made, the more power and knowledge he was able to acquire.

In this totalized system of Wild's the London middle class and gentry had become complicit[10] and for the usual reason: by its very nature regulated crime is more predictable and easier to deal with than unregulated crime. In Wild's London the victim of a theft had a very fair chance of seeing the goods returned for a reasonable charge, perhaps twenty percent of its replacement value, if the crime was committed by one of Wild's gangs, and of seeing the rogue hanged if it was committed by an independent. Propertyowners were in effect better off in Wild's heyday than they had been under his clumsier predecessor in corruption and thieftaking, the London Under-Marshal Charles Hitchen.[11] Those who administered the system of justice could point to what looked like extraordinary efficiency, comparatively speaking, in arresting and convicting serious criminals. The law had to be complicit in more serious ways than the ordinary citizens: Wild's thieftaking required a number of tame magistrates, who were undoubtedly paid well for their cooperation. And when Wild finally fell, theft in London continued, though it did dramatically cut the number of thieves who were tried and convicted (Howson, 253).

The massive social complicity in the system Wild had devised made it hard to draw the usual set of morals from the facts of his career. This, at least, is how I read a great deal of the "factual" journalism that followed on Wild's execution. Far more than in the usual Tyburn journalism, the authors seem to be straining to find the usual things to say. One way of handling the problem was to distort the facts so that the usual things could be said: to misrepresent what it was that Wild had done or had been punished for, in such a way as to bring his case into the scope of the contemporary ideology of crime. Another was to find a moral in his downfall by any available means, by main force if necessary.[12]

The journalism of the time has such loose standards of factual accuracy that one is forced to guess without much grounds for precision which misstatements are mere inadvertencies and which ones are done with malice aforethought, but one has to assume that truly pointless errors are made in all innocence. The pamphlet *Weighley, alias Wild*, for example, has Wild executed on 1 June rather than 24 May, the previous Monday, probably on the erroneous assumption that condemned criminals had a minimum of two weeks to repent after the death warrant came down. Similarly, Alexander Smith reports that Wild was apprenticed to a trunkmaker rather than a bucklemaker as most other sources seem to agree.[13]

It is less clear, though, that Alexander Smith's report of Wild's trial has no ideological motive in misreporting what Wild was condemned for:

> About this Time, *Thomas Butler*, who had been formerly convicted for Robbing a Person at the *Feathers* Tavern in *Cheapside*, and who had been again lately taken up in *London*, and committed to *Newgate*, for privately stealing about fifty Guineas from a Widow Goldsmith at *Winchester*, obtained his Majesty's most gracious Pardon for the last Offence, and gave Bail on *Saturday* the 27th of *February* 1724–5, to plead to the same. This *Butler* made a long Information against *Wild*, charging him, among many other Crimes, with having seen in his Custody a Pocketbook, which had been stolen from a Corn-Chandler in *Gilt-Spur-Street*, and that *Wild* did commit the same to the Flames: So that these, and other Matters, being laid to his Charge when he came upon his Tryal, the Jury found him Guilty of the Indictment, and he was justly Condemned for the same.[14]

What do "these and other Matters" refer to? Smith's report manages to suggest that Wild was merely a common thief by associating him with his accuser Butler, whose larcenous misdeeds are represented in detail; it mystifies us by the implication that Wild had become so irrational as to burn up his booty. But having in one's custody a stolen pocketbook was not a capital crime,[15] and it was not at all what Wild was condemned for:[16] he was sentenced to death under sections five and six of the 1719 "Transportation Act" for having taken £10 reward after returning £50 worth of lace stolen from Catherine Stetham, a Holborn dealer.

Weighley, alias Wild also attempts to turn Wild into a mere common thief: In this narrative, Wild begins his career as a sneak thief in his native Wolverhampton, where he robs a visiting "chapman" of "two gold watches and a considerable sum of money" (33). This occasions his flight to London, where

> when Stock run low, he took a trip into the Country, to make a Visit to some Honest Money'd Man, whether Gentleman, or Tradesman, and that he was obliged to wait their Leisure, and his own Opportunity. This Course of Life he followed a considerable time undiscovered, until he happen'd to rob Sir Joseph Jekil, at that instant an eminent Councel, and a Gentleman of Interest and Fortune; for this Robbery he was Apprehended, Committed, and Convicted, March 1704–5; but Pardon'd by the Intercession of Friends, and May 1705 pleaded to a Special Pardon, and got his Liberty. [35–36]

This episode seems to be made out of whole cloth: no evidence for it exists in the Public Record Office. The record shows no brush of Wild with the law before 1709, when he was imprisoned for debt in the Wood Street Compter. That was where he met his second wife, Mary Molineux (usually misspelled Milliner) with whom he began his career as the second party at the game of "buttock and twang."[17]

If Howson is correct, Wild in fact was an extraordinarily cautious criminal, who deftly managed to inveigle others into criminal activities rather than acting himself. Even as "twang" Wild committed only misdemeanours, though the female thief herself was liable to capital penalties. The journalists' misrepresentations of Wild suggest to the contrary that he had done himself what most of those had done who suffered at Tyburn, at some time or other, regardless of what act a London jury had condemned him for.

Weighley, alias Wild's most suspicious alteration is in Wild's commencement of his major career. N. P. proposes that, after Wild's fictitious brush with the gallows following the robbery of "Sir Joseph Jekil,"

> Jonathan . . . hir'd a small House and kept a Brandy-shop; whither he invited the Brothers of the Quill. Those Gentleman of Fortune are willing to embrace any offer, where they may be private, and therefore frequented his House. He had a pretty good Trade; because where-ever they come, they Drink plentifully, and value not their Money, provided they can have the good Opiniovn of their

> Landlord; so they flock'd to him; and whatever they stole, that was valuable, they gave him the first offer: He bought the richest and best at low Prices, and left the Rest to their own disposal. By these indirect Means he got Money, and such an universal Acquaintance among the Thieves, that there was scarce a Robbery, but he immediately had Information of the Fact, the Time, and the Persons that committed it. . . . (36)

The way Wild learned his trade was not as the independent owner of a dramshop frequented by criminals; Wild had been under-lieutenant to Charles Hitchen, the Second Marshal of London, whose operations as both fence and thieftaker were tolerated until the crudity with which he blackmailed thieves and returned stolen property for a price became an embarrassment to the London judicial administration, and he was suspended in his post. *Weighley* thus prevaricates about the most embarrassing aspect of Wild's career: that the secret of his success was that he had in effect privatized thieftaking by doing with efficiency and style what his more gently born predecessor had done clumsily and vulgarly.

Weighley is in fact a massive tissue of fantasy from beginning to end,[18] and most of N. P.'s stories are not innocent of implication at all. *Weighley* begins with an elaborate discussion of Wild's years as an apprentice to a Wolverhampton bucklemaker, and the stories are designed both to present an etiology of the criminal and to serve as a warning to youth. Wild begins as an industrious apprentice to a master bucklemaker, his master is noble and good and, when Wild falls in love with a local widow with a bit of capital, he spends his own capital so that a marriage can take place. All goes well until the "fatal glass of beer":

> After they were marry'd, [Jonathan] liv'd with her in Unity and Friendship; he set up for himself, wrought hard, and liv'd in good Repute; 'till one Day he met some of his old Acquaintance, and People of a slender Character, with those he associates; and Jonathan being naturally prone to Vice, they pervert his Principles, and byas'd his Inclinations; they met often, sate long, and spent profusely; and if Wild at any time wanted to go Home to his Family, would scornfully reply, Thank God I have no Wife to follow me to an Ale-house; that I can say, I am Master of my self, and am not afraid of a brawling Daughter of Eve. . . . (31)

Stung in his pride, Jonathan adopts the idle habits of his companions and begins the familiar rhetorical path later etched by Hogarth that leads downward, ultimately to Tyburn.

But even the more factually responsible histories of Wild had trouble deciding what the moral of his career was. Indeed, one contemporary biography basically decided that there wasn't any moral to it. This was H. D.'s *Life of Jonathan Wild from His Birth to His Death*, originally published by Applebee in 1725. While it might be going too far to say that he is sympathetic to Wild's purposes, H. D. is clearly taken with Wild's immense personal zest and vitality and deeply impressed by his craft and cunning and by the machiavellian subtlety of his operations. Some of the narrative episodes, the story of Wild's collaboration with the female quack, the story of the Queen Square house emptied of its furniture and fixtures by a confederate of Wild's, or that of the amateur campanologists fleeced out of £300, are told with the moral ambiguity of a Hollywood caper flick, where we sympathize in spite of our bourgeois sensibilities with the cleverness of the rogue as he foils the helplessly inadequate dupes. The only place where H. D. seems to judge Wild, he judges him a damned fool: the occasion is over returning Mrs. Stetham's lace after his arrest and incarceration: to have contravened the "Jonathan Wild Act" whilst in Newgate, H. D. supposes, can be only the imprudence of a madman, and he quotes the Latin proverb *Quem Iupiter vult perdere prius dementat* (68). There *is* a final bit of italicized moralizing that, after a seventy-page narrative, seems completely perfunctory:

> We shall conclude with observing that whoever had seen him in the Gaiety of his Life, when all his Rogueries were successful; and had also been witness of his deplorable State of Mind after his Condemnation, might have drawn a Lesson of Morality from it, which might have been of use to an Atheist. I say to have seen one remarkable for the Gaiety of his Temper, for a vast Depth of Cunning, as well as Hardness and personal Courage, so chang'd at the Apprehensions of his approaching Death, and the great Account which is to follow; to have seen him under the greatest Distractions and Horrors of Mind, that human Nature is capable of suffering, wou'd be convinc'd, that *Virtue only can give true Tranquillity, and nothing can support a Man against the Terrors of Death but a good Conscience*. (70–71)

H. D.'s biography of Wild is unique in its amoral attitude to its subject, but an insistent question, given the inchoate state of the genres of narrative at the time, is whether it is to be read as a factual biography at all. On the one hand, H. D. gets the basic sequence of Wild's career right, and the episodes that can be checked against the factual record (such as Wild's vow to bring the murderers of Mary Knap to justice) do check out. On the basis of this, Gerald Howson is willing to authenticate the H. D. life as essentially reliable—and he may indeed be right. But on the other hand it troubles me that the vast majority of H. D.'s stories cannot be checked out, and read like generic examples of the art of the thief (such as Defoe had collected in *Moll Flanders*), or as what I suppose are mere fantasies, like the notion that Wild planned to go into the theft insurance business after the passage of the Transportation Act.

Many of the stories that apply only to Wild's career seem to be universalized into fictions. The most wonderfully told is the story of the broken cheesemonger whom Wild recruits from the debtors' haven of the Southwark Mint, turns into a highwayman, then pursues when he defects from his organization and murders in cold blood, picking his pockets of fifty guineas and sending the local magistrate's men to pick up the dead body. But its narrative detail is sometimes full, sometimes strangely lacking (the cheesemonger is not even named), and some of the details could have come only from the cheesemonger, others only from Wild. Both from its substance (it is the archetypal Wild story about his double-crossing his partners in crime) and from its manner of representation, the narrative reads as a plausible fiction.[19] My own reading of the H. D. pamphlet is that it is a strange amalgam of truth and fiction, a combination of reportage and invention based on an authentic core of Wild's career, alternating actions Wild actually performed with stories of bold confidence games that he or his confederates *might* have enacted that could be plausibly joined to his legend by accretion.

The most accurate of the Tyburn biographies, Defoe's *Life and Actions*, is also the most sophisticated about Wild's career. Defoe seems to admire, in spite of himself, Wild's business acumen, the way his indirect mode of operation circumvented the law against both theft and receiving stolen goods. After describing a hypothetical case in which Wild encourages a thief to return to its owner, for a fee, a piece of stolen merchandise, Defoe asks:

> What can Jonathan be charged with in such an affair as this? I must confess I do not see it; no, nor if the thief sends him a present of

> four or five guineas out of the money. . . . Nor . . . does the treating for delivering the goods . . . give any room to fix anything on Jonathan. . . . Indeed, I do not see why he might not have carried on such a commerce as this with the greatest ease, I do not say honesty, in the world, if he had gone no farther . . . (258).

Defoe argues that by later taking a more active role, by "impudently taking the goods of the thief, sending the porter himself, taking the money, and then capitulating with the thief for such a part of the reward," Wild made himself liable to punishment; "so that, in a word, Jonathan's avarice hanged him" (259). Defoe also comments on the perverse effect the passage of the "Jonathan Wild Act" (part of the Transportation Act: 6 George I c. 23 §5 and §6) has on Wild's business:

> This Act was so directly aimed at Jonathan's general practice, that he could not be ignorant enough to see it; but lest he should, a certain honourable person, too just to favour him, and yet too human not to warn him of the danger that he might avoid it, gave him notice that this very Act was made against his unlawful practice, and therefore in time warned him, in few but significant words, to take heed to himself, and avoid the consequence by leaving off the trade of thief-catching, as it is unjustly called—that is, of compounding for the return of stolen goods. But good advice to Jonathan Wild was like talking gospel to a kettle-drum, bidding a dragoon not to plunder, or talking of compassion to a hussar: he that was hardened above the baseness of all cautionary fear, scorned the advice, and went on in his wicked trade; not warily and wisely as he had formerly done, but in short with more impudence and shameless boldness than ever, as if he despised laws and the governors, and the provoked justice of the nation . . . He now not only took rewards for returning goods stolen, but even directed the stealing of them; and making himself a party to the very robberies themselves, acted a part of the thief and the receiver also. . . . But one felony being fully proved was sufficient and upon a full hearing he was convicted in so evident a manner, that he really had nothing to say on his own behalf. . . . (266–67)

Defoe is seeking a set of standard morals: "love of money is the root of all evil"; "the first step into crime eases all the rest"; "the pitcher goes too often to the well"; "the hardened criminal is deaf to the voice of Providence." But the portrait isn't just: Howson gives no indication that Wild became a bolder crook than when he began his operation, nor that the offense for which he was condemned was one in which he dealt with conspicuous avarice or carelessness. Defoe's own narrative confirms that Wild was eminently cautious right to the last: his prosecutor, Mrs. Catherine Stetham, testified that, having paid the £10 to a hired porter with no provable connection to Wild after he returned her £50 worth of lace, she afterwards asked Wild, lying under arrest in Newgate,

> 'What must you have for your trouble?' 'Not a farthing,' says he, 'not a farthing for me. . . . As for the piece of lace that is missing, I hope to get it for you ere long, and I don't know but I may help you not only to your money again but to the thief too . . . And as you are a good woman and a widow and a Christian, I desire nothing of you but your prayers, and for them I shall be thankful. I have a great many enemies, and God knows what may be the consequence of this imprisonment.' (270–71).

Defoe's immediate commentary, "this is a black story indeed," seems smoke without fire.[20]

But the main source of moral confusion here is over the dating of the Jonathan Wild Act. Defoe's presentation of the way Wild ignored the timely warning of the "honourable person"[21] suggests strongly that Wild's 1725 prosecution followed directly on the passage of the Act. But this was not so: the Act had been passed in 1719, so that Wild was not prosecuted under it for another six years—in fact during most of his career as self-styled Thieftaker General he operated under the law designed to put him out of business, a law that was treated almost entirely as a dead letter until the day Wild was prosecuted under it.[22]

The other area where Defoe lets out all the moral stops is in accusing Wild of being an even more horrid version of Dickens's Fagin *avant de la lettre*:

> I have several stories . . . of children thus strolling about the streets in misery and poverty, whom he has taken in on pretence of providing for them, and employing them, and all has ended in this, viz., making rogues of them. Horrid wickedness! His charity has been to breed them up to be thieves; and still more horrid! several of these, his own foster-children, he has himself caused afterwards to be apprehended and hanged for the very crimes which he first taught them to commit. . . . To see him take up an unthinking youth in the street, covered with dirt and rags, and willing on any terms to get out of his misery; to see this superlative wretch pretend charity to

> the child, and tell him he will provide for him, and thereby engage the lad to him as a gentleman that intends to do him good, and then, instead of providing for him, lead him by the hand to hell-gates, and after that, like a true devil, thrust him in! First to attempt and then accuse, which is the very nature of the devil; first to make some poor desolate vagabond boys thieves and then betray them to the gallows! Who can think of such a thing without a just abhorrence? who can think it to be any less than the worst sort of murder? Such was the life and practices of this wretched man. . . . (267–68)

It is possible to wonder if Defoe is here on strong factual ground. Despite Wild's having made public a list of those he had brought to justice, Defoe does not go on to detail as betrayed protégés any of the hanged thieves from that list except Joseph Blake ("Blueskin"), who does not fit the picture very well. It is true that Blake at one time worked with Wild, then rebelled against his rule, after which Wild took all possible steps to destroy him. But Blueskin—who tried to cut Wild's throat with a blunt penknife at the assizes—had by no means been introduced to crime by Wild.[23] But leaving aside the truth of Defoe's specific accusation,[24] what of its motives? What would Defoe's audience of respectable tradesman think about thieftaking?

For the London mob, Wild's thieftaking activities were probably the reason he was the most detested criminal of his time, why he was pelted with rocks all the way to Tyburn. For reasons that are made clear in *Albion's Fatal Tree*, *The London Hanged*, and other sociological sources, working-class Londoners felt that the victims of Augustan justice were their class brethren rather than their social enemies, and were apt to be sympathetic to almost any but the most brutal of criminals.[25] Conversely, Wild, as the man who had caused dozens of proletarian thieves to swing at Tyburn, was a class enemy to the London mob, even though as a bucklemaking son of a provincial carpenter he was of the same class as themselves. But the tradesmen who made up Defoe's audience were unlikely to be sympathetic to thieves and gangsters, and more likely to favor those who brought them to justice. Hence Defoe's story about Wild as Fagin, which presents him as a an enemy to the values of the middle class: as a false and conniving master who exploits his apprentices instead of behaving as he should, in loco parentis. . . .

Thus the contemporary "factual" narratives about Wild strain against their own conventions and ideology, seeking a way of accommodating the sort of criminal he actually was. By contrast, the two canonical representations of Wild that are explicitly fictional, which not only neglect but intentionally distort the factual details of his life and death, seem to understand better the nature of the beast, the way he had "regulated" crime in London during his heyday. I shall be able to comment only very briefly here on *The Beggar's Opera*, by John Gay, and on Fielding's *Jonathan Wild*.

If what was unique about Wild's career was the totalization of his dual role as crook and crook-catcher, it comes out in the very first line of *The Beggar's Opera*:[26]

> PEACHUM: A Lawyer is an honest employment, as is mine. Like me too he acts in a double capacity, both against Rogues and for 'em; for 'tis fitting that we should protect and encourage Cheats, since we live by 'em. (1.1.488)

Like Wild, Peachum goes through his list of thieves, marking some of the lazier rogues down for death for the sake of the £40 reward, others more industrious to be gotten off by perjured witnesses for the sake of further gain. But the key to Gay's understanding comes in the scene between Peachum and his "brother" Lockit, the turnkey of Newgate:

> LOCKIT: In this last affair, brother Peachum, we are agreed. You have consented to go halves in MacHeath.
> PEACHUM: We shall never fall out about an execution.—But as to that article, pray how stands our last year's account?
> LOCKIT: If you will run your eye over it, you'll find that 'tis fair and clearly stated.
> PEACHUM: This long arrear of the government is very hard upon us! Can it be expected that we should hang our acquaintance for nothing, when our betters will hardly save theirs without being paid for it? Unless the people in employment pay better, I promise them for the future, I shall let other rogues live besides their own.
> LOCKIT: Perhaps, brother, they are afraid these matters may be carried too far. We are treated too by them with contempt, as if our profession were not reputable.
> PEACHUM: In one respect indeed, our employment may be reckoned dishonest, because, like great Statesmen, we encourage those who betray their friends.
> LOCKIT: Such language, brother, any where else, might turn to your prejudice. Learn to be more guarded, I beg you.

> When you censure the Age
> Be cautious and sage,
> Lest the courtiers offended should be:
> If you mention vice or bribe,
> 'Tis so pat to all the tribe;
> Each cries—That was levell'd at me. (2.10.510–11)

The first night audience of 1729 stared up at Sir Robert Walpole's box in the theater when Lockit's ballad was sung because, as every viewer of *The Beggar's Opera* realized, Peachum and Lockit were not only Jonathan Wild and Spurling the governor of Newgate, but Walpole and his partner Lord Townshend going over the patronage rosters,[27] and that the operations of Wild's establishment in the Little Old Bailey were parallel with those of Walpole in Whitehall.[28] Was there much to choose, Gay in effect was asking, between Wild's totalized control over crime and the totalized system that Walpole had established, whereby his exclusive control over court patronage and its rich emoluments could be turned into the power of the first genuine prime minister England had known, while loyalty to the government was assured by the money and influence Walpole could bring against dissenters and opposition? For both Walpole and Wild, power could be turned into money, which could be used to secure more power.

In Fielding's novel, the process of abstraction of character into ideology goes even farther.[29] Here Fielding is explicit that he is not presenting a factually accurate biography of Jonathan Wild, who, we need to remember, was executed when Fielding was a teenager. "My design," Fielding argued in the preface to the *Miscellanies*, "is not to enter the lists with that excellent historian who from authentic papers and records, &c. hath already given so satisfactory account of the life and actions of this great man. . . . My narrative is rather of such actions which he might have performed, or would, or should have performed, than what he really did; and may, in reality, as well suit any other such great man, as the person himself whose name it bears."[30] As Lennard Davis put it, Fielding "is . . . different [from the earlier crime reporters] because he both admits his work is fictional and yet seems to be speaking about public events more openly than most earlier novelists."[31] My own take is that, as a good Aristotelian, Fielding creates a representation of the "Great Man" as "Prig," a person to whom other persons are not ends in themselves but means to his own enrichment, pleasure and advancement, in order to give us an anatomy of Priggism that will implicitly contain a sense of the entire political process, in which great men rise, struggle with one another, and fall.

Like Gay, Fielding presents Wild as using the law from both directions: exercising power on thieves by virtue of his connections with the court of the Old Bailey and imposing on the law-abiding public by virtue of his power over thieves. This seems one function of the deliciously overcomplicated episode of Heartfree's banknote (Book Two, chapter five), which is stolen by Wild's accomplices; the theft is blamed on a dupe in Wild's gang named Thomas Fierce, whom Wild assures he will get off at his trial, all the while conspiring with the actual thieves, Straddle and Sly, to get Fierce hanged; the entire charade is, of course, part of a larger scheme to keep Heartfree's trust so that he can defraud, cheat, and bring Heartfree himself ultimately to Tyburn. Fielding sums up the performance as the way "GREAT" men "know how to play with the Passions" of others, "to set them at Variance with each other, and to work his own Purposes out of those Jealousies and Apprehensions . . . by Means of those Arts which the Vulgar call Treachery, Dissembling, Promising, Lying, Falshood, &c., but which are by GREAT MEN summed up in the collective Name of Policy, or Politicks, or rather *Pollitricks*. . . ." (78).

By the end of the novel, however, Fielding lets the allegorical identification of Wild with Walpole slide away. Intentionally, it would seem, for it would have been easy to have rewritten the messy episode of Book Four, chapter three, in which Wild displaces Roger Johnson,[32] the previous chieftain of the Newgate prigs, to create a consistent allegory.[33] The fact is that by this point it no longer matters very much which "GREAT MAN" is running the show. The Newgate election chapter underscores what the "chapter of hats" had earlier hinted at: that politics is a totalized mechanism, in which power is turned into money, which can be reconverted back into power, rather than a clash of principles that could matter to the world at large. Fielding's representation of the Newgate Debtors, the outsiders who have nothing to gain or lose by a change in governance among the place-hunting prigs, passionately taking sides in the squabble and ranging themselves on Johnson's side or on Wild's, becomes a savage indictment of the folly of the public who wanted to believe that the fall of Walpole could mean an end to the system of public corruption he had perfected.

Fielding knew that thieftaking too went on long after the London mob had exulted at the sight of Jonathan Wild dangling in a noose. Once it had been systematized, priggism continued with different, rather less efficient beneficiaries, until Fielding in 1751, now a barrister and a judge, proposed in one of his last official acts (in *An Enquiry into the Causes of the late Increases in Robbers*) a system of undercover police to contain it. These were the Bow Street Runners, a countersystem put into practice by his blind half-brother Sir John Fielding, and the ancestor of Scotland Yard. Fielding died before the system could be established, and was long dead when in 1816, six of his official Bow Street thieftakers were hanged for conspiring to take thieves' booty in order to sell it while using their police power to frame the innocent, in a scheme worthy of Jonathan Wild himself.[34] Fielding would have been morally outraged, of course, but I suspect that the irony would not have been lost on him.

Notes

1. On the dating of *Jonathan Wild*, see Martin C. Battestin with Ruthe R. Battestin, *Henry Fielding: A Life* (London and New York: Routledge, 1991): 281–2. On the curiously unnovelistic quality of *Jonathan Wild* explained by its creation before Fielding read *Pamela*, see Ralph W. Rader, "The Emergence of the Novel in England: Genre in History vs. History of Genre," *Narrative* 1 (January 1993): 69–83.

2. In this paper I am going to be differentiating between "fiction" and "factual literature" in a very rough-and-ready way. I am taking Fielding's *Jonathan Wild* as "fiction" despite the factuality of the protagonist, because of Fielding's explicitness about his manipulations of fact: as he says in the preface to the *Miscellanies* (1743), "my Design is not to enter the Lists with that excellent Historian [probably Defoe] who from authentic Papers and Records, &c. hath already given so satisfactory Account of the Life and Actions of this great man. . . . My narrative is rather of such Actions which he might have performed, or would, or should have performed, than what he really did; and may, in Reality, as well suit any other such great Man, as the Person himself whose Name it bears" (Henry Fielding, *The Life of Jonathan Wild the Great* (London: Basil Blackwell at the Shakespeare Head): 255. Similarly, Gay's *Beggar's Opera*—where Wild is represented as Peachum—is a dramatic fiction, not a chronicle play or docudrama. Not having made any independent attempt to verify or refute its narrative, I have accepted Gerald Howson's recent biography of Jonathan Wild as representing what is currently verified about Wild's life and criminal operations. This is hardly an absolute

standard of truth against which to measure the pamphlet literature—if, indeed, such a standard could exist. But it serves at least to demonstrate the discrepancies between two horizons: what our own age considers a plausible narrative about Wild, and what the narratives generated in his own day presented. See Gerald Howson, *It Takes a Thief: The Life and Times of Jonathan Wild* (London: Cresset, 1987).

3. See Lincoln Faller, *Turn'd to Account: The Functions and Forms of Criminal Biography in Late Seventeenth- and Early Eighteenth-Century England* (Cambridge: Cambridge University Press, 1987), and Ian Bell, *Literature and Crime in Augustan England* (New York and London: Routledge, 1991). See also the long introduction to Philip Rawlings, *Drunks, Whores and Idle Apprentices: Criminal Biographies of the Eighteenth Century.* (New York and London: Routledge, 1992).

4. Lennard Davis, *Factual Fictions: The Origins of the English Novel* (New York: Columbia University Press, 1983).

5. Most of the dozens of fugitive pieces are in the British Library and the Guildhall in London and were not available to me for this paper. I am basing these remarks on the following contemporary texts: Alexander Smith, *Memoirs of the Life and Times of the Famous Jonathan Wild* (London: Sam. Briscoe, 1726), reprinted in photocopy in the *Foundations of the Novel* Series (New York and London: Garland Publishing, 1973); *The Malefactor's Register or New Newgate and Tyburn Calendar* (London: Alex Hogg, 175?); N. P., *Weighley, alias Wild, a Poem in Imitation of Hudibras, to which is annex'd a more genuine and particular Account in Prose, than any yet publish'd, of the most remarkable Events, and Transactions of his Life, from the Time of his Birth to his Execution. Also Jonathan's last Farewel and Epitaph, with a Song, never before Printed* (London: J. Roberts, 1725); Daniel Defoe, *The Life and Actions of Jonathan Wild* (1725), reprinted in *The Works of Daniel Defoe*, ed. G. H. Maynadier (New York: George D. Sproul, 1905), 16:231–75; *The Life of Jonathan Wild, from his Birth to his Death . . .* by H. D., Clerk to Justice R——— (London: Thos. Warner, 1725; also reprinted in Ben Franklin's *New England Courant* for 9 October–18 December 1725); The *Weekly Journal* or *Saturday's Post* for 1725. *Mist's Weekly Journal* for 1725; The most accurate source of the day is *Select Trials at the Sessions House at the Old Bailey for Murder, Robberies, Rapes, Sodomy, Coining, Frauds, Bigamy, and other Offences, To which are added, Genuine Accounts of the Lives, Behaviour, Confessions and Dying Speeches of the most eminent Convicts*. 4 Vols. London: J. Applebee, 1742.

6. The difficulties of making clear what was unique about Wild appear also in the broadsheets that appeared after Wild's death. One rare woodcut in the New York Public Library that represents "The Several Degrees taken by Ionathan Wild; Pupils from their commencement, under his Tutorship to their final Promotion at Tybourn" clearly is engaged with the question of Wild as an employer and "tutor" of thieves. But the large plate containing seven smaller pictures would be read sequentially

as describing the basic career of the idle apprentice: a man is shown on trial, then being whipped at the cart's tail, then in the pillory, then aboard a transportation ship. Two more pictures show Wild in the condemned cell offering the Devil "forty or fifty more" in his place if he contrives Wild's escape and the devil insisting that "tis in vain" to take poison, for "they'll cure you first and hang you then." (Wild had attempted to anticipate the hangman by overdosing on laudanum.) The final cut shows a man, probably Wild, being turned off at Tyburn.

7. John J. Richetti, *Popular Fiction before Richardson: Narrative Patterns 1700–1739* (Oxford: Clarendon Press, 1969), 35.

8. In the case of the Waltham Blacks, hanged for murder in 1723, the Newgate Calendar moralized that "idleness must have been the great source of their lawless depredations. . . . No man, however successful in the profession, can expect to get as much profit by deer-stealing, as by following his lawful business" (73). The sequence of idleness leading to petty crime leading to murder is parodied in De Quincey, "If once a man indulges himself in murder, very soon he comes to think little of robbing, and from robbing he comes next to drinking and Sabbath-breaking, and from that to incivility and procrastination." In "On Murder Considered as One of the Fine Arts," in De Quincey's *Collected Writings*, 14 vols. (Edinburgh: A. and C. Black, 1889–1890), 13:56.

9. An extra £100 was added when the thief was caught within five miles of Temple Bar, so Wild's take was often as much as £140.

10. The chief disadvantage of organized crime is precisely the complicity it forces the law-abiding citizen into and the corruption it presumes and breeds in official quarters. Bernard de Mandeville's *Enquiry* reminded readers of the *British Journal* of the ancient crime of "theft-bote"—compounding a felony by paying a thief for return of his booty—and expressed his outrage at how London had become implicated in Wild's system. See Bernard de Mandeville, *An Enquiry into the Causes of the Frequent Executions at Tyburn* (London: J. Roberts, 1725) which had originally been published as articles in the *British Journal.*

11. Corruption was built into the process of justice in a number of ways exemplified by Hitchen's career. Justices and marshals were forced to pay for their offices, and expected to reimburse themselves through the fees of the justice system. While justices were paid for writs and warrants, the easiest way for a marshal to make money was to take booty from thieves in exchange for not prosecuting them, then turn the booty into specie by returning it, for a finder's fee, to the original owner. Wild began his career as a thieftaker in Hitchen's service; his innovation was to do suavely what Hitchen had done crudely, and to do as a private citizen what had previously been done, in the way of official corruption, by a government employee: to privatize thieftaking, as it were.

Hitchen survived Wild by only two years. In April 1727, he was arrested for sodomy in Covent Garden and spent a horrible two hours in the pillory, where he was brutally manhandled by the mob, whose motives may have had more to do with his career as a thieftaker than with homophobia. Hitchen survived the pillory and the six months' imprisonment in Newgate but died in poverty not long after his release.

12. I don't mean to suggest that Wild was in any way unique in having his life distorted by the Tyburn journalists. Lincoln Faller has chronicled the ways in which certain "myths" of the gallant highwayman, the violent crime within the family, and the brutal thief produced standardized narrative formats into which the procrustean journalist stuffed the facts at hand, fabricating factoids at will to jazz up the account. But the particular sort of criminal Wild had been was not one of the usual mythic categories, and challenged some of the contemporary ideas about crime and its nature. The result is a reshaping even more creative (or defensive) than is usual among the type characters Faller has studied.

13. *Weighley, alias Wild*, 48; Smith, 2.

14. Smith, 17.

15. It was no crime at all unless it could be proved one knew it was stolen.

16. Defoe's *Life and Actions of Jonathan Wild* refers to Mr. Tidman the corn-chandler's pocketbook as a further accusation the Recorder had up his sleeve to try Wild on if the Stetham prosecution had failed (271). So Smith's pocketbook is not mythical, just irrelevant to the actual criminal proceeding against Wild.

17. Or "whore and bully." The "buttock" would relieve the mark of his valuables, give a signal to her "twang," who would come and rough up the gentleman for long enough to allow the "buttock" to make her escape with the loot.

18. Howson gives N. P. credit for making up his own fantasies rather than copying those already in press (319).

19. If the story *is* an inside narrative, the fictionmaker providing inside views of the cheesemonger might not be H. D. but rather Wild himself.

Could the story be an inside narrative? In places, the narrator seems to be simultaneously an intimate of the London Recorder and of Wild. This would have been possible, if H. D. was, as he advertises, clerk to one of the Lords Chief Justice. The end of H. D.'s narrative has a genuine insider's note. He knows and tells what Wild was tried and hanged for, but to H. D., the real reason for Wild's fall (the First Cause of which is perfunctorily ascribed to Providence) was that, after the seizure of one of his lockups for the storage of stolen goods, he had the effrontery to bring an action (via a confederate) to have the goods returned. This impudence, H. D. states, "put certain Persons upon finding out Means of bringing so sturdy a Rogue to Justice" (68). The suggestion in H. D.'s sequence is that the action finally alienated the London Recorder, who after six years of tolerating Wild was finally driven to action when Wild tried to use the law in all its majesty to recover his ill-gotten booty. The strangest passage of all is this paragraph:

> But vengeance at length overtook him, and from the Minute of his being seiz'd, his Sense and Resolution fail'd; nor was he spirited up by the Hopes of a Reprieve, which some People endeavour'd to flatter him with, and industriously spread such a Rumour about, whilst they were trembling, lest it shou'd be so; because, he and they are suppos'd to be no Strangers to each other's Practices. (70)

If one reads past the mumbling, H. D. is telling us that it was "vengeance" rather than justice that overtook Wild, that rumors of a reprieve were industriously spread around in the hope that Wild would believe them and not queer the pitch for royal mercy by opening his mouth and accusing people in high places who were "no strangers to each other's practices." This accords with the historical record: if Wild did actually believe that a reprieve would be coming, he kept silent until it was too late to talk; his last recorded words in the cart on the way to Tyburn, according to Howson, were "What a queer rig they run on me," meaning "what a strange trick they played on me"(Howson 253)—"they" being the officers of the court who had profited in reputation if not financially from Wild's thieftaking activities, but had known how to destroy him when they needed to.

20. Possibly Defoe's outrage is at Wild's hypocrisy, his pretending to sympathize with a widow in a theft he had himself planned out, but hypocrisy had always been the mainspring of his business. But it seems obvious that Wild's language, in rejecting any personal reward and suggesting a possible future prosecution of the thief, is seeking to avoid the terms of the law under which he was convicted.

21. In his very differently toned account, H. D. gives the name of the "honourable person" as William Thomson, the London Recorder himself (61).

22. A minor criminal named John Thomson from Durham (no relation to William Thomson of Durham, the London Recorder) was prosecuted under the act in 1721 and condemned to death, which Howson feels Wild must have known about and which ought to have given him pause (Howson 98–99).

23. Joseph "Blueskin" Blake was a "highwayman" footpad noted for his connection with Jack Sheppard, in whose gang he worked. Howson describes him as "twenty-four years old [when he was hanged], and if early stage representations of him are anything to go by, he was a large, fat, lazy young man of coarse sensibilities. He was . . . an incurable gaol-bird, having been in and out of every prison, workhouse, and House of Correction in the Metropolis since the age of twelve, and it was generally believed that he owed his continued survival to Jonathan Wild" (Howson 190–91).

24. Howson presumes that the accusation was probably just but notes that "the other pamphleteers either ignored the matter or treated it with irony. The employment of children as pickpockets was as old and universal as theft itself, and Wild was simply following an ancient tradition.

Under-Marshal Hitchen was just as bad, and, to go back to the time of the 'Black Dogs of Newgate' if no further, there is a famous letter from Recorder Fleetwood to Lord Treasurer Burleigh, in which he describes how Wooten, an impoverished gentleman, had set up a school for young thieves behind his alehouse in Smart's Key, near Billingsgate." (Howson 124)

25. On the sympathy of the London mob, see Douglas Hay, et al., *Albion's Fatal Tree: Crime and Society in Eighteenth-Century England* (New York: Pantheon, 1975); on the class basis of the sympathy see the recent social analysis in Peter Linebaugh, *The London Hanged: Crime and Civil Society in the Eighteenth Century* (London: Penguin Press, 1991). Lincoln Faller's *Turn'd to Account* comes to a somewhat different conclusion: that any form of criminal organization was unpopular. His extensive study of criminal biography notes that, while "practically all notable highwaymen were members of gangs,"this fact is suppressed or downplayed in their biographies, particularly in the case of highwaymen like Dick Turpin and Jack Sheppard that had a "Robin Hood" appeal. "Organized crime appears to have been offensive to the popular imagination, or at least to the imaginations of those who wrote and read about crime. . . . Highwaymen typically were shown acting as lone gunmen, it would seem, because they were at their best and most entertaining when they stood outside *all* bodies politic" (179).

26. John Gay, *Poetical Works* (New York: Russell and Russell, 1969).

27. The song "When you censure the age" has been ascribed to Gay's friend Jonathan Swift. See Swift's *Poems*, ed. Harold Williams (Oxford: Oxford University Press, 1958) III, 1131. Bertrand Goldgar, in *Walpole and the Wits: The Relations of Politics to Literature 1722–1742* (Lincoln and London: University of Nebraska Press, 1976) presumes that "Peachum and Lockit are Walpole and Townshend" (69). Goldgar assumes that Walpole was unpopular with the wits primarily because he was not a "Maeceneas" opening his purse to them, as they had hoped. But Wild too was loathed even by those who tolerated his system, even by those who profited from it themselves.

28. The public exposition of parallelism between Wild and Walpole begins not with the Tory wits but with the Opposition newspapers. *Mist's Weekly Journal*, in a set of articles beginning a fortnight after Wild's execution suggests, without mentioning Walpole's name, how much the two great men had in common: "I call [Jonathan Wild] both Statesman and Politician, because I do not understand them to be synonimous Terms; for, I conceive, it is well known to many Persons, still living, that there have been some Statesmen in the World who never were so much as suspected of being Politicians, as well as an infinite Number of Politicians who never were Statesmen.—But the extraordinary Person, of whom we are Writing, was an Instance of both. . . . The Historian has curiously enough accounted by what sort of Arts Jonathan made himself considerable, and drew the Eyes of the admiring World upon him, he has given

many instances of his deep Fetch in Politicks, when he describes that Form, or rather that System of Government which he established over the Thieves." (12 June 1725, 1)

29. I am adopting the suggestion of Goldgar and others that *Jonathan Wild* originated in 1739 or 1740 as a Menippean satire on "greatness" using the career of Wild as its structure, that the plot of Wild against Heartfree was a later addition, and the digressions involving the travels of Mrs. Heartfree were added when Fielding was attempting to pad out *Jonathan Wild* to make a complete volume of the *Miscellanies* in 1743. It takes no faith in a "higher criticism" to see these layerings of intention in *Jonathan Wild*.

30. Henry Fielding, *Jonathan Wild* (Oxford: Basil Blackwell Shakespeare Head Press, 1926): 225.

31. Lennard Davis, *Factual Fictions: The Origins of the English Novel*. (New York: Columbia University Press, 1983): 196. Davis is surely right that Fielding's novels "are less like newspapers, but also more like them; these works make no claim to being actual documents but do claim to report on public events from an ideological and political viewpoint" (197). I disagree with Davis only in his insistence that "Fielding's aim is superscribed by the hidden aim of assigning an allegorical interpretation to a work in which Jonathan Wild stands for Horace [*sic*!] Walpole" (196). By the end of the novel, the Wild-Walpole analogy has already stretched into Aristotelian universals.

32. The name of Wild's actual agent for his fencing operation in Holland.

33. He could have done this either by exchanging their physical characteristics or by having Johnson displace Wild. The problem with the episode as it stands is that either we have to read the large and lusty Johnson as Walpole and the paltry Wild as Lord Wilmington, the mediocrity who replaced him in 1742 (which makes the allegory read backwards), or read Wild as Walpole and Johnson as Townshend (whom Walpole ditched in 1730), which makes nonsense of the physical characteristics of the two men.

34. Howson, 283–84.

David H. Richter is Professor of English at Queens College and the City University of New York Graduate Center. His most recent book is *The Progress of Romance: Literary Historiography and the Gothic Novel*. He is currently at work on two books, a cultural approach to true crime fiction and a study of difficulty in Biblical narrative.

Form and Ideology

in Cultural History

The Question of Ideological Form: Arthur Young, the Agricultural Tour, and Ireland

Ina Ferris

> But travelling upon paper, as well as moving amongst rocks and rivers, hath its difficulties.
>
> Arthur Young, *Travels in France* (1792)

To think about the question of form and ideology via the late eighteenth-century genre of the agricultural tour is to turn from an inquiry into literary forms and their implication in ideology (the concern of most of the essays in this volume) and think instead about ideology and its formal implications. As practiced by Arthur Young, the most celebrated agriculturalist of his day, the agricultural tour was an openly ideological writing rather than simply a writing operating within an ideology, for it actively set out to promulgate the idea of scientific agriculture as synonymous with the public good. On the issue of a rationalized agriculture Young was, as his modern editor put it, a "monomaniac," a point about his temperament made rather more tactfully in his own day by the *Edinburgh Review* in 1812 when it referred to him as "that restless, rambling, meddling, bustling, adventurer in Economics, who by his ardent spirit and unwearied labour, and perhaps even by his bold blunders, has for forty years usefully contributed to give a wholesome activity and a rational direction to the public understanding."[1] Committed to the agricultural interest as the foundation of the nation and convinced of the benefits of an "improved" husbandry, Young traveled around England, Ireland and France, making copious notes and pioneering the collection of statistics on the agricultural sector.[2] These, incorporated into his tours (published between 1771 and 1792), helped to consolidate his reputation in both Great Britain and on the Continent, and Young went on to a distinguished career devoted to the agrarian interest, serving as Secretary of the new Board of Agriculture, editor of the *Annals of Agriculture* (1784–1815), and member of numerous scientific societies, as well as continuing to produce reports, pamphlets and other texts on agrarian matters. Young thus exemplifies a writing that understands form as secondary, as simply the reflex of a primary ideological content. But a consideration of both the ambition and the curious collapse of Young's first tour outside English space, *A Tour in Ireland 1776–1779* (1780) points to a more complex dynamic at work even in so apparently straightforward a case.

The late-eighteenth-century agricultural tour draws useful attention to how ideologies (in the sense of ideas about the public good to be acted upon rather than simply reflected on) may find themselves confounded by way of the very forms in which they are invested. As a system of ideas an ideology not only has a formal logic of its own but itself implies certain forms for articulating and communicating its premises and allegiances, as in the empirical forms of writing chosen by agricultural writers such as Young. But the forms spun off by an ideological system—the forms through which adherents promulgate an ideology—are not always symmetric; hence a certain friction may occur, threatening ideological coherence and confidence. Moreover, ideological genres like the agricultural tour have to contend with form in another sense as well: as a mode of public writing, the agricultural tour enters a discursive field in which it must establish authority and find an audience.[3] It thus operates in a space shaped by the pragmatics of response and rivalry, and in this space form becomes importantly a matter of address and no longer just a question of the "fit" between an idea and its material figure (the printed text). Here too frictions may occur, especially when, as in the case of the late-eighteenth-century agricultural tour, we are dealing with a new and hybrid genre entering a literary field itself disturbed by the pressure of a whole set of emerging genres and discourses jostling for position (e.g. the novel, political economy, natural science).

In such a context the ideal transparence of form and idea posited by an ideological genre is necessarily unsettled, not least by the self-consciousness about questions of authority and audience it induces in authors. It is not incidental that Young's *Tour in Ireland* is framed by a lengthy "Author's Preface" that raises precisely the question of the relation of form to ideology, as Young sets out to clear a space for his tour-text and to define its ideal reader. To explain "the design"of his work, Young situates his text against nonempirical forms such as theory and fiction, and aligns it with empirical forms of practical reason.[4] "Husbandry," he writes, "is an art that has hitherto owed less to reasoning than I believe any other. I know not of any discoveries, or a single beneficial practice that has clearly flowed from this source. But every one is well acquainted with many that have been the result of experiment and registered observation" (1:10). Up to now, according to Young, agrarian writing has not reflected this fact, driven as it has been by theory. Its deductive, didactic works have provided no sense of the "actual state" of agriculture in any country, for such actual knowledge depends on "detailed descriptions" from a writer who has traveled and seen for himself. "Of little consequence must precepts, maxims, and directions for a better conduct appear," writes Young, "unless we really know the evils that are to be remedied, and the practices that are to be condemned" (1:2–3). Most agricultural writers have been unwilling to make the effort, preferring to remain within the standard, deductive model, not least because it offers the attractions of unified and capacious form which please both writer and reader: "[the writer's] views are great, his work comprehensive, round, and complete, and every reader finds something that suits him" (1:1). The success of such comprehensive treatises with the public, along with "the good reception of well written, though erroneous theories," confirms for Young that in the marketplace "the *agreeable* [bears] away the palm due to *the useful* alone" (1:1). So it is that a writer (like Young himself) who "aims simply at utility, must expect his productions to give place to those of a more amusing turn" (1:2).

Young pulls sharply apart the poles of pleasure and utility conventionally invoked in eighteenth-century travel writing so as to establish his credibility as an agricultural traveler, one whose work is the more useful precisely because it is less pleasing.[5] Such a move was standard in the period for texts seeking cognitive authority, but Young pushes the repudiation of pleasure to an unusual degree.[6] From the outset he advertises the tedium of his text: "The details of common management are dry and unentertaining; nor is it easy to render them interesting by ornaments of style." Moreover, he stresses that agricultural reports inevitably take the shape of "chains of repetition, which tire the ear, and fatigue the imagination" (1:2). By the final pages of the preface, the motif of the text *ennuyant* has become insistent:

> Part of these enquiries may be uninteresting to those who do not reside in the country . . .
>
> I have determined to explain them as fully as I was able, tedious as they may appear to those, who read rather for amusement, than information . . .
>
> The registers of such journies . . . must necessarily be exceedingly dull to those who read for pleasure . . . (1:10–11)

As such formulations indicate, the insistence on tedium has as much to do with defining a proper reader as legitimating the author. To be sure, Young is anxious to assert the experiential base of his writing and to dissolve distinctions between form and idea in his text. So he declares at one point that if he were *not* tedious, he would have failed to accomplish the goal for which "I have travelled, practised, and written," a formulation that identifies the three spheres of activity (travel, farming, writing) as simply different forms of the same end.[7] But he leads into this defence by a turn to (on?) the reader: "Perhaps there would be no impropriety in prefixing to all the productions I venture before the public, this caution: I have been reproached for being tedious" (1:10). Only the hardiest or most virtuous souls will keep reading after this.

And that of course is the point. Young aims his writing at readers like himself, serious and committed members of what John Barrell has called the rural professional class.[8] He thereby underlines the generic ambition of the agricultural tour (and the institutions linked to it) to achieve political authority by discounting literary and claiming scientific status. This means ruling out certain readers, in particular those who represent the "idle" present age and its search for pleasure. Such readers demand the pleasures of fiction even when they turn to nonfictional genres, and Young attributes the success of certain histories to the fact that their "charms of stile rendered them as amusive as a romance" and made them akin, not to other histories, but to the sentimental novels of Richardson and Rousseau (1:11). By contrast to such self-indulgent readers, he seeks for his writing readers (gendered male) "who are willing to sacrifice their amusement to their information" (1:2). Eschewing pleasure for instruction, such readers will constitute an elite minority not simply because of their virtue but because of their analytic ability to perceive in the "seemingly inconsiderable" details of farm management the foundation of the state. "It may be dry," Young comments, "but it is important, for these are the circumstances upon which depend the wealth, prosperity, and power of nations" (1:2). To recognize this is also to recognize that the only knowledge with "real utility" takes the form of comparative generalizations based on all the facts one can procure: "To men thus scientific, too many facts can never be published" (1:12). It is to these readers that he directs his work on Ireland, a work that aims to produce a "general view of the kingdom" which will "throw Ireland into that just light, in which she has not hitherto appeared" (1:9).

Adopting a severe and aggressive approach to the reading public, the "Author's Preface" defines the agricultural tour through a strict opposition between literary pleasure and scientific knowledge in which only the latter yields political and public good. Interestingly, Young was to relax the severity of this stance by the time he came to publish his best-remembered book, *Travels in France During the Years 1787, 1788 & 1789* (1792), and one reason for the change was precisely the reception of his uncompromising Irish *Tour*. Like the earlier tour, the French *Travels* are prefaced by a self-reflexive discussion of the form of the work, this time titled, "Travels &c." After outlining the two methods of travel writing (a register of the journey, a set of reflections on the journey) and defining his text as a combination of the two, Young brings in a version of the Person from Porlock to explain a feature of his work not strictly consonant with its official civic and scientific tenor. He recounts that when cutting his manuscript for publication, he initially excised "a variety of little circumstances relating to myself only, and of conversations with various persons which I had thrown upon paper for the amusement of my family and intimate friends." But an unnamed "friend" declared this a serious mistake, saying that Young had expunged "the very passages that would best please the mass of common readers," and he urged the author to restore them and to treat the public "like a friend." In direct discourse, the friend then tells Young that a writing "guided by the importance of the subject" is not as "pleasing" as "a careless and easy mode of thinking and writing" without a view to reputation or serious theme. And he cites as proof the Irish *Tour: "Your Tour of Ireland* (he was pleased to say) *is one of the best accounts of a country I have read, yet it had no great success. Why? Because the chief part of it is a farming diary, which however valuable it may be to consult, nobody will read."*[9] Young would now clearly prefer to be read rather than simply consulted as a source of information, despite the argument put forward in the earlier tour, and he is also willing to admit a broader readership and hence a less uniform model of reading. So he follows the friend's advice to keep the itinerary "just as it was written on the spot"; at the same time, he advises those readers who find the journal "trifling" and wish "to attend only to subjects of a more important character" to move directly to the reflections in the second part.[10] The tour-text now accommodates at least two kinds of readers, and the question of form emerges as a more dialogic matter, the result of ongoing negotiation with the words of others, as well as the embodiment of an a priori set of assumptions.

But if form and ideology begin to fold less readily into one another when placed in the matrix of the larger discursive field, the core ambition of the agricultural tour, as articulated in the preface to the Irish *Tour* and reflected in the two-part structure Young helped to make standard, remains constant throughout Young's career. Based on several journeys around Ireland in the late 1770s and on a period in residence as agent of Lord Kingsborough in Mitchelstown near Cork (the same estate, incidentally, where ten years later a young Mary Wollstonecraft would serve as governess), the Irish *Tour* is made up of two volumes. Volume 1 consists of "Minutes of the Tour," providing the "particulars" of agricultural practice in different regions of Ireland. The "particulars" generally assume the abstract, visual shape of sets of tables, lists of figures, and compilations of sets of statistics. They are embedded in a largely impersonal journey narrative that concentrates on economic matters but includes the occasional pointed comment on political subjects and frequently stops to describe the landscape, descriptions which often (but not always[11]) underline the benefits of enclosure and cultivation. The bulk of the volume, however, is devoted to more mundane details of crop rotation, types of manure, rental rates, returns on the linen manufacture, roads, and so forth. From these "particulars" Young then derives the "general facts" proffered in Volume 2, which is divided into short essays on matters like "Of the Tenantry of Ireland," "Timber-Planting," "Manures—Waste Land—Bogs," "Absentees," "Population,"and "Revenue—Taxes."

Improvement is the grand theme of the whole, both in the technical agricultural sense and in the more philosophical sense of historical time as progress. Indeed the work itself embodies the particular idea of progress it affirms: first, it amasses empirical details that will correct the misrepresenting generalizations of the past and then, enabled by such details, it moves to a renovated and improved level of generalization. The generalizations on Ireland include some strong liberal critique, as in Young's attack on the Penal Laws and his characterization of the Ascendancy as a "domineering aristocracy of five hundred thousand Protestants [who] feel the sweets of having two millions of slaves" (2:66). Such comments were rapidly picked up by those agitating for Irish reform, but the political generalizations offered by Young depend less on the "particulars" garnered by travel than do the general remarks on economic matters like the state of the labouring poor, land use, taxation, and so on. Witness his handling of an old English topic: the Irish cabin.[12] Young does not overturn the dominant English view of the cabin as a miserable hovel; indeed, his eye remains firmly English throughout, and he concludes Volume 1 by imagining the whole of Ireland as so "improved" that it resembles "the richness of an English woodland scene" (1:470). But having traveled through the countryside and taken a special interest in the living conditions of the poor, he replaces the generic cabin found in most travel writing with a series of differentiated cabins, detailing such matters as the variety of roof coverings, the gradations in cabins, the different materials used for building, the specific cost of different types of cabins in different regions, and so forth. In Young, all cabins are not collapsed into the same cabin, as they are, for instance, in the Irish travels of his contemporaries Richard Twiss and Thomas Campbell.[13] Moreover, he takes the cabin seriously as a living space and does not see it as simply a sign of savagery or misery. He notes, for example, that well-built mud cabins are warmer than English clay cottages and argues that, contrary to English opinion, potatoes must be wholesome food, given the healthy Irish bodies he has seen (2:48, 2:43). Young thus makes a case for particular experience as a correction to received views, and his generalizations gain in the process, emerging as more authoritative than those of fellow travelers (not to mention past writers on Ireland) because they are more inclusive and possess superior explanatory power.

And it is explanatory power that is at stake. As Barrell has pointed out, agrarian writing of the period sought "to *explain* the countryside, open it out, and to make each particular place more available to those outside it."[14] Barrell stresses how such an "opening" of the countryside involved both attaching the local place to a larger unit (nation, empire) and detaching it from local knowledge in the interest of a general rationality. Such a procedure, in turn, depended on an itinerant viewpoint, the mobile viewpoint of a stranger passing through: one must see with one's own eyes, but those eyes cannot become entangled in the place. Young's tours are exemplary on all counts, but at the same time they embody a telling ambivalence about the traveling that makes them possible. Even as Young maintains the importance of travel, he gives it an oddly secondhand status, making the empirical form he espouses rather less sure than it seems.

Despite its argument on behalf of the agricultural tour as a writing "on the spot," the "Author's Preface" to the Irish *Tour* ends up defining the form as a substitute for a more primary form. It turns out that the preferred kind of agrarian writing for Young would be that of "resident gentlemen"; in fact, had resident gentlemen published accounts of what fell within their sphere of observation, "such journies as I have registered and published, would have been perfectly unnecessary." Residents can provide "a far better and more particular account of every circumstance than it is possible a traveler should procure," but in the absence of such accounts Young offers his traveling account as the best alternative. Its strength, he emphasizes, lies in that it was "taken on the spot, from the mouths of gentlemen or farmers who reside in the districts, they describe" (1:3). The same contrast between resident and traveler periodically surfaces in the tour-text itself as well, as when Young observes that a traveler to Ireland who passes through "without making any residence" can make only crude distinctions of class, whereas one who has resided there will have a more differentiated sense of the social order (2:146). And he frequently draws attention to the advantages of his own residence in the country ("a much longer residence there enables me to exhibit a very different picture," [2:144]). It is noteworthy that such claims to the status of resident appear in Volume 2 in support of the generalizing mode of the essay featured in this volume. In the diary form of Volume 1, by contrast, the author usually appears as simply a traveler; moreover, he is a traveler whose journey is marked by lacunae, as Young repeatedly reports that someone he seeks was "not at home." Since the tour-text is enabled by the meetings of traveler and resident, the missed meetings that punctuate the text underline the gaps and absences inevitable in a traveler's account.

The moments contrasting resident and traveler may signal conventional modesty and caution (although Young was not known for either), but there is also a sense in which they point to the empiricist's desire for a writing that coincides with what it writes: a longing that a "writing on the spot" merge with the "spot" itself. Inevitably, however, such writing comes up against its own secondariness, especially when, as in the case of Young's tour, such writing knows itself to be dependent on explicit mediation. Young may report what he sees in Ireland, but the larger part of his travel diary is a report of what others told him: he is not only a traveler but one heavily reliant on informants, a double distanciation. His account may be "taken on the spot," but (to recall the suggestive formulation of the preface) it is taken "from the mouths" of others. To be "on the spot" is not therefore necessarily to be closer to its truth (however that they may be defined), and Young goes on to draw the obvious caution: "that the accounts are however perfect, cannot be expected—they are proportionally so to the sagacity, information, and experience of the person who speaks" (1:3). He carefully notes that he did "not trust entirely" to the reports of country gentlemen but spoke as well to "common farmers" and to "cottagers"; and as for the information on manufacture and commerce, it too was also "chiefly gained on the spot" and was not (he reassures the reader) provided to him with any intention to deceive.

But suspicion of deceit has nevertheless surfaced, and it is striking how often the invocation of empirical form ("on the spot") produces anxiety or at least equivocation. The legitimating move, that is, works as much to undo as to confirm the credibility of the text, highlighting the extent to which the "particulars" on which this credibility rests are a matter of hearsay. Volume 1 constantly identifies sources:

> The following particulars of agriculture I had from General Cunninghame, who took every means of having me well informed. (1:95)

> Waited on the bishop, who was so obliging as to procure me several valuable particulars concerning the neighbourhood. (1:220)

> As to its commerce, the following particulars I owe to Robert Gordon, Esq.; the surveyor-general. (1:332)

Through such reiteration, "particulars" come to seem *essentially* secondhand, so much so that Young indicates when they come under firsthand observation: "In several particulars, which I saw myself, Mr Pepper appears an excellent farmer" (1:109). Even here Young seems wary about the signification of those particulars he sees (Mr. Pepper "appears" an excellent farmer). All the same, he generally trusts his eyes more than the word of some of his informants. Volume 2, for example, announces that Young found gentlemen inadequate sources of information about the conditions of the laboring poor not only because of their "surprising inattention" to such things but because many gentlemen, "infected with the rage of adopting *systems*," used the inquiry about the poor as an occasion to expatiate on their favourite social idea. "When truth is likely to be thus warped," Young declares, " a traveler must be very circumspect to *believe*, and very assiduous to *see*" (2:35).

But the problem is that what Young can see is very limited in relation to what he wants to know, in large part because as a traveler he cannot see a place through time. He is limited to the present moment, but he wants to know the present as part of the flow of time, with time understood as productivity. Even as Young's tour lays out Ireland on a static, spatial grid, it is motivated by a temporal idea: the narrative of history as progress. To be sure, he can attach Ireland to this narrative in certain ways himself. He can look at the composition of the soil in a particular area, for example, and project a possible future cultivation on the basis of the possibilities of this soil. But he cannot see the past, and so he cannot know exactly how to connect present and past productivity for a more confident projection of the future. For such vital information, central to his concern with the trajectory of the Irish economy, he has to rely on the reports of others:

> This town [Newry] appears exceedingly flourishing, and is very well built; yet 40 years ago, I was told there was nothing but mud cabbins in it. (1:116)

> Their circumstances [the poor in Kerry] are incomparably worse than they were 20 years ago; for they had all cows, but then they wore no linen. (1:369)

> In general I was informed that the trade of the place had increased considerably in ten years, both the exports and imports. (1:406)

So it is that the intangibles of belief and trust, along with the irrationalities of guess and gossip and legend (Young was later ridiculed for believing stories that the Irish attached horses to ploughs by the tail) play as large a role in writing "on the spot" as do the concrete work of the eye and the inferential processes of empirical reason.

To further complicate matters, the ideology of improvement generates both macro- and microforms, and these may not always yield congruent representations. Framing the tour-text is the overarching grand narrative of progress, but the tour-text itself (like the microforms of experiment, table, and report it includes) is one of the smaller, specific forms spun out of the grand narrative. These smaller forms not only have their own formal imperatives but deal with microtemporalities that often operate unevenly. The macrolevel may smooth out any unevenness that appears—and it usually does—but the potential for destabilization remains, for the point of representation at the microlevel is to chart the differentiation of "particulars" within the general field. That is, Young travels about asking the same general questions (what type of crop rotation is used in this area? how are rents paid here? what is the state of trade?), but through these general categories he indicates the specificity of distinct regions. The years 1772–73, for instance, witnessed a depression in the Irish linen market, but that depression did not take the same shape in every place. In Strangford, for example, Young reports that the decline was "not felt in the trade of this place" (1:142). In Armagh, however, there was a "great decline" in the linen manufacture, a decline that continued into 1774 until May of that year when there was a sudden rise. Young reports that this rise, having to do with events in America, Spain, and Germany, has continued ever since (1:123). The point is that while Armagh is placed within modern, rational time and linked to the macrospace of international trade, it nonetheless has its own distinctive experience of that time. Through such calibrations of prosperity, decline, and change in the country, Young's *Tour* seeks to specify the particular workings of the Irish economy, countering the static and atemporal depictions current at the time. This does not mean that Young had any interest in difference or in history as we understand these terms. He did not conceive of an Irish people or culture or entertain other views of time and place, as did many antiquarians of his day. But he did have a great deal of interest in specificity in the sense of the specification of conditions posited by his general model. And, ironically, the very ideological investment in this specificity threatened in the end to undermine the whole project of his agricultural tour.

In the remarkable—and little-noticed—final pages of *A Tour in Ireland* the entire enterprise verges on collapse, and it does so in a way that is highly suggestive for the question of ideological form in general. Arthur Young had planned to close his *Tour* with the chapter on "General State of Ireland," a chapter whose final paragraphs sound a ringing note of optimism: "Upon the whole, we may safely determine that, judging by those appearances and circumstances, which have been generally agreed to mark the prosperity or declension of a country, Ireland has since the year 1748 made as great advances as could possibly be expected, perhaps greater than any other country in Europe" (2:258).[15] Less than a page later, however, he opens a new, additional section by declaring: "The preceding sections have been written near a twelvemonth; events have since happened, which are of an importance that will not permit me to pass them by in silence, much as I wish to do it" (2:260). Young does not provide a detailed account of the events that have altered the planned shape of his book, but he does note at the start of the section that "the minds of men are in ferment"and that "the distress of the kingdom" has been engrossing the attention of the Irish Parliament, which has demanded a free trade in remedy. Not until fourteen pages later does he also mention the "armed association" that is part of the matrix of agitation. What Young is responding to in these pages is the economic and political crisis in Ireland in 1778–1779 indirectly generated by England's war with its American colonies. These years witnessed a depression in the linen trade, widespread unemployment, and a credit crisis for the Irish government. To bolster employment, a series of non-importation agreements, keeping out English goods, were put in place; at the same time, the Irish Parliament demanded a free trade, seeking an end to restrictions on both exports and imports imposed by Britain. The demand for free trade—and this is the point that most disturbs Young—was made in the context of increasing militancy by the Irish Volunteers, the "armed association" of Irish Protestants permitted by England in 1778 when it had to withdraw its own troops for the American war. The Volunteers, who had put on an aggressive display in November 1779, rapidly became a potent national symbol manipulated by Ascendancy patriots like Henry Grattan, so that in 1779, as a recent economic historian puts it (echoing Young's own phraseology) the "non-importation agreements and the Volunteer Movement caused a ferment"[16]

This "ferment" ran counter not only to the general tenor of Young's account but to his specific prediction about a steadily increasing Irish prosperity. In the year since he finished writing his analysis, a dramatic gap had opened up between the microtemporality of Ireland in 1779 and the macrotemporality of gradual European progress within which he had placed the country. This gap had to be addressed, and the imperative to do so was a double one, each in a sense a formal imperative even as it constituted a response to historical events. The first imperative derives from form understood as internal to a system: the empirical allegiance to events and circumstances demanded by Young's model meant that he could not simply ignore the issue. As he himself put it, given the "picture" of Ireland provided by the preceding sections, he had to "enquire into the circumstances of a situation which seems to have changed so suddenly, and to so great a degree" (2:260). The second imperative pertains to form understood as a function of the discursive matrix of publication and reception: the contract with readers implicitly established in the "Author's Preface" meant that Young would lose credibility if he failed to comment. He would have preferred to remain silent, "but, as a dead silence upon events of such importance would look either like ignorance or affectation, I shall lay before the reader the result of my own researches" (2:260).

With the authority and integrity of the *Tour* at stake, Young scrambles in the final section to shore up his massive work. Drawing on the resources of economic method, he produces tables to show that the decline in Irish revenue has come only from certain sectors, affected mostly the higher classes, and in general has not been quite so precipitous as reported. Moreover, the decline that *has* occurred has been the result of the non-importation agreements, themselves "a forced artificial measure" (2:263). But Young is curiously uncertain in his tone and argument, and the section includes a series of uncharacteristic authorial notes, as if to underscore that the crisis spills over the regular bounds of the text (these notes range from a sardonic report of an item in the

1779 Irish national accounts for rebuilding old churches in parishes where no services had been held for twenty years to a passionate defence of why the landed interest should not now unite with the commercial and manufacturing interest). Repeatedly, Young denies there is a serious problem in Ireland and claims the distress is only temporary; but, equally repeatedly, he indicates bafflement and a suspicion that there may be more to the situation than he can recognize—or interpret. Thus he states that the decline in some articles of import "induces me to think there must be more distress than appears from others," and the same page notes a sharp decline in many export articles as well: "enough to convince any one that all is not right in that country" (2:265). Statistics themselves tend to become elusive, almost surreal. Young is puzzled, for example, by the marked decline in Irish beef exports, and the only way he can begin to account for it is to say he has been told that for the past two years all government contracts for beef have not been entered in the customhouse books by order of the surveyor-general: "if this is the fact, it accounts for one of the heaviest articles in this declension" (2:266). Whatever the case with the vanishing beef entries, however, Young has seen for himself that the accounts tabled by the English House of Commons "do not admit the same conclusions as the Irish accounts, owing probably to some circumstances with which we are not fully acquainted" (2:266). Not surprisingly, he eventually gives up trying to mount an argument from particulars, even as he continues to maintain the superiority of "figures" over "anecdote" and "*assertions*" (2:270). Young shifts to a more general level of analysis—and a wider temporal perspective—by choosing to connect the question of current distress in Ireland "with the general state of the Kingdom rather than peculiarly to the present moment" (2:270), citing seven basic and long-standing factors that impede Irish prosperity.

It is not just the particulars of the Irish economy in 1779 that unsettle Young's project but the eruption of agitation, especially that represented by the Irish Volunteers, those "armed associations, which have made too much noise in England" (2:274). Policy issues like free trade have moved out of the properly public sphere of rational discussion and argument, become subject to physical coercion: a matter of noise rather than rational articulation. Over and over again in the final pages, the motif of noise surfaces: "the present noise of distress," "the violent cry for a free trade," "clamours of distress," "loud complaints." The danger, as Young sees it, is that what should be won on principle will be won by force, a policy like free trade granted as part of "a series of concessions, not given to reason, but to clamour" (2:275). Young's response to all this is rather curious for a propagandist: he urges the landed interest to fall silent. "It is always a benefit of the landed interest TO BE QUIET," he writes. "Let merchants and manufacturers complain, riot, associate, and do whatever they please" (2:273). Moving to an even higher level of generality and temporality, he links silence and stillness to the universal form of progress, clamour and agitation to limited—and dubious—local forms of change. At this point micro- and macrotemporalities begin sharply to diverge, and in the final paragraphs Young declares that the Irish should not look to political policies for relief since "the silent progress of time is doing that for them, which they are much too apt to look for in statutes, regulations and repeals" (2:279). With a certain desperation Young now seeks to align his garrulous text with "the silent progress of time," to erase the very timeliness on which he had based its positive value. In these final pages, the asymmetry of the forms generated by Young's ideology opens up a gap that he attempts but fails to close. And his text thereby underlines a central point: that even when ideologies condition forms, they do not contain them. And because they do not, certain openings occur through which the possibility of a new thought may emerge.

Notes

1. Constantia Maxwell, introduction to *Travels in France During the years 1787, 1788 & 1789*, by Arthur Young (1792; reprint, Cambridge: Cambridge University Press, 1950), xix; [James Macintosh], review of *An Account of Ireland, Statistical and Political*, by Edward Wakefield, *Edinburgh Review* (November 1812) 20: 347.

2. Economic historians continue to take Young's statistics with some seriousness even when they dispute his conclusions. See, for example, Robert C. Allen & Cormac Ó Gráda, "On the Road Again with Arthur Young: English, Irish, and French Agriculture During the Industrial Revolution," *Journal of Economic History* 48 (1988): 93–116.

3. I draw on Bourdieu's increasingly well-known notion of "field." The usefulness of this notion, which posits relatively autonomous fields of cultural production largely structured by struggles for legitimacy, is

that it bypasses the binary division of "internal" versus "external" explanations of texts. The early formulation of the concept appears in his "Intellectual field and creative project," *Social Science Information* 8 (April 1969): 89–119. For Bourdieu's analysis of the literary field in particular, see *The Rules of Art: Genesis and Structure of the Literary Field*, trans. Susan Emanuel (Stanford: Stanford University Press, 1996).

4. Arthur Young, *A Tour in Ireland 1776–1779*, ed. A. W. Hutton, 2 vols. (1780; reprint, Shannon: Irish University Press, 1970) 1: 12. Subsequent references to this edition will appear in parentheses within the text.

5. On the negotiation of pleasure and instruction, see Charles L. Batten, Jr., *Pleasurable Instruction: Form and Convention in Eighteenth-Century Travel Literature* (Berkeley: University of California Press, 1978).

6. On the antirhetoric trope in travel writing, see for example Michael McKeon, *The Origins of the English Novel 1600–1740* (Baltimore and London: Johns Hopkins University Press, 1987) and Anthony Pagden, *European Encounters with the New World* (New Haven: Yale University Press, 1993).

7. In a related point, Katie Trumpener shrewdly notes that Young's preface argues for "agricultural reclamation, scientific investigation, and the reading of his own *Tour* as parallel forms of labor," *Bardic Nationalism: The Romantic Novel and the British Empire* (Princeton: Princeton University Press, 1997), 38.

8. See John Barrell, *The Idea of Landscape and the Sense of Place 1730–1840: An Approach to the Poetry of John Clare* (Cambridge: Cambridge University Press, 1992).

9. Arthur Young, *Travels in France*, 3. Young's biographer reads the incident as an actual event, speculating that the friend may have been Dr. John Symonds, see John G. Gazley, *The Life of Arthur Young 1741–1820* (Philadelphia: American Philosophical Society, 1973), 282. Charles Batten, however, inclines to a fictional reading, noting the close resemblance to a similar story in Boswell's *Account of Corsica* (1768), see Batten, 34.

10. Young, *Travels in France*, 3.

11. On this point, see Barrell, 81–83.

12. For English views of the Irish cabin, see the final section of Andrew Hadfield and John McVeagh, *Strangers to That Land: British Perceptions of Ireland from the Reformation to the Famine* (Gerrards Cross: Colin Smythe, 1994).

13. Thomas Campbell, *A Philosophical Survey of the South of Ireland, In a Series of Letters to John Watkinson, M. D.* (London, 1777), 144–48; [Twiss, Richard], *A Tour in Ireland in 1775. With a Map, and a View of the Salmon-Leap at Ballyshannon* (London, 1776), 29–30.

14. Barrell, 84.

15. At such moments, Young nicely exemplifies John Harrington's point that the characteristic eighteenth-century English view of Ireland derived largely "from the English visitor's own general ambience of prosperity, optimism, and benevolence." See his introduction to John P. Harrington, comp. and ed., *The English Traveller in Ireland: Accounts of Ireland and the Irish through Five Centuries* (Dublin, 1991), 17.

16. L. M.Cullen, *An Economic History of Ireland Since 1660*, 2nd ed. (London: B. T. Batsford, 1987), 76.

Ina Ferris is Professor of English at the University of Ottawa. Her most recent book is *The Achievement of Literary Authority: Gender, History, and the Waverley Novels*. She is currently working on the Romantic national tale and the question of Ireland.

Form as Meaning:
Pope and the Ideology of the Couplet

J. Paul Hunter

Alexander Pope has never been an easy poet to like, not in his time, not in ours. Some of the reasons reside in his prickly personality and righteous preoccupations: zealous moralists and cultural dictators are never easy to take, especially for those with different standards or contrary views, and when the lawgiver is himself obviously flawed it is tempting to sneer and dismiss. Thousands of readers have done so quietly, and hundreds of critics, following John Dennis's lead, have justified their own reactive rage, often noisily and at some length. For modern readers, as well as for Pope's contemporaries, there is much to dislike, and differing opinions—about morality, art, philosophy, politics, class, and gender—are fair enough grounds for disagreeing and castigating. Given the tendency to prefer confirmation to challenge, readers often choose to avoid books they expect to be disagreeable, and Pope at several points in reception history has tended to make the lists of the Famous Unread. Undiscriminated hostility toward Pope seems less prevalent now than it was a decade ago, but the traditional resistance to his ideas and forms of argument remains strong.[1]

The readers I seek in this essay are not those who genuinely and legitimately disagree with the historical Pope, but rather those who react to the constructed Pope of literary history, a "Pope" who seems to me to have been badly served by foe and friend alike who have made him both more complacent and more consistent than his poetry proves him to be. Pope is himself partly responsible for that construction, of course, having done more than nearly any poet to construct himself in his poems. But there are other constructions and constructionists too, not all of them so conscious, explicit, and historically informed as Pope himself. One of the most powerful indirect forces involves received ideas about poetic tradition and form—traditional conceptions of metrics, rhyme, poetic form, and craft generally and (more specifically) expectations of the heroic couplet. Commentators on Pope invariably remind us of Pope's careful attention to craft, usually invoking the famous mentoring conversation with the aging William Walsh and noting that Pope sought the only "slot" seemingly left for greatness in poetry at the start of the eighteenth century, that of the "correct" poet. From there to an understanding of the iambic pentameter couplet—especially given its daunting male epithet of "heroic"—as rigid, arrogant, showy, conservative, and predictable—is but a short distance, and a lot of readers, including many learned ones who should know better, tend to find in Pope's choice of verse form a confirmation of his wicked, narrow, and manipulating ways. What I want to suggest here is that to read couplets this way is historically to misunderstand how couplets worked in Pope's time and to ignore how, and why, Pope used the verse form as he did. It is also to ignore the values and structures of thought that tend to inhere in verse forms in particular historical contexts and thus to fail to employ important theoretical aids to negotiating meaning in poems. To misread the implications of form—or to ignore how ideologies may be implicit in formal structures—is not only to misunderstand individual poems and to make Pope both more monolithic and less interesting than he in fact is but also to misconceive much of the way poetry worked culturally in the eighteenth century.[2]

What does it mean to speak of the "ideology" of a verse form, a professedly neutral vehicle waiting to be employed by a conscious rhetorical manipulator? The ideology of individual people, yes, though often less coherently and predictably than some theorists may wish. And—even more surely—of groups of people with common backgrounds or coherent interests. And genres, perhaps, may have ideologies of their own: the arguments can be fierce about what they are, witness the ongoing debates about the novel. But forms? Can we plausibly think of verse forms as having ideologies? Are patterns of rhetoric, thought, and value so fully built into structure that one can speak usefully of what a particular form represents culturally or what kinds of work it can do? To a committed historicist and constructionist like myself, the answer must obviously be *no* in an absolute sense. But verse forms—like genres—primarily exist in time and practice (why it is tricky to assign an ideology to genres or species that shift and turn and change as much as the novel), and traditions of usage create poets with habitual assumptions and readers with particular expectations, so that it may be possible—even obligatory—to think practically about the ideology of form in particular historic moments and for particular groups of authors and readers. This essay is an attempt to think through the ideology for the heroic couplet at the beginning of the eighteenth century,[3] when its traditions of usage were well established and when it was far and away the dominant verse form in Anglophone poetry and perhaps the characteristic form of verbal discourse in English. Absolute and unbending loyalties or essential values for the heroic couplet as a verse form may be impossible to establish, but expectations, patterns, leanings, tendencies, and appropriate formal associations can all be culturally described so as to make it easier to see why individual passages and poems work the ways they do. Such a strategy—as a working procedure, if not as an utter commitment—has at least the advantage of setting the workings of individual couplets against the contexts of contemporary functions and habits rather than against later retrospective views of what the couplet, from a modernist perspective, must have been like to satisfy our presentist sense of its oddness, for its former popularity is a major mystery to the modern mind and ear. At a minimum, such a procedure shifts the grounds of generalization onto a historical basis—what genre and verse form really are, merely frozen moments in the historical process of ideational and aural organization, rather than some kind of essential category described by Plato but ultimately set in the mind of God.

I

Couplets, especially for modern readers unused to rhyme and the intricacies of measured verse, are easily misread by amateurs who do not hear the cadences or see the implications of symmetrical or oppositional structures. And even experienced readers may be overmatched without knowing it because they fail to observe the rules of the game, ignoring for example the way the argument is built and qualified by couplet-upon-couplet structures or the way key terms are defined and redefined by their syntactic positioning. That is, they may know neither the theory of the form nor its history of use and therefore fail to see either how individual poets used it or how it tends to shape (and limit) thoughts and values. Couplets in Pope's time are both more complex and more formally determined than is usually recognized, and many of the mistaken views of eighteenth-century poetry—both old and new—derive from misconceptions of what is at stake in this, one of the subtlest and most demanding of verse forms where oppositions are set up for purposes of refinement and complication, not to enforce the power of one at the expense of the other. For values can be at stake in verse forms. The question is, just what values are implicit in a particular form, and what demands—formal, philosophical, and rhetorical—does a particular verse form, poetic kind, or genre make on writers and readers alike.[4]

Alexander Pope—slippery in all kinds of ways on many kinds of issues—was himself extremely clear (and often explicit) about how the couplet worked and what kinds of propositions, arguments, and conclusions it could illustrate, support, and argue. Easy critics of the couplet and glib readers of Pope—those who wish to distance themselves politically from what they take to be the rigid social propositions Pope uses couplets to make—tend to talk about the couplet's central features in broad theoretical terms, emphasizing balance, symmetry, and closure as essential features, as if the terms themselves coded an authoritative and fixed universe. They invoke these terms easily and unproblematically, without examining why balance is used or to what uses it is put, whether symmetry is a value or a strategy of analysis, and whether the "closure" of an individual couplet really means "end" in any real sense. The crucial question is not what such terms may suggest in the abstract but how they work in practice, what happens in actual poems when a particular feature like symmetry or juxtaposition or end rhyme is introduced for a particular effect.

II

One example of perceptive criticism weakened by a misreading of formal features is Laura Brown's analysis of Pope's poetic lists.[5] Brown is excellent as a close reader when she describes Pope's many lists. I had always thought Wordsworth the master of poetic lists, as he is the great poet of many prosaic, mundane, and undiscriminated gray values. But Brown persuades me by copious and well analyzed examples that Pope is simply the best poet (as Swift is the best prose writer) at listing things that must be tested as equivalences in order to be properly understood. The fact that Pope's lists are almost always satirical is relevant but, as Brown cleverly sees, less than definitive: his assertion of parallels makes claims that may damn those with opposing values but may also taint Pope: "Puffs, powders, patches, Bibles, billet-doux" may characterize refusals to make distinctions by Belinda, her companions, and her patriarchal models, but it also raises questions about Pope's own hierarchies. In implying the equality of items in the list, does Pope tell us more than he means to about his own equations, something about the way satiric attack and satiric norm tend to merge regardless of target and intention? And Brown often clarifies the grounds of Pope's equivalences, noting allegiances that he himself might have questioned or denied but that seem nevertheless persuasive. Regarding Pope's lists as functionally the same as the lists of J. Jocelyn in *An Essay on Money and Bullion* and thus in the service of a mercantile or capitalist hegemony involves, however, a huge analytical leap and an assumption that lists, like other apparent symmetries, always work in the same way. Lists may involve accumulation or acquisition or annexation, but they can also involve leveling, equation as well as territoriality or imperialism: the critical choice of what category or categories to apply involves more than Pope's conscious choice, of course, but also cannot be simply the critic's.

The difference between lists and couplets as forms of rhetoric and formulators of value is in what they do with tradition; lists depend on a history of use, too, of course, but their primary allegiance is to structure, a process of comparison implied in the thing itself. Lists do not have a history of application that involves intentional, conscious, and contractual choice, as couplets do; they may assert equivalances, as they tend to do in Wordsworth where qualities are flattened out and evened up, but they may also imply inappropriate comparisons that blur distinctions, as they tend to do in Swift (though Swift typically works the device both ways, sometimes at once). The point is that one simply cannot tell from a list per se just what kind of comparison is going on; lists mean one kind of thing in a recipe and quite another in a political pamphlet (but even in a recipe, the initial flat list is typically elaborated and inflected by later narratives of how the seeming indiscriminateness needs to be carefully, step by step, discriminated and applied). And of course sometimes multiple kinds of things go on simultaneously, even contradictorily. What determines the category or categories is the context, sometimes including the definitions provided by genre or form.

Heroic couplets *imply* in their structures, though they do not determine or necessarily limit. They suggest—and tend to advocate—certain kinds of values and meanings. It is not possible to say that couplets always argue for balance and the golden mean or (contrariwise) that they never imply absolute choices, but there is in Pope's time a predisposition in the form—because of the history of its use—to set up oppositions and then add in qualifications that refuse to allow the antinomies first implied. There are of course coupleteers who do not understand this basic point—and much of the mediocre poetry of the couplet-rich period from 1650 to 1750 displays their limitation and illustrates the dullness of what happens when distinctions are binary and simple. Pope does not fall for such simplicity, even when easy answers tempt him, and his most talented contemporaries seldom do either. Had he built his *Dunciad* simply to show the haves and have-nots in couplet verse, he might have made a far more coherent statement about form than he ever made explicitly, but (typical of Pope) he was not satisfied to make a formal point apart from a cultural one, and therefore the issues in his most important sorting poem have to be sorted out by modern readers in both aesthetic and social terms at the same time, an issue that has to be sorted out carefully by anyone who begins from premises different from Pope in either poetic or political terms.[6]

Brown's analysis turns on where Pope's values lie and how his self-knowledge works; what she believes she sees in Pope is self-contradiction, an adamant embracing of certain views that are silently undercut by assumptions he can be shown to hold elsewhere. Her Pope is dogmatic, unbending, mistakenly righteous, and egregiously lacking in self-awareness, and it is true that these features are sometimes to be found in Pope, especially the later Pope. But Brown does not see Pope's hesitancies—his uncertainty, his sense of divided public and personal loyalties, his worry about the fact that his values are in genuine conflict—because she does not see the way he reacts to categories. In a way, she takes too literally the later exasperated Pope who, genuinely disturbed that he is not being listened to, does try to command the world to moral attention according to his own hardening cultural analysis.

But the Pope of "The Rape of the Lock," caught up in the luxury and elegance of his society even at the moment he sees that its values are corrupt and demeaning to everyone concerned, deliberately implicates himself as well. Here Belinda, the Baron, Sir Plume, Queen Anne, the court generally, the Catholic gentry, jurymen, the political establishment, the social consensus on gender values and sexual behavior, and Pope himself are all included in the indictment, the latter by creating so epic a celebration of so gorgeously and intricately corrupt a culture; the very beauty of the poem is a crucial part of its satire. Such a reading, derived from modern theoretical tools, seems more accurate biographically and historically than interpretations based on long-discredited (by both deconstructionist and historicist theory), older-fashioned commonplaces about mock-heroic providing one clear standard, one clear violation. The Pope that then emerges is neither trapped in his own contradictions nor unconscious of his position. As a conscious worker in the couplet tradition, he is concerned to discover subtleties, rather than occlude them, and to find rather than suppress his own culpabilities.

Let me illustrate further the problem of values on a purely thematic and affectual level, this time by looking at "Windsor Forest," a difficult but very revealing poem—revealing both about Pope and the nature of the couplet. Pope is not at his best here as a political thinker—he was too caught up in a political and rhetorical act among his friends, and he tried desperately—too desperately, it seems to me—to put together fragmentary notions he had been wrestling with for several years. Some of Pope's very best—and most complicated—poetry is included in "Windsor Forest," and the exercises in perspective that he there incorporates show him struggling nobly with a recalcitrant patriotism that he cannot ever quite suppress or get control of. On a purely thematic level, one might see contradiction here, but by manipulating perspective and working to refine readerly judgment, Pope manages to show just how complicated and qualified his allegiances are, even those to personally admired authorities and ways of thinking.

III

One of the lasting accomplishments of deconstruction is to have established how attack is to admiration near allied, and Pope often—not just in "The Rape of the Lock"—admires, at some level, that which he lashes mercilessly: Walpole is a convenient human example, Luxury an abstract one. It has long been a useful commonplace that Pope admires (and uses) political expediency and manipulation even as he distrusts (and vilifies) it, just as he loves the delicacy, sensuousness, elegance, and grandeur of the Hampton Court society that he excoriates for its insensitivity, materialism, triviality, and flattening of values. And Pope is, in fact, very much tied to the loyalties of English nationalism, imperialism, and tradition, even as he suspects the corruptions of power and commerce. "Windsor Forest"—in its apparent celebration of the Peace of Utrecht, of unregulated trade and cultural exploitation, and of British ethnocentrism—is a very problematic poem; it has always been problematic for readers, and it was problematic for Pope himself, as the story of its composition, occasion, and publication plainly show. But to see "Windsor Forest" as an unabashed defense of British commerce and conquest, totally insensitive to the pain and destruction wrought by colonial and imperial sway, is to ignore not just the formal implications of the verse but also the plain words of the poem and the perspectives that it forces upon the reader. The complexity of its sympathies, for oppressor and oppressed, is remarkable. In one of the most powerful emotional maneuvers in the poem (a passage in which he is celebrating the "progressive" national history of England), Pope shows himself highly sensitive to the human cost of imperialism, and he tries to force a recognition of complexity onto the reader. The passage shifts radically in sympathy, from victor to victim, from England to England's encircled enemies. The misleading allusion to "small" and "great" signals the shift not only from abstract to particular but also from power to powerlessness. From a moment when we are asked to share the perspective of a hunter who "meditates the prey," we are abruptly switched to the point of view of victims who feel the net sweeping over them. And the larger "patriotic" point is emphasized by the swift move to national analogy in which we are asked to feel what it is like not to be Albion, but Albion's "prize."

Ye vigorous swains! while youth ferments your blood,
And purer spirits swell the sprightly flood,
Now range the hills, the gameful woods beset,
Wind the shrill horn, or spread the waving net.
When milder autumn summer's heat succeeds,
And in the new-shorn field the partridge feeds,
Before his lord the ready spaniel bounds,
Panting with hope, he tries the furrowed grounds;
But when the tainted gales the game betray,
Couched close he lies, and meditates the prey;
Secure they trust th' unfaithful field, beset,
Till hovering o'er 'em sweeps the swelling net.
Thus (if small things we may with great compare)
When Albion sends her eager sons to war,
Some thoughtless town, with ease and plenty blessed,
Near, and more near, the closing lines invest;
Sudden they seize th' amazed, defenceless prize,
And high in air Britannia's standard flies.
ll. 92–110

The raising of Britannia's flag in this context of shifting perspectives between victor and victim involves one of the most bathetic patriotic celebrations in verse. The brilliant shifts in referent for "they" decenters the affect and leaves us uncertain of where we stand—with hunter? prey? man? beast? victor? vanquished? Britain? or the "thoughtless town" Britain conquers? And the two following paragraphs repeatedly elaborate the pathos of loss and victimhood as the "whirring pheasant . . . feels the fiery wound" and the "mounting larks . . . leave their little lives in air"—lines in which sympathy for prey entirely subverts any lingering identity with victors, but also entirely diverts our attention, consciously at least, from nationalistic and human issues, pretending that we have left the military and imperialist issues behind in a mere metaphor. The delicate balance of emotions here, the radical repositioning from heroic celebration to sympathy for victimization, helps us to see on a thematic level the way Pope characteristically employs the natural loyalties of the couplet to their fullest advantage.

So far, I have suggested the complexities of Pope mainly through content, monitoring his sympathies by exploring his tones to show that he knew what he was doing (admirably or not) when, on the one hand, he satirizes luxury, accumulation, and commodification, and on the other celebrates a nationhood and national identity based on conquest and commercial exploitation. But I'd like to make the case more fully on the basis of the couplet form and the traditions of value it embraces and privileges, or at least predisposes. To do so, I want to look in more detail at the value structures of not only "Windsor Forest" but also "The Rape of the Lock," poems that Pope worked on almost simultaneously and put into what he thought of as their final shape in 1713–14, when he was about twenty-five years old and trying hard to find and stick to a firm set of personal, philosophical, social, and political loyalties. In many respects, the poems are complementary in their sorting among values and in their longing for greater purity than they can manage. Though the earlier poem is mainly political in its thrust and the latter involved primarily with social and sexual customs and mores, both poems roam (typically of Pope) across personal and public categories and explicitly expose human contradictions and inconsistencies, including Pope's own. Both are assertive poems and in some ways pretentious and grand ones, but they are also ultimately modest and just in their moral and psychological claims.

"The Rape of the Lock" makes the case for perspective just as well as does "Windsor Forest," but it makes it on a personal level. It is, in fact, there that the fish and game from Windsor Forest—killed or devoured to satisfy the greed or ambition for conquest of hunters and anglers, or to displace human destructive desires so that humans are not killed—become human sacrifices: "wretches [who] hang that jurymen may dine." Cannibalism has a significant symbolic place in the self-indulgent world of "The Rape of the Lock" because the intervening system of mythic displacement has been eliminated in the urbanized world and "lower" forms of life no longer absorb the aggressive human urges. Instead, the human protagonists here—the Baron and Belinda, as well as the Queen and the jurymen—fail to recognize symbolic structures at all, stage a real battle of the sexes instead of a displaced one, and create a world in which treachery, physical brutality, and rape replace banter, negotiation, and sexual acceptance. The complex indictments and entrapments proceed out of formal commitments as well as personal ones. I do not want to say that Pope's use of the couplet dictated the nature of his conclusions, for it may well be the other way around: that he found the couplet so congenial a form because of the nature of his own commitments and modes of thinking. But the formal commitments of the heroic couplet—its ideology, so to speak—are not what older kinds of formal analysis, based on predispositions to find ordered absolutes, once led us to see and that (oddly) are still preserved in readings like that of Brown and of the hostile '80s more generally. The couplet now is for most traditionally trained readers, as it is for Brown, an excessively neat, aphoristic, and rigid form; but in fact it is not so in its nature, was not usually used that way in Pope's time, and tends not to be at most historical points of its application because of the tendencies of its structure.

IV

Let me make (briefly) three basic points about the nature of the couplet and the way it was understood by Pope and the other coupleteers who made it the representative verse form of those complex years from the mid-seventeenth century to the mid-eighteenth—when everyone longed for some simple binary choices, though only fools and innocents could actually believe in them.[7] First, couplets formally involve a careful pairing of oppositions or balances but no formal resolution. There is a notable absence of Hegelian forms of dialectic, and the opposing units are kept in formal tension, rather than being resolved. Rather than privileging one half or the other of the conflict or negotiating a successful compromise, the closed couplet tends to privilege the balancing itself—the preservation and acceptance of difference rather than a working out of modification or compromise: from the Civil Wars to the American Revolution, Anglophone poets consistently used it that way and found its structural properties useful to express such values. This principle of creative tension is signaled by the harmony of rhyme in which opposites are yoked together by a convenient—but often logically invalid—similarity of sound. As W. K. Wimsatt demonstrated long ago (though I think he got the politics of his analysis all wrong, possibly part of the reason more recent critics react so intemperately), rhyme is part of the essential grammar of couplets, and implicitly the paired sounds at the ends of lines invite a comparison of function and meaning of the words themselves.[8] Often, the force of a couplet hangs on our noticing the conflict between the words. Practically any couplet in "The Rape of the Lock" illustrates the tendency: eyes/dies; reveal'd/conceal'd; resort/court; Race/Place; sign/dine. A pretty good close analysis of what is going on in the poem on a value level could be done just on the basis of rhyme words, irrespective of normal syntax or even of plot. Here, for example, are the eight rhyme words in the four couplets characterizing Sir Plume—vain/ Cane; Face/Case; Devil/civil; Pox/Box—pretty much a summary of "the nice Conduct of a Clouded Cane" and his stammering attempts to articulate the values of a classist and sexist patriarchy so that the habitual superficiality can continue. Pope seems to have understood this principle better than most other couplet poets, but whether this means that he saw more clearly than anyone else the tendencies inherent in the couplet form or was just a more complicated poet who exploited the form to its fullest extent is debatable.

But the couplet is far more complicated architecturally than any syntax of rhyme can hint at. Each couplet involves (and this is my second point) a structure of four fundamental units—in effect, four terms, for not only do the two lines play off against each other, but also the first and second halves of each line—divided rhetorically by a caesura and syntactically by some crucial grammatical relationship that implies cause/effect—also play against one another. Ordinarily there is one dominant term in the first half of the line, searching for some relationship to cause and meaning, and another term in the second half of the line. Often the two are linked, usually by a verb that states causality, but sometimes the link is frustrated and held over into the second line in which, again, two terms exist in search of relationship. Sometimes term 1 is a cause and term 2 is an effect, sometimes the reverse. Often term 3 (that is, the first term in line 2) and term 4 parallel the relationship of the first line, but sometimes they reverse it. Exactly how the terms relate to one another in any given instance is less important than the fact that they all are questing for connection, and the couplet encloses them (in an apparently—but really only temporarily—closed world) so that they have to find in-house relationships, however temporary—that is, mates within their own small structure. In effect, we have four "floating" key terms in each couplet (there are exceptions, of course, especially those lists in which all terms refuse to be privileged), and they are trying to find their appropriate place and establish one or more meaningful relationships. The net effect of the destabilizing of terms is that the key verbs, crucial to setting the initial statement of relationships, are nearly cancelled when the nouns realign. In other words, the literal syntax of the passage is cancelled out by the larger structural grammar of the form.

Here, for example, is the very first couplet in "The Rape of the Lock," the summary statement of what the poet is about to sing:

> What dire offence from amorous causes springs
> What mighty contests rise from trivial things.

Here the four key terms (dire offence/amorous causes; mighty contests/trivial things) invoke the subject matter of the *Iliad* and "The Rape of the Lock," and while comparing the ancient to the modern, war to card games, and the important to the insignificant, they keep all four terms fluid: they do not belittle Belinda by comparison with Helen but demonstrate that one result is just like the other: the terms "float" for connections, and all the actions in both poems and both worlds are at once trivial and mighty, am'rous and dire. Again, in the four-part structure as in the rhyme, there is a notable refusal of the third compromising, resolving, or clarifying step—no Hegelian synthesis.

Third, the couplet, though sometimes mistakenly regarded so, is not (in the early eighteenth century, at any rate) a verse form but a rhyme scheme. Its stanza unit is, in poets from the early seventeenth century onward, not a pair of lines but rather a paragraph, as the print typography of the time makes visually clear. Pope's poems, like Dryden's and like those of almost any poet between Cleveland and Byron, always develop through a careful building, unit by unit. At first glance, the distinction may seem trivial but it is mighty. Pope's thinking is never—NEVER!—complete in a single couplet, except when he writes only a single couplet; and even in single-couplet poems, like his famous epitaph for Newton, the lines refuse to stand alone in their simplicity, reaching beyond themselves through echo or allusion or some other referential device to imply something quite different from their seeming statement, something far more refined and complex. Pope is not an epigrammatist, and when his great memorable lines are quoted in misguided isolation—"Fools rush in," "True wit is nature to advantage dressed," etc.—they parody his ideas, refusing the qualifications, complications, and explanations Pope carefully builds into the several lines that follow, part of a central definitional process. That is because such witty memorable lines form, in a Pope paragraph, only an opening gambit—an attention-getting device, a title-page promise, a sweeping generalization—which is then refined and complicated by the rest of the paragraph. Brown's isolation of the "True wit" couplet as the key to Pope's (and his whole century's) thought is thus doomed from the start, and her literal, single-dimensional analysis of the dressing metaphor is seriously misleading about both Pope and his culture.

Look, for example, at the way Pope refines his "little learning is a dangerous thing" canard, not only illustrating the process of making learning more extensive, arduous, and complex, but also forcing readers almost literally to experience the difficulties of the task—mountain-climbing as intellectual discovery as growth of the imagination. The metaphors here, derived both from classical mythology and contemporary experience—education as movement through space—are incredibly intricate: they allude, overlap, intertwine, and complicate; and reading the passage almost seems to produce physical weariness and aging, even as we negotiate perspective and discover our limits of knowing.

> A little learning is a dangerous thing;
> Drink deep, or taste not the Pierian spring;
> There shallow draughts intoxicate the brain,
> And drinking largely sobers us again.
> Fired at first sight with what the Muse imparts,
> In fearless youth we tempt the heights of arts,
> While from the bounded level of our mind,
> Short views we take, nor see the lengths behind;
> But, more advanced, behold with strange surprise
> New distant scenes of endless science rise!
> So pleased at first the towering Alps we try,
> Mount o'er the vales, and seem to tread the sky,
> Th' eternal snows appear already past,
> And the first clouds and mountains seem the last:
> But, those attained, we tremble to survey
> The growing labours of the lengthened way,
> Th' increasing prospect tires our wandering eyes,
> Hills peep o'er hills, and Alps on Alps arise!
> *Essay on Criticism*, ll. 215–232.

Again the direction is antisynthetic. We move not toward compromise or resolution but rather deeper into human examples and distinctions, farther and farther into the uncertain and the unknown. Critics want to clarify, theorists want to generalize, but Pope wants to complicate; and the couplet refuses to resolve.

V

You may be surprised to hear so committed a historicist as myself making this plea for the interests of formal integrity, and indeed there are important distinctions to be made about temporal constraints upon form, as well as categories to add of cultural, contextual, and biographical analysis. But form, as John Freccero has argued persuasively for terza rima, does make demands and have implications;[9] verse forms are not decorative afterthoughts or neutral frames for messages. Theory has a crucial place, but that place must be tested against historical and cultural categories before we try to utter the final synthetic word that Pope and couplets themselves systematically refuse. Still, one has to find a theory appropriate to the text, and that may also involve finding an appropriate theory for the form.

Notes

1. The mid-1980s, partly in reaction to Maynard Mack's eloquent defenses, were especially hard on Pope. See for example Ellen Pollak, *The Poetics of Sexual Myth: Gender and Ideology in the Verse of Swift and Pope* (Chicago: University of Chicago Press, 1985) and Laura Brown, *Alexander Pope* (Oxford: Blackwell, 1985). More recent assessments have tended to regard Pope's ideas and poetic practices more sympathetically. See especially Valerie Rumbold, *Women's Place in Pope's World* (Cambridge: Cambridge University Press, 1989); Claudia Thomas, *Alexander Pope and His Eighteenth-Century Women Readers* (Carbondale: Southern Illinois University Press, 1994); and Helen Deutsch's *Resemblance and Disgrace: Alexander Pope and the Deformation of Culture* (Cambridge: Harvard University Press, 1996).

2. The best account of Pope's ideology (though not from the perspective of verse form) is Brean Hammond, *Pope* (Atlantic Highlands, N.J.: Humanities Press International, 1986), especially chapter three.

3. It is also part of a larger project on the cultural history of the couplet from the sixteenth to the nineteenth century.

4. Most of the major work on the couplet as a form dates from the 1930s. See for example Ruth C. Wallerstein, "The Development of the Rhetoric and Metre of the Heroic Couplet, Especially in 1625–45," *PMLA*, 50 (1935), 166–210, and George Williamson, "The Rhetorical Pattern of Neo-Classical Wit," *Modern Philology*, 33 (1935), 55–82. William Bowman Piper harvests most of the best of previous formal analysis and extends it somewhat in *The Heroic Couplet* (Cleveland: Case

Western Reserve University Press, 1970), and Paul J. Korshin demonstrates a variety of couplet complexities in "The Evolution of Neoclassical Poetics: Cleveland, Denham, and Waller as Poetic Theorists," in *ECS*, 2 (Winter 1968): 102–38. More recently, the best work on the couplet has been done in analyzing individual poets; see, for example, John Jones, *Pope's Couplet Art* (Athens: Ohio University Press, 1970) and Pamela Slate Liggett, "Pope's Phonetic Triangles: The Heroic Couplet in The Rape of the Lock," *New Orleans Review*, 15 (Winter 1988): 17–22. A number of important studies of metrics and versification more generally (especially by Paul Fussell, John Hollander, and Percy Adams) have useful things to say about couplet techniques, and among recent more comprehensive books on eighteenth-century poetry, by far the most suggestive about couplets is Margaret Anne Doody, *The Daring Muse: Augustan Poetry Reconsidered* (Cambridge: Cambridge University Press, 1985).

5. See Brown, pp. 8–15.

6. I have suggested the complexity of some of Pope's commitments in his later poetry in "From Typology to Type: Print Technology and Ideology in *The Dunciad* and *Tristram Shandy*," in *Cultural Artifacts and the Production of Meaning: The Page, the Image and the Body*, ed. Katherine O'Brien O'Keeffe and Margaret J. M. Ezell (Ann Arbor: University Michigan Press, 1994), pp. 41–69.

7. The literal-minded interpretation of much primitivist, Golden Age, and Utopian rhetoric of the late seventeenth and early eighteenth century—involving such diverse writers as Behn, Swift, and Johnson, seems to me to ignore well-established traditions of argument and assume that rhetorical stances, adopted for comparative purposes, represent historical beliefs.

8. See his classic "One Relation of Rhyme to Reason," *Modern Language Quarterly* 5 (1944), 323–38, reprinted in *The Verbal Icon* (Lexington: University of Kentucky Press, 1954), 153–166.

9. See *Dante: The Poetics of Conversion* (Cambridge, Mass.: Harvard University Press, 1986).

J. Paul Hunter is the Barbara E. and Richard J. Franke Professor and Director of the Franke Institute for the Humanities at the University of Chicago, and the Senior Advisor in Literature for the Andrew W. Mellon Foundation. He is currently at work on a cultural history of the Anglophone couplet.

The Rules of the Game; Or, Why Neoclassicism Was Never an Ideology

Trevor Ross

My subject is the historical moment when literary form ceased to be valued as a vehicle of political ideology. In his contribution to this volume, J. Paul Hunter suggests that, insofar as literary conventions may become invested with certain values within historical formations, we can plausibly speak of an "ideology" of a verse form such as the couplet.[1] There have been, it is true, a number of occasions in literary history when the advocacy of specific formal principles was motivated by ideological sentiments, from the longing for an imperial antiquity that lay behind the failed humanist attempt to replace accentual with quantitative meter, to the reactionary politics that gave rise to modernist experiments in poetic fragmentation. That literary practices may become associated at times with certain constellations of thought should not, however, obscure the fact that, between the Renaissance and the modern era, the status of culture underwent a fundamental change, wherein artistic production was gradually identified as a separate sphere of human activity defined by its relative freedom from external social, political, or religious interests. This process of cultural "autonomization," as Pierre Bourdieu has termed it, culminated only in the late nineteenth century with the advent of aestheticism. Before then, the process was ambiguous, though literary historians have long celebrated the individual struggles for creative independence waged by the "heroes" of literary professionalism, Pope and Johnson.

The process is indeed inseparable from the rise of the professional author. It is, as Bourdieu has explained, "correlative with the constitution of a socially distinguishable category of professional artists or intellectuals who are less inclined to recognize rules other than the specifically intellectual or artistic traditions handed down by their predecessors, which serve as a point of departure or rupture. They are also increasingly in a position to liberate their products from all external constraints, whether the moral censure and aesthetic programmes of a proselytizing church or the academic controls and directives of political power, inclined to regard art as an instrument of propaganda."[2] In England, this process began as early as the Renaissance, when the competitiveness of an emergent print market compelled authors to assert their uniqueness by vaunting their literary pedigree. A prime example is Ben Jonson, whose espousal of a formal classicism enabled him to elevate his laureate professionalism above commercial authorship, as well as to declare his artistic autonomy from powerful influences, Jonson announcing himself to the court as "thy servant, but not slave."[3] Classicism, a formal movement often equated with the rise of political absolutism in Europe, was thus in the first instance an attempt by artists to discharge themselves from being directly answerable to a dominant class, and to create a legitimate space for their own activity by invoking the authority of an antique cultural inheritance. Though I will refer to Jonson again, my chief concern here is the extent to which this reliance on classicism as a badge of independence was still operative during its later history, when classicist prescriptions were so loudly proclaimed as to acquire the force of law. My aim is not to rehearse the familiar story of "the rules"—decorum, the unities, poetic justice, and the rest—but to apply Bourdieu's model for a sociology of modern aesthetics to this formative period in the history of the cultural field. Literary production during this period increasingly becomes a self-enclosed caste where poets and critics could legislate their own styles of practice, transforming culture into a game in which participants had to play by the rules or else risk losing their legitimacy as artists, a legitimacy formerly available to them only through the beneficence of their patrons or the church.[4] This transformation, I shall argue, was a crucial stage in the process whereby the literary activity frees itself from external constraints, on the way to becoming in the next century a separate field centered on a nascent ideology of the aesthetic.

Received accounts of the period tell a different story. Civil war and its aftermath, it is said, made for a polemicization of poetics more intense than had been possible before or since, with authors declaring with marked conviction that literature was subordinate to politics. Even publishing a collection of Cavalier tributes to Jonson during the Republican era could land an activist in prison for inciting rebellion.[5] For Davenant, in what is usually taken as the manifesto for a renewed classicism, his preface to *Gondibert* (1650), poetry took its moral patterns directly "from Courts and Camps," and was therefore "fit to be imitated by the most necessary men; and the most necessary men are those who become principall by prerogative of blood."[6] With the Restoration, poets would continue to maintain this polemicization, at least in principle, with Dryden among others ascribing the source of symbolic capital "to the Court; and, in it, particularly to the King, whose example gives a law to it."[7] Johnson, notoriously, would lament Dryden's prostrations before the powerful as degrading to the "dignity of genius," but the structure of belief that would uphold an independent cultural field, with its own source of value located in such imponderables as genius, began to be formed only late in Dryden's age.[8] At most, national poets like Jonson or Dryden could assert a degree of ethical independence, without which their praise of the state and its worthies could seem vitiated by the corrupting influences of sect, money, or other interests. Classicism, with its Horatian or Juvenalian postures of detachment, could offer the male poet the means to present himself as a public-minded verbal artist sufficiently free of self-interest to contribute genuinely to the common good. Classicism in this way, as I have argued elsewhere, was the cultural analogue to the ideology of civic humanism, with the national poet being equivalent to the statesman who practised autonomy in the confined space where he met with equals; the neoclassical poet saw his cultural practice as self-governing, yet integral to the state in its circulation of symbolic capital, itself conceived in terms of the civic humanist values of honour, fame, and devotion to the public realm.[9]

What is to be stressed in this formulation, however, was that classicism promised a cultural order that was only *analogous* to order in a political sphere. From its inception, classicism had been a cultural discourse and not a political ideology. Its legitimacy may have been owing to its applicability as a model of political harmony—"fit to be imitated," as Davenant insisted—yet it could not in itself provide a basis for social power, which in principle lay in the prerogatives of birth and property. As in previous campaigns of verbal refinement, beginning in England with the Lancastrian canonization of Chaucer as the first "perfecter,"[10] classicism may have been promoted as a means to enhance the language of political signification; certainly its proponents were successful in making it seem a vital element in a broader effort to reinforce social distinctions through the polishing of manners. It could be indeed argued that classicism in its later form represented an attempt to supplement a faltering political absolutism with a new cultural absolutism, as if methodizing aesthetic practices could somehow compensate for an increasing loss of conviction about the source of value in society. *Neo*classicism, which may be defined as a classically inspired formal practice that was submitted to a distinctly unclassical systematization, seemed to promise a purity and coherence increasingly unavailable from an existing social reality. But the relation of cultural to political order remained an artificial one, and this arbitrariness was all the more difficult to overlook the more critics sought to codify classicist practice in precepts that any author could observe. Not only was the belief in the suasive force of analogy, the episteme of similitude that had dominated Western thought for centuries, being broken down by the onslaughts of empiricism and analytical reason. But, equally, the more the advocates of classicism attempted to insist on the legislative force of their precepts (that is, as laws to be enforced by statutory fiat rather than as values that emanated from an origin inherent within the social structure), the more these precepts seemed like a cultural imposition, without their own immanent source of socially harmonizing power.

This arbitrariness had been evident from the start, since classicism was originally the creation of the schools, an effort by humanists like Ascham to gain a measure of power by dictating standards of speech, behavior, and erudition. To many of its early opponents, classicism was merely a pretentious essay at social control. Popular authors complained that it was designed to discourage literary expression among the lower orders, as though "none may be allowed of to write, but such as have bene trained at schoole with Pallas"; Puritan reformists saw the vogue for Latinisms as a ploy by elites to mystify their discourses of power, as though "truth cannot be delivered but in unknowen words and termes farfet."[11] But the most vocal opposition to classicism came from Tudor courtiers, who saw the humanists' program as an illegitimate encroachment upon their customary authority over cultural production. Its narrow prescriptions, Puttenham feared, threatened "the alteration or peradventure totall destruction" of those medieval forms such as rhyme or the chivalric romance for which the courtiers felt a nostalgic attachment.[12] Classicism was thus equated at its inception with an emergent class of professional intellectuals, who sought to appropriate aristocratic traditions of *courtoisie* and patriciate ritual, to refine them in accordance with a consensus ostensibly reaching back through the ages, and to disseminate them in pedagogical treatises in furtherance of their own group interests. Such appropriation, the first in a series of borrowings, opened up the possibility of social advancement through a studied impersonation of antique craftsmanship, whose symbolic power could potentially match the authority of courtly grace. Accordingly, classicism could have strong normative appeal for a low-born poet like Jonson, as it offered him a legitimizing cultural lineage reaching back to revered ancient *imperium*, an enabling revisionist narrative of refinement by which to define his modernity, and the prestige of being able to contribute to the cultural enrichment of the state as fully as any noble peer.

Its arbitrariness was nonetheless difficult to suppress, as evidenced by the attacks upon Jonson's "labored" writing and untiring self-promotion—what one literary historian has called his "constant, sweaty effort to mark a difference."[13] However much authority it may have furnished them among their colleagues, classicism could not endow authors with true distinction because it was a species of formalism that could be learned or flaunted only with a disabling show of effort. To gain distinction, one cannot be seen to be striving for it; dominant agents within a social order, as Bourdieu has noted, appear distinguished by manifesting "their difference without needing to want to, that is, with the unselfconsciousness that is the marks of so-called 'natural' distinction."[14] Thus the courtier, Castiglione declared, did not burden himself with "any kind of order, rule, or distinction of precepts."[15] It was not until the early seventeenth century, then, that classicism began to gain a foothold in the cultural imaginary with the rise of the French *salons*, where the prestige of displaying a classical polish in wit and conversation could be enhanced by a further appropriation of aristocratic values, this time of the courtly art of occultation. Though sanctioned by the rhetorical doctrine of concealment, dissimulation as practised by the courtiers had less to do with styles of oratory than with an entire cosmology of being, where the performing self was so skilfully fashioned as to make his artistry, in Puttenham's words, appear not "to proceed from him by any studie or trade of rules, but to be his naturall."[16]

It was this cosmology which the *salonniers* hoped to recreate within their circle by requiring their members to play by the rules, in terms of writing well-crafted verses or behaving with achieved gentility and yet doing all with an air of spontaneity. The original of these *salons*, the one led by Malherbe that convened at the Hôtel de Rambouillet, has long been identified as the progenitor of the neoclassical doctrines of decorum and *politesse*, though its most interesting historical feature was that it was formed by the marquise de Rambouillet as an intellectual refuge from the French court, whose crass manners she found repellent.[17] Its ideal of the *honnête homme*, whose precise yet seemingly effortless deployment of the arts of pleasing permitted him to succeed within diverse social encounters, presented an image of the free-floating intellectual who, like the courtier, spurned "specialization, trades, and techniques" including humanist pedantry, yet who could also define himself in contrast to the excesses of the court by embodying a sophisticated cultural discourse that was "more conducive to the indefinite niceties of the games of distinction."[18]

The ideal could not last, however, since it did not imply an alternative vision of political order.[19] By their gestures of disavowal, of opposing themselves to the court or the trading classes, the *salonniers* were only confirming how much their self-definition was contingent upon an existing social hierarchy: one could float "freely" only because others could not. Their classicism was thus played out as a game, as a set of behavioral norms that had little authority outside of their own circle. By their art of concealment, they had merely transposed the arbitrariness from the rules themselves to their own existence as a group. This explains why neoclassicism could later become enshrined as a cultural dominant only thanks to the express endorsement of the king. In a reverse appropriation, Louis XIV recognized the utility of neoclassical discipline in manners and the arts as a mechanism of hegemonic control, insofar as it could make more precise the task of social distinction-making. Like the *salonniers*, courtiers had to learn this discipline and to perform it with disguised artistry. Yet this now high-stakes game could be legitimized as an expression of absolutist order. It did not in itself amount to an ideology, and the artificiality of its rules was to some degree assumed since they required the stewardship of an *Académie*. Yet any arbitrariness was ultimately shrouded within the all-encompassing universe of belief that sustained the mythologies of kingship and rank.

The comparative weakness of monarchic rule in England made for a corresponding doubt about the value of neoclassical precepts. The French model had shown that the aesthetic could perform an important ideological function in heightening the symbolism of political hegemony. Neoclassicism presented poets with a clear aesthetic program which could secure them a recognized role in elite society—and at the same time could render them directly subservient to a dominant order. This subservience, as I have said, was upheld in principle by English authors, who observed it by adhering to the general values of decorum, refinement, and concern for the antique properties of genre. These formal values, in turn, seemed amenable to a politics of conservative moderation. Yet without a comparably strong centralized power or rigid social hierarchy by which to authorize the observance of any *particular* neoclassic formula, it remained unclear to English authors how much symbolic capital, for themselves or the state, might be gained from following this or that rule. Davenant may have felt that, at a time of crisis for the aristocracy, the aesthetic was a suitably safe ground from which to launch his vision of renewed hierarchy, but he was little interested in translating the dicta of French neoclassicism into English practice, preserving for himself the prerogative of modernity: the poet, he announced, "is no more answerable for disobedience to Predecessors, then *law-makers* are liable to those old Laws which themselves have repealed."[20]

For Dryden in the *Essay of Dramatic Poesy*, the French had simply gone too far in politicizing their stage conventions. Because of their heavy reliance upon declamatory speeches, Neander protested, their dramatic works ought "not so properly to be called plays as long discourses of reason of State." Likewise, their rule of making "one person considerable in their plays" led to a restrictive concentration on the mysteries of rank at the expense of the mobilities of worth. By contrast, a variety of "shining characters" permitted English dramatists to suggest "that greatness may be opposed to greatness, and all the persons [may] be made considerable, not only by their quality but their action."[21] The idea that greatness could be either innate or achieved may have implied a different and perhaps shakier set of ideological beliefs than those which prevailed in France, where courtiers "did not discuss the reasons for their election."[22] Arguably, though, it was not necessarily the case that Royalist poets like Davenant or the early Dryden were assuming a greater poetic license in accordance with a greater English liberty in a political sphere—though later opponents of the rules such as Farquhar would, under considerably altered circumstances, make such a correlation.[23] It was rather that the political applications of specific formal conventions were not so definitively established in England as they were in France. Hence the rules seemed to English authors to involve choices that were relatively more formal than ideological in nature, and this led to a certain doubt as to their utility, what Michael McKeon has called a "nagging, neo-Aristotelian suspicion" that neoclassicism was not entirely consonant with political discourse.[24]

For many Restoration authors, the status of the rules was therefore similar to that which had earlier obtained within the French *salons*. Playing by the rules might gain the poet some respect within literary circles, if not always commercial success in the theater. The critics could likewise invoke the rules as a credible judicial frontier for their own discipline, or at least as recognized terms for participation within it. This encouraged a greater self-reflexivity within the literary sphere, the sense that the styles of literary production could be legislated solely by reference to the history of literature, without direct oversight from political and religious authorities. Literature was still supposed to heighten belief in a social structure, in reinforcing, say, class determinations of speech and behaviour through the formal principles of decorum and propriety. And of course few literary producers could get by without some form of patronage. Yet no matter how deeply political and economic concerns continued to inform cultural work, the rules were being heralded by critics as a set of gestures for empowering the critical act with the symbolic authority of disinterestedness—"if people are prepossest," Rymer declared, "we can never have a certainty."[25] This was thus the first significant occasion in English critical discourse when cultural activity as a whole, and not simply the work of isolated artists like Jonson, was being valorized through disavowals of partiality or external influence. By their gestures, critics were inaugurating the formation of a separate cultural field, one that could be defined by its relative autonomy from other spheres of human activity.

What impeded this formation in the short term, however, was a failure to agree upon any particular source of value for cultural work. For critics, the rules offered the certainty of method and an apparent evaluative independence, yet could not help them to identify what was so distinctive about literature as to justify its autonomy as a self-regulating field. In the absence of such a theory of aesthetic value, belief in the cultural game could not be generated from within a literary field, but only prescribed arbitrarily as a condition of entry. Thus Sir Robert Howard scoffed at the critics who sought to transform culture into a charade in which a participant had "to be perswaded into a power of believing, not what he must, but what others direct him to believe."[26] Without an expectation of specific rewards, in other words, there was no real incentive either to internalize obedience to the rules as a determining disposition ("what he must"), or to grant their force as a harmonized set of presuppositions ("a power of believing") that could make sense of either experience or specific formal choices in the arts. Nor could this belief extend far beyond intellectual circles since, without clear ideological foundation or linkage to social power, the rules did not seem to possess much legitimacy. For those with a stake in the social hierarchy, the arbitrariness of the critics' designs was most evident whenever they presumed to assert that their edicts could have political import, as in Gildon's claim that his proposed academy of letters could determine which English families were worthy enough to be memorialized in poetry.[27] The several schemes for an English academy, in the view of conservatives like Temple, were the pipedreams of Minims who had deluded themselves into thinking that they could exercise political influence through their "laws." In reality, Temple declared, Richelieu had set up his *Académie* merely "to amuse the Wits of that Age and Country, and divert them from raking into his Politicks and Ministry."[28]

The appeals for an English academy also revealed the arbitrariness of the intellectual's own social position. Evelyn's scheme involved identifying the many causes of linguistic corruption, with the implication that the academician could stand outside all of these historical conditions by a vigilant effort of disavowal: "victories, plantations, frontieres, staples of com'erce, pedantry of schooles, affectation of travellers, translations, fancy and style of

Court, vernility & mincing of citizens, pulpits, political remonstrances, theatres, shopps, &c."[29] That these proposals came to nothing reflected the fact that disavowal alone could not lend the intellectual any positive social identity. It could lead only to an endless struggle to mark out a relative position in society or in a literary field—hence the persistent conflicts among poets and critics of the period, who, vying for distinction, set themselves against one another with such hostility as to undermine the possibility of consensual self-regulation, and to confirm that any attempt to claim critical authority was largely a matter of self-assertion.[30] There was nothing inherent within the rules that could be a basis for social distinction. The "grounds" of criticism were themselves ideologically ungrounded in that they served no particular political order. On the contrary, critics could happily point out that anyone could play the game. Since the rules were said to be ultimately founded on common sense, a staunch advocate like Rymer could put forward the provocative notion that even "*Women-judges* . . . left to their own heads" could evaluate literary works with rightness and certainty.[31]

Of course, writers and critics keenly sought to authorize their practice, rule-bound or not, by referring to the objective conditions of reason, nature, classical precedent, native temperament, or other essence. Yet citing such determinisms, however much they seemed founded in the concrete, was largely ineffective because these determinisms did not naturalize the relations of power *enough*, either within a cultural field or without. On the one hand, in being justified by an appeal to nature and common sense, the rules could not be long enforced before they began to be challenged by differing perceptions of experience and the real state of sublunary nature. In containing subjective aspirations and desires too objectively, they soon seemed illegitimate to authors who felt inhibited from writing anything truly new. On the other hand, in not being tied to a particular order of social values, the paradigms of reason, nature, and the rest could be too easily invoked on either side of a critical debate, and too easily recontextualized on behalf of any cultural or political mythology.[32] In sum, the arbitrariness of all these ostensible determinisms could be neither misrecognized nor occluded—as Dennis famously remarked of Pope's central trope in the *Essay on Criticism*, the poet ought to have told his readers "what he means by Nature, and what it is to write or to judge according to

Nature."[33] The solution, then, in the eighteenth century was to develop a new set of foundational theories that could certify a structure of value by which to enforce social distinctions, and yet at the same time were functionally ambiguous enough to sanction the expression of subjective desire vital to the renewal of the cultural field. For art to provide an alternative basis for moral and social authority, critics had to devise and refine a new aesthetic essentialism that, as Wittgenstein noted of the semantic category of "game," was itself completely resistant to essentialist definition.

Thus the third and most decisive appropriation of aristocratic properties occurred when critics began to fix their evaluations in the imponderables of taste, genius, the sublime, and *je ne sais quoi*. This last notion, first used in English by Suckling as a courtly alternative to Jonsonian rigor,[34] openly announced the arbitrariness of value choices in manners and the arts, but like the other concepts consigned this arbitrariness to a realm beyond rational understanding and hence beyond questioning. That realm had once been occupied solely by the providential signifieds of divinity and kingship, yet from Castiglione onwards courtiers had been engaged in secularizing this affective power and assigning it to their own performing selves. Yet in so doing, they had loosened it from its essentialist moorings in religious or immemorial authority, and made it increasingly a function of discourse. Influential guides like Castiglione's may have sought to mystify gentility as a "natural" manifestation of the courtier's right to social eminence, but they also laid out potent representations of courtly conduct that any aspirant could learn to emulate. By thus equivocating over nature and nurture, the courtiers had rendered this source of value flexible enough to be eventually appropriated on behalf of an emergent ideology of the bourgeois self. The idea of taste, initially championed by alienated aristocrats like Temple and Saint-Evremond who hoped to preserve their cultural hegemony from the encroachments of the critics, was seized upon by Addison and others for its enabling vagueness, the fact that it could be at once proposed as the defining essence of cultural activity, and promoted as a category of social capital in which distinction could be keyed to self-improvement. Taste, Addison famously declared, "must in some degree be born with us," yet equally it had to be cultivated or else "it will be very uncertain, and of little use to the Person that possesses it."[35] By this equivocation, Addison could justify a separate realm of the aesthetic as the basis for a new social hierarchy, one that promised clear rewards of personal enrichment and advancement, yet whose source of value could be deemed beyond interrogation.

I need not describe how eighteenth-century philosophers developed this idea into an ideology, in which the aesthetic experience was said to refine an innate moral sensibility into something that could underpin civil society as a whole—this is another story that has been told before.[36] I do, however, wish to comment on how authors in the first half of the century reacted to what they sensed were two serious consequences of forsaking neoclassical order for the perceived irrationalities of taste, sublimity, and *je ne sais quoi*. First, neoclassicism had at the least furnished precise models for composition: norms of correctness and propriety, protocols of genre, and ancestors to imitate. No doubt, too, the continuing popularity of the rules among critics had to do with the high degree of specificity that the rules lent to the business of tallying up a work's beauties and faults. Such models and criteria were unavailable from the newer aesthetic discourses. Though these discourses recognized opportunities for enrichment through consumption, of cultivating taste or modulating the passions through the experience of art, they had little to offer on the subject of production. Attempts were made to draw up Longinian handbooks on affecting the sublime but their cheesy expedients were quickly ridiculed in satires like *Peri Bathous*. Though poetry could still be written according to established conventions, Addison noted, "there is still something more essential, to the Art," which, by definition, could be neither defined nor codified.[37] Not even the poet, Shaftesbury argued, could explain this unintelligible essence and thus, like readers, could be left "feeling only the effect whilst ignorant of the cause."[38] The thought, then, of abandoning neoclassical virtues in favour of a poetic compulsion that came with no rational guidelines for composition evoked the frightening prospects of writing without any sense of structure or tradition, of submitting wholly to the vagaries of the market, or of surrendering art to the perturbations of unreason. Indeed, when the ongoing autonomization of culture finally compelled poets like Gray to reject neoclassicism and the civic-mindedness it entailed, they were left scrambling for alternative poetic fathers in Spenser or Milton, and to experiment with a broad array of vernacular and classical genres, from ballads to Pindaric odes, in search of a defining order for their poetry. Yet none was available since the source of poetic value had been relocated from an imitable practice equated with the ancients, to a providential mystery that could be identified only by its effects. At the same time, the weakening of rational principles of form opened the way for that most antigeneric of genres, the novel.

Second, the new aesthetic discourses seemed to deprive artists of their traditional roles as servants to the king and state. These discourses could empower cultural activity, making it appear integral to the moral welfare of the nation and its citizens. But in freeing poets from external constraints, the new discourses left them without any specific ideological function to perform. Shaftesbury had sensed this possibility when he heralded the poets' new freedoms: "in early days, poets were looked upon as authentic sages, for dictating rules of life, and teaching manners and good sense. How they may have lost their pretension, I cannot say. 'Tis their peculiar happiness and advantage not to be obliged to lay their claim openly."[39] By the later decades of the century, the romance of the solitary genius had evolved to the point where poets were being celebrated for their unsuitability for participating in public life, and even for their lack of conventional manners.[40] For Augustan writers like Pope and Swift, this marginalization of artistic labor could benefit them morally by legitimizing their stances of opposition, but they resisted the role that the new discourses would assign to poets, the role of being nourishers of the private sensibility, since this role would preclude them from intervening directly in social and political affairs. It seemed instead to confirm the arbitrariness of the poet's place in society.

Their response was complex, even conflicted. At the start of his career, Pope entertained a number of identities, both traditional and modern: the great correct poet, the wit who waged warfare upon earth, the purveyor of a grace beyond the reach of art. By its end, Pope was toying with mythologies of compulsion ("I lisp'd in Numbers, for the Numbers came"), and engaging in strenuous acts of disavowal by which to position himself at once in and out of society: grandly declaring that his singular honesty could "redeem the land" while spurning allies in the fragmentary *One Thousand Seven Hundred and Forty*, relinquishing culture to the dunces, and resolving to publish no more.[41] Throughout, however, Pope held on to the formal values, thought-structures, and ethical coordinates of neoclassicism. Pope, and certainly Swift and Fielding, may have understood at some level that neoclassical order was nothing more than a fiction, an ideal of order rather than the thing itself, a belief to be proclaimed even as its relation to a social and political reality could be called into question. Their art of "couplet-rhetoric," as Claude Rawson has designated it, may have implied certain ideological assumptions, about an ordered universe or the civic responsibilities of the artist.[42] Yet it appealed to them, as it did to earlier authors like Jonson, primarily because its apparent certainties could be justified by reference to a time-honored and specifically literary tradition that did not oblige them to defer directly to religious, political, or economic powers. That tradition provided them with rules and an artistic bearing by which they could believe themselves to contribute actively to the circulation of symbolic capital in society, while remaining relatively detached from the perplexing realities, dark psychic energies, and pervasive external interests that continually threatened to undermine judgment. They may have vigorously confronted such realities, energies, and interests in their work, but the fact that they answered these threats with ironies that inevitably revealed the author's own frustrations and doubts indicates that their classicism never fully cohered into an ideology that could protect them from such doubts. If anything, the greatest literature of the period—by Swift, Pope, Fielding, and others— was devoted to exposing shams, and this would not have been possible had its authors failed to recognize an element of artifice in what they themselves were doing.

In hindsight, it is apparent to many of us that their formal choices were in fact propelled by ideological imperatives deeper than any they could have possibly imagined. But my point is that, in sensing this measure of artifice, the Augustans came face to face with what we now call the problem of mediation, of not knowing for certain what form does to content. Being aware of such arbitrariness, they could not wholly subscribe to the old and fast-eroding structure of conviction that had once posited a clear correspondence between specific rhetorical formulas and their effects upon an audience. On the contrary, they took advantage of this disjuncture between form and meaning for the purposes of ironic critique—in mock forms, modest proposals, romance parodies, and the like. Yet the disjuncture left them without any definitive sense of the relations between art and ideology, relations which the new aesthetic discourses threatened to occult or perhaps sever altogether.[43] The problem of mediation may have therefore appeared to them intractable and insoluble, as it remains for us. In any event, their response was one of mixed feelings, of being, in effect, torn between ideology and form. The traditional and modern roles for the poet each presented its own rewards and limitations: whereas the old order accorded poetry a prestigious ideological function while rendering it directly subservient to powerful interests, the pursuit of an aesthetic purity in form and the imagination promised the poet a new liberty and a new source of specifically cultural power, yet at the severe cost of denying poetry its former centrality within the social and political economy of the state. In the face of such a difficult choice between two equally compromising roles, perhaps the most honest response open to the Augustans was to adopt a position of ambivalence.

So it is, or should be, with us. We may now question an inherited ideology of the aesthetic but we continue to benefit by its rewards and freedoms. Even as we yearn to reinvest our work with a greater social relevance, we have fortified our borders by requiring degrees and professional protocols that are designed to keep the uninitiated out. As ever, we argue over the rules of the game, as formalists contend with historicists over how best to understand literature, though in reflecting more generally over the value and purpose of the game, we may recognize that these rules are to a degree arbitrary. Neither formalism nor historicism is in this sense an ideology, though diverse political values have been attributed to each. What these rules are meant to provide us with are conventional discourses by which we may choose to describe how cultural forms mediate meaning and value within and between works, traditions, authors, readers, and history. Yet, as the problem of mediation remains unabatably complex, so these rules never seem entirely satisfactory for very long, and we regularly feel compelled to revise them in an attempt to come up with a better answer to the problem. In view of this, my own penchant for historical synthesizing, which may be construed as a kind of historicist formalism whose object of enquiry is the literary field as a whole, is not unqualified by doubt, and I am disinclined to making strong claims for it. "Those of us," as David Simpson (rightly, in my view) suggests, "who still think that it is not redundant to historicize have to do so with a certain suspension of belief about what exactly such historicizing can achieve."[44] By extension, I also refrain from fully endorsing Bourdieu's project, whose subject is precisely the operation of belief, since it can itself be criticized for its failure to interrogate its own interests and assumptions. In holding out an idealistic promise that our understanding can "escape (however slightly) from history" while all but collapsing value into interest, Bourdieu's scientism is not without contradiction or arbitrariness, and so its insights, powerful though they often are, will ever be only partially satisfying.[45] Yet this is about as much as we ought to ask of any intellectual endeavour if it is not to become an ideology.[46]

Notes

1. Hunter cautions that we cannot speak "in an absolute sense" of literary forms "as having ideologies." At most, he suggests, a form such as the heroic couplet can become linked within certain periods to a host of "expectations, patterns, leanings, tendencies, appropriate formal associations" that are tantamount to an ideology ("Form as Meaning," 149). I do not dispute the theoretical point. My aim in this essay is, rather, a historical one: I wish to consider the kinds of linkages that, during the later seventeenth and early eighteenth centuries, were drawn between neoclassical formal practices and larger social ideologies. In particular, I examine the critical discourse of the period for early signs of what in time would become an "ideology of the aesthetic"—that is, the belief, usually associated with Romanticism, that culture represents a separate field of activity, which, because of its autonomy from political or other worldly interests, is uniquely suited to providing the private sensibility with emotional and imaginative enrichment. If the purpose of the present collection of essays is to debate the relation of literary form to ideology, my concern is with how this relation first became a subject of debate, with how it was that some English authors began to perceive literary form as being to a degree independent of political ideology.

However, I am also implicitly advancing a larger claim, one that may make for confusion (as it did, apparently, for an anonymous reader for the press) since it requires me to rely on two divergent notions of ideology. When I speak of how art began to be seen as independent of "ideology," I am using the word in its narrow sense as denoting a consciously held set of political doctrines. Yet when I speak of an aesthetic "ideology," I am using the term in its broad sense as denoting a complex of ideas, beliefs, and procedures that govern the "spontaneous" self-experience of groups or individuals. The latter definition of ideology has of course been much contested: Slavoj Žižek has noted that, just as the theory of ideology appears to be making a comeback, the concept of ideology has become so expansive as to be in danger of losing its analytical precision (see "Introduction: The Spectre of Ideology," in *Mapping Ideology*, ed. Slavoj Žižek [London: Verso, 1994], 1–33; this collection also includes an interview between Bourdieu and Terry Eagleton ["Doxa and Common Life," 265–77], in which Bourdieu declares that he finds the concept of ideology too vague to be of much use.)

I am nonetheless prepared to risk confusion because I wish to argue that, historically at least, neoclassicism was not an "ideology" in *both* senses of the term. Beginning in the late seventeenth century, some authors began to see their art as not being entirely commensurable with political discourse, with the result that the relation of literary form to ideology (in its narrow sense) became problematic. At the same time, neoclassical practice, despite the efforts of its defenders to legitimize it as reflecting the dictates of nature, was never fully naturalized as part of a prevailing ideology (in its broad sense) of social conduct. Ernesto Laclau has helpfully suggested that ideology, broadly defined, ought to be seen as a kind of horizon where, by a "logic of equivalence," divergent ideas and practices become tied together in a larger incarnation. Laclau cites as an example the theory of evolution: in itself, the theory is not an ideology but, when it is transformed into a larger operative paradigm for many aspects of scientific thought and human behavior ("Darwinism"), it acquires the dimensions of an ideological horizon ("The Death and Resurrection of the Theory of Ideology," *MLN* 112 [1997]: 303). In this sense, neoclassicism was not an ideology because there occurred a failure of misrecognition: the arbitrariness of many neoclassical precepts could not be concealed, and so its norms could not be transformed into a larger ideological horizon of human thought and activity.

The reasons for this failure I can only hint at within my argument. Neoclassicism, it seems, was a transitional cultural logic that served two incompatible socioeconomic orders: the early market capitalism of the professional intellectuals who first promoted neoclassicism as a sign of their independence, and the feudal absolutism of the French court that appropriated neoclassical edicts to consolidate its hegemony within a cultural realm. This incompatibility essentially made it impossible to set neoclassicism within a chain of equivalence that would have linked it to one particular social order (even though either side promoted neoclassical practice on the basis of similar ideological assumptions, notably the belief that the ancient empires were the supreme paradigms of civilization). Only once market capitalism had displaced courtly hegemony was it possible to transform professional literary practice into an ideological horizon—the ideology of the aesthetic—that could serve the new prevailing order. This ideology may have inherited from neoclassicism a belief in artistic autonomy, but such a belief could now be fully legitimized since it accorded with the capitalist division of labor into separate spheres of activity.

2. Pierre Bourdieu, *The Field of Cultural Production*, ed. Randal Johnson (New York: Columbia University Press, 1993), 112–13.

3. Ben Jonson, *Works*, ed. C. H. Herford, Percy Simpson, and Evelyn Simpson, 11 vols. (Oxford: Clarendon Press, 1925–1952), 4:33.

4. Hunter uses the phrase "the rules of the game" to refer to the appropriate learning or competence required to decipher the full implications of couplet structures ("Form as Meaning," 149). I use the phrase to recall Bourdieu's more abstract notion of the cultural "game," which he defines as an internalized structure of belief that predisposes agents within the cultural field to behave in accordance with deeply tacit rules: not only are competent readers, for example, expected to possess a certain level of learning but equally to abide by norms of competence, to uphold the value of these norms, to seek personal distinction through a display of such competence, to accept as given the legitimacy of the collective order and internal workings of the cultural field—in sum, to believe "in the value of the game and in its stakes" (*The Rules of Art: Genesis and Structure of the Literary Field*, trans. Susan Emanuel [Stanford: University of California Press, 1996], 172–73).

5. See Derek Hirst, "The Politics of Literature in the English Republic," *The Seventeenth Century* 5 (1990): 133.

6. Sir William Davenant, preface to *Gondibert* (1650), in *Critical Essays of the Seventeenth Century*, ed. J. E. Spingarn, 3 vols. (Oxford: Clarendon Press, 1908), 2:14.

7. John Dryden, *Of Dramatic Poesy and Other Critical Essays*, ed. George Watson, 2 vols. (London: J. M. Dent, 1962), 1:181.

8. Samuel Johnson, *The Lives of the English Poets*, ed. George Birkbeck Hill, 3 vols. (Oxford: Clarendon Press, 1905), 1:398–99.

9. See my "'Pure Poetry': Cultural Capital and the Rejection of Classicism," *MLQ* 58 (1997): 437–56, which condenses material from later chapters of *The Making of the English Literary Canon: From the Middle Ages to the Late Eighteenth Century* (Montréal: McGill-Queen's University Press, 1998). The present essay reworks some of the evidence I consider in the book, though I have attempted to extend my original thesis about the relation of classicism to cultural autonomization. On civic humanism, see J. G. A. Pocock, *Virtue, Commerce, and History* (Cambridge: Cambridge University Press, 1985), 37–50.

10. According to John H. Fisher, evidence suggests that the refinement of the vernacular "was encouraged by Henry IV, and even more by Henry V, as a deliberate policy intended to engage the support of Parliament and the English citizenry for a questionable usurpation of the throne. The publication of Chaucer's poems and his enshrinement as the perfecter of rhetoric in English were central to this effort" ("A Language Policy for Lancastrian England," *PMLA* 107 [1992]: 1170).

11. Barnabe Rich, *Allarme to England* (London, 1578), sig. *3_v; John Jones, *The arte & science of preserving bodie & soule in healthe* (London, 1579), 2.

12. George Puttenham, *The Arte of English Poesie* (London, 1589), 86.

13. Richard Helgerson, *Self-Crowned Laureates: Spenser, Jonson, Milton and the Literary System* (Berkeley: University of California Press, 1983), 183.

14. Pierre Bourdieu, *In Other Words: Essays Towards a Reflexive Sociology*, trans. Matthew Adamson (Stanford: Stanford University Press, 1990), 11.

15. Baldassare Castiglione, *Il Libro del Cortegiano* (1528), as cited in Jacques Revel, "The Uses of Civility," in *A History of Private Life*, vol. 3: *Passions of the Renaissance*, ed. Roger Chartier, trans. Arthur Goldhammer (Cambridge, Mass.: Harvard University Press, 1989), 190.

16. Puttenham, 253.

17. Thomas Kaminski rehearses the standard account of the Rambouillet circle's influence on a later neoclassicism in "Rehabilitating 'Augustanism': On the Roots of 'Polite Letters' in England," *Eighteenth-Century Life* 20 (1996): 49–65.

18. Pierre Bourdieu and Jean-Claude Passeron, *Reproduction in Education, Society and Culture*, trans. Richard Nice (London: Sage Publications, 1977), 130.

19. Or rather, the ideal went into abeyance, to be revived later in the century in the notional spaces of a Republic of Letters and a public sphere. This is not the occasion to determine whether such a public sphere ever existed, but clearly the idea of a conversational space, free from the distorting effects of power, had gained enough legitimacy by the early eighteenth century that it could be meaningfully proclaimed by Addison and others as a normative value. On how the idea is based on the assumption that the literary and political fields had to be kept separate lest rational discourse devolve into ideology, see Neil Saccamano, "The Consolations of Ambivalence: Habermas and the Public Sphere," *MLN* 106 (1991): 685–98.

20. Davenant, in Spingarn, 2:20. Stephen N. Zwicker suggests that Davenant and his respondent Hobbes were concerned with neoclassical prescriptions only as a means to politicize poetics: "Davenant and Hobbes may have fostered neoclassicism, but they aimed beyond aesthetics, arguing broadly to the social, spiritual, and political realms." Yet, as Zwicker acknowledges, by implying that "the aesthetic might be foundation of the political," Davenant and Hobbes were reversing the priorities of an earlier courtly culture that had stressed the primacy of the political in all matters (*Lines of Authority: Politics and English Literary Culture, 1649–1689* [Ithaca: Cornell University Press, 1993], 23).

21. Dryden, 1:60–61.

22. Revel, "The Uses of Civility," 195.

23. "An English play," Farquhar insisted in his *Discourse upon Comedy* (1702), "is intended for . . . an English audience, a people not only separated from the rest of the world by situation, but different also from other nations as well in the complexion and temperament of the natural body as in the constitution of our body politic" (in *Eighteenth-Century Critical Essays*, ed. Scott Elledge, 2 vols. [Ithaca: Cornell University Press, 1961], 1:92).

24. Michael McKeon, "Politics of Discourse and the Rise of the Aesthetic in Seventeenth-Century England," in *Politics of Discourse: The Literature and History of Seventeenth-Century England*, ed. Kevin Sharpe and Stephen N. Zwicker (Berkeley: University of California Press, 1987), 45.

25. Thomas Rymer, *The Tragedies of the Last Age* (1678), in Spingarn, 2:183.

26. Sir Robert Howard, pref. to *The Great Favourite* (1668), in Spingarn, 1:107.

27. Charles Gildon, *The Post-Man Robb'd of his Mail: or, the Packet broke open* (London, 1719), 333.

28. Sir William Temple, "Of Poetry" (1690), in Spingarn, 3:102.

29. John Evelyn, letter to Sir Peter Wyche (20 June 1665), in Spingarn, 2:310.

30. On this point, see Paul Trolander and Zeynep Tenger, "Criticism Against Itself: Subverting Critical Authority in Late-Seventeenth-Century England," *PQ* 75 (1996): 311–38.

31. Rymer, in Spingarn, 2:183. Rymer, of course, did not have in mind *all* women, regardless of rank. It is nonetheless indicative of a significant cultural transformation that he should believe that his claim could be a credible gesture by which to assert the independence of the critical act. On how French intellectuals of the 1690s, seeking to detach culture from a failing monarchic order, relied on similarly gendered claims to establish a public sphere, see Joan DeJean's polemic, *Ancients Against Moderns: Culture Wars and the Making of a Fin de Siècle* (Chicago: University of Chicago Press, 1997).

32. Trolander and Tenger note that, in the criticism of the period, "legal, political, and moral discourses used to bolster the authority of critical discourse served contradictory ends: to establish or subvert the validity of a critical pronouncement, to vindicate or arraign an author's practice, to inaugurate or unseat critical authority" ("Criticism Against Itself," 326).

33. John Dennis, *Critical Works*, ed. Edward Niles Hooker, 2 vols. (Baltimore: Johns Hopkins University Press, 1939–43), 1:403.

34. On Suckling's use of the phrase, see Michael P. Parker, "'All are not born (Sir) to the Bay': 'Jack' Suckling, 'Tom' Carew and the Making of a Poet," *English Literary Renaissance* 12 (1982): 366 and note.

35. Joseph Addison, *Spectator* 409, in *The Spectator*, ed. and introd. by Donald F. Bond, 5 vols. (Oxford: Clarendon Press, 1965), 3:529.

36. See, among others, Howard Caygill's *Art of Judgement* (Oxford, 1989), and Terry Eagleton's *The Ideology of the Aesthetic* (Oxford: Basil Blackwell, 1990).

37. Addison, *Spectator* 409, in Bond edition, 5:530.

38. Anthony Ashley Cooper, Earl of Shaftesbury, *Characteristics of Men, Manners, Opinions, Times*, ed. John M. Robertson, 2 vols. (Gloucester, Mass.: Peter Smith, 1963), 1:214.

39. Shaftesbury, 1:104.

40. William Duff offered perhaps the most extreme account of the unsociable "temper" of genius in his *Critical Observations on the Writing of the Most Celebrated Writers and Original Geniuses in Poetry* (London, 1770), 338–66.

41. Pope, *Epistle to Dr. Arbuthnot*, l. 128, and *One Thousand Seven Hundred and Forty*, l. 98, in Twickenham edition, ed. John Butt, 11 vols. (London, 1939–1969), 4:105, 337.

42. See Claude Rawson, *Henry Fielding and the Augustan Ideal Under Stress* (London and Boston: Routledge and Kegan Paul, 1972), 35–66.

43. In actuality, the disjuncture had always existed, since the traditional division between rhetoric and logic stipulated no intrinsic connection between thought and the particular form of its expression. Yet the disjuncture had been held in check by ideology: so long as it was understood that both the delights of form and the teachings of content were to serve the larger goal of circulating symbolic capital in society, there was felt no need to say how a poem's expression might relate to its meaning. Such a need arose only when it became possible for poets to assert a measure of autonomy from prevailing interests, since justifying this freedom required them to define what it was about their art that could not be rendered serviceable to such interests. Thus it was no coincidence that Dryden was writing at the height of neoclassicism when he became the first English critic to propose a theory of organic unity, in which form and content were said to be fused in the author's consciousness and "particular turn of thoughts and of expression, which are the characters that distinguish and, as it were, individuate him from all other writers" (1:271–72). As Bill Readings has noted, the historic significance of Dryden's organicism will continue to be overlooked as long as literary historians abide by the standard account of neoclassicism as a species of formalism; see Readings's entry on Dryden in *The Johns Hopkins Guide to Literary Theory and Criticism*, ed. Michael Groden and Martin Kreiswirth (Baltimore: Johns Hopkins University Press, 1994), 216–19.

44. David Simpson, *The Academic Postmodern and the Rule of Literature* (Chicago: University of Chicago Press, 1995), 165.

45. Bourdieu, *The Rules of Art*, 310. A number of critics have taken Bourdieu to task for refusing to acknowledge his own political position; see, for example, John Frow, *Cultural Studies and Cultural Value* (Oxford: Oxford University Press, 1995), 27–47, 166–68. In Bourdieu's defense, John Guillory has brilliantly shown how the sociologist's work may in fact propose a model for social action, but a model that "is complex in the same way that making or consuming art is complex" ("Bourdieu's Refusal," *MLQ* 58 [1997]: 397).

46. My final plea should not be taken as an endorsement of the idea of aesthetic autonomy, whose prehistory I have sought to analyze in this essay. I am speaking in my conclusion on behalf only of the value of doubt. By analogy with the ambivalence of the Augustans over the relation of their art to ideology, I am suggesting that criticism ought to be informed

by doubt over its assumptions and promises. In saying this, I have in mind all critical approaches, though especially what others in this volume call "ideological criticism." Doubt, it seems to me, aptly describes the situation of tension that, according to Žižek, is necessary to keep the critique of ideology alive: "ideology is not all," Žižek writes, since "it is possible to assume a place that enables us to maintain a distance from it, *but this place from which one can denounce ideology must remain empty, it cannot be occupied by any positively determined reality*—the moment we yield to this temptation, we are back in ideology" ("Introduction: The Spectre of Ideology," 17). The moment we cease to value doubt, I would similarly suggest, we fall prey to the ideological temptations of quietism or cynicism, of an unreflective postmodernist resistance to totalizing narratives, or of the easy comforts of moralizing reduction.

Trevor Ross, Associate Professor of English at Dalhousie University, is the author of *The Making of the English Literary Canon: From the Middle Ages to the Late Eighteenth Century*. He is currently working on a history of how the English began to interpret their own literature.

Desire and Mourning: The Ideology of the Elegy

George E. Haggerty

In vain to me the smiling mornings shine,
And reddening Phoebus lifts his golden fire:
The birds in vain their amorous descant join,
Or cheerful fields resume their green attire:
These ears, alas! for other notes repine,
A different object do these eyes require.
My lonely anguish melts no heart but mine;
And in my breast the imperfect joys expire.
Yet morning smiles the busy race to cheer,
And new-born pleasure brings to happier men:
The fields to all their wonted tribute bear;
To warm their little loves the birds complain.
I fruitless mourn to him that cannot hear,
And weep the more because I weep in vain.[1]

These lines, Thomas Gray's "Sonnet on the Death of Richard West" (1742), allude to a tradition of elegiac verse that is rich in its ability to express grief, the kind of grief that a man may feel when he loses a friend whom he loves. Gray is mourning his friend in conventional terms that are also deeply personal—as Roger Lonsdale points out, "the poet is mourning the only friend that could have understood and shared such a grief"[2]—and in that process he also configures his own desire for his departed friend. In Gray's case the desire is intensely physical and erotic, but within the elegy it can only be expressed as loss. Loss is finally what this poem is about: the blank and the frustrations of loss.

As elegiac writing, the poem is probably most celebrated because it was so importantly condemned by Wordsworth for its artificial language—"Gray . . . was at the head of those who, by their reasonings, have attempted to widen the space of separation between Prose and Metrical composition, and was more than any other man curiously elaborate in the structure of his own poetic diction."[3] I have elsewhere offered a reading of this poem that suggests that its "curiously elaborate" structure works to refigure as elegiac loss what for Gray is actual physical longing and frustrated physical desire. The octave expresses a distinctly physical longing that is no longer available—"In vain to me the smiling mornings shine" (note that "me" is the object of loss here rather than its subject), and the sestet answers by developing this contrast. By mourning to West (rather than *for* him), Gray underlines the personal quality of the loss—just what it means to him—and explains the loop of grief which the last line expresses. With West finally out of reach, at the end of the poem Gray withdraws—as the man of feeling must—into the privacy of his own misery. "I . . . weep the more because I weep in vain": Gray must stop short of breaking through the language of grief to something (or someone) outside himself. "I" is the source of grief, that is, rather than "he" or "you."[4]

Wordsworth finds these lines, as well as lines 6–8, "of . . . value" because "the language of these lines does in no respect differ from that of prose."[5] For me, their cultural "value" lies in this ability to figure desire as loss. At the same time that these lines commemorate desire, and perhaps its fulfillment, they use conventional imagery to hide their personal intensity. Every line reveals as much as it conceals, and poetry itself, decorous and allusive, becomes the vehicle for private longing. Gray's melancholy stems from the failure of the elegy to lead him to an encounter with anything more than his own private emotion. "Friendship" involves an internal contradiction and self-confrontation that West's death now make inevitable.[6]

Wordsworth notices none of this; or, more precisely, he notices something powerful here, but he is not certain what it is. In this essay I will argue that something even larger than one poet's private grief is at issue here, and that Wordsworth's response is culturally inevitable. In "Mourning and Melancholia," Freud talks about the elaborate contours of grief and suggests that within the "economics of pain" that comprises mourning, "a turning away from reality takes place and a clinging to the object through the medium of a hallucinatory wishful psychosis." He adds that "it is really only because we know so well how to explain it that this attitude does not seem to us pathological." Furthermore, for Freud, "each single one of the memories and expectations in which the libido is bound to the object is brought up and hypercathected," as Gray's elegy suggests. Gray's grief in this poem would seem "pathological" in more conventional terms as well, if it were not clear that the desire he expresses is already experienced as loss.[7] The expression of male-male desire does not challenge cultural prerogatives, in other words, it almost seems to reaffirm them.

It is of course no secret that the elegy is the poetic form concerned with the erotics of mourning, as recent critics have suggested, and that nowhere more importantly than in the period between Milton and Tennyson, when a half dozen of the most famous poems in our language were written to commemorate one man's erotic grief at the loss of another. If within the confines of this essay I talk about only a few important examples of this form—Gray's *Elegy Written in a Country Churchyard* (of course) as well as Milton's *Lycidas*, and Shelley's *Adonais*—I hope to be able to show how the ideology of the elegy form itself functions both to carve a space for male-male desire at the same time that it reinscribes that desire within the contours of hegemonic cultural practice. In the end, not desire but loss becomes the most recognizable feature of male love.

In his recent study of the modern elegy, Jahan Ramazani argues that while the "most canonical English elegists had depicted mourning as compensatory," modern elegists, in contrast, "tend to enact the work not of normative but of 'melancholic' mourning," which, following Freud, he calls "unresolved, violent, and ambivalent."[8] It is no criticism of the depth and thoughtfulness of Ramazani's own study to suggest that this account of the early modern elegy tradition overstates the power of consolation in poetry written before the twentieth century. What is Gray's *Elegy*, after all, if not a melancholic account of the poet's own subjectivity? I will discuss this point in detail below. For now, however, it will be helpful to pause momentarily over this depiction of the seventeenth- and eighteenth-century elegy as "compensatory."

Peter M. Sacks connects compensatory mourning to the oedipal resolution: "at the core of each procedure is the renunciatory experience of loss and the acceptance, not just of a substitute, but of the very means and practice of substitution. In each case such an acceptance is the price of survival, and in each case a successful resolution is not merely deprivatory, but offers a form of compensatory reward. The elegist's reward, especially, resembles or augments that of the child [in the oedipal model]—both often involve inherited legacies and consoling identifications with symbolic, even immortal, figures of power."[9] I hope to consider the psychological and social implications of the elegy more directly as I proceed. I would observe here in passing, however, that the compensation that Sacks offers is (always already) flawed, tentative, and in danger of imminent collapse in the face of forces greater than those that the elegist can control. Sacks himself moves on to a discussion of the Lacanian "mirror stage" as a way of explaining a split consciousness: "the child's relation to this mirror is dyadic, remaining within a condition of primary narcissism but now revealing a preliminary split in, or we might say *for*, the constitution of the self."[10] But this theoretical move seems to me superfluous; for within the elegy itself self-projection is constituted in lack that perforce alienates the speaker from his own experience of grief at the loss of his friend. This lack can be realized in individual psychoanalytic terms or, equally plausibly, in broader cultural ones. If I move in the direction of the latter, it is not to ignore individual psychology but rather to attempt to understand some of its more puzzling features, as evidenced particularly in these few elegies.

Sacks talks about "the alienating displacement of the inchoate self during the mirror stage" and the degree to which "the child's instinctual renunciation requires a symbolic self-castration."[11] His Lacanian child is warding off the "threatening figure of the father," and in doing so he resigns sexual agency to a paternal order as an elaborate defense against mortality. As Sacks argues, "the work of mourning . . . is largely designed to defend the individual against death. . . . Once again, a forced renunciation prevents a regressive attachment to a prior love-object, a potential fixation on the part of the griever, whose desire in such cases for literal identification with the dead is another force very much like that of the death wish. Melancholia usually involves a lasting return to [a] kind of regressive narcissism, . . . often including an identification between the ego and the dead such that the melancholic tends toward self-destruction."[12] I find this argument persuasive, but I would also insist that this paternal order may be cultural, as well as personal, as even various Lacanian accounts have made clear. The "death wish" may not be the most harrowing feature of private desire in a heteronormative cultural situation, nor are "narcissism" and "identification" always the richest sources of melancholy. The "threatening figure of the father," as Žižek and others have argued, may be internalized as "Law" so as to rewrite desire with a traumatic and "senseless" normalcy.[13] But perhaps normalcy is precisely what these elegies are attempting to resist.

Another way to look at the particular process of grieving that an elegy represents is to see the cathexis between the living poet and the dead friend not as a trajectory of failed identification but as a trajectory of desire. Michael Moon has completely rewritten the concept of loss in his essay on Whitman's "Drum Taps." In an essay that was delivered at the first AIDS panel at the 1986 MLA convention (and later published in *Professions of Desire*), Moon argues that "if we are to make, read, and teach memorials to the dead in the light of models of mourning that do not contain and repress urgent needs and feelings, as the traditional elegiac model does by presenting the process as a set of conventional tasks with a preordained beginning, middle, and end, where are these models to come from?"[14] The ideological implication of these remarks are clear. The "conventional tasks" that Moon describes are based loosely on the paradigms that Freud outlines in "Mourning and Melancholia": "Mourning is work for Freud," Moon says, "but there is a payoff at the end of the job: acceptance, reintegration, the 'fresh woods, and pastures new' that Milton holds out at the end of 'Lycidas.'" The language of "work" and "payoff" are being used with full reference to the capitalistic system that they imply, and Moon makes this point even more explicitly in a passage that follows:

> There are of course other ways of understanding work besides the capitalist ones that have long predominated in American culture, but one of the things that seem most wrong with the notion of grief and mourning that informs Freud's idea of "working through" is the considerable degree to which that idea is constructed under the signs of compulsory labor and the cash nexus. One must dig one's way out of grief, advisers in Freud's tradition say, to be rewarded by a return to "normalcy."[15]

"Normalcy" in this analysis, and especially in the context of AIDS laments, is an ambivalent ideal at best, and the moves that replace the extreme emotions of grief with a rational consolation are the moves to reassert what Kaja Silverman calls the "dominant fiction," in which cultural prerogatives are given the ascendancy that the ideological state apparatus presupposes. In her attempt to read Althusser through Freud and more particularly Lacan, Silverman reopens the concept of "interpellation" to include the notion that the "state apparatus" itself is only a "dominant fiction," rather than anything "real." She argues further that "it is only by defining what passes for 'reality' at the level of the psyche that ideology can be said to command the subject's belief."[16] Silverman also argues, with the help of Lacan and other French theorists such as Laplanche and Pontalis, that the dominant fiction is consequently more real than any details of concrete reality. For Silverman, no writer completely escapes the force of the dominant fiction within which she or he constructs imaginative fictions. In other words, elegiac writing is already ideologically charged: the form of consolation reins in emotion and refuses to allow the encounter between the living poet and his dead friend to be anything but tidy and respectable. The dominant fiction insists on consolation, that is, precisely because the alternatives are too threatening to the contours of bourgeois individuality.

Moon offers Whitman an alternative model of mourning established loosely on Freud's concept of the fetish: "What if instead of focusing on bodily deficiency in thinking about our own mourning practices, we focus on bodily abundance and supplementarity? Resisting thinking of the deaths of others as the making deficient of our own bodies or body parts and resisting thinking of death as absolutely rupturing the possible erotic relation of a living person to a dead one may make an important difference to our mourning practices."[17] He uses this perception to examine a few of the poems in Whitman's *Drum-Taps*, poems such as "The Wound-Dresser," "a poem not only about literally shattered flesh but also about the shatterings—not least of all erotic shatterings— one can experience in response to flashes of flesh, the unexpected uncoverings and re-coverings of desired or beloved flesh that are as much a part of the everyday of the sick as they are of numerous other quotidian practices."[18]

This reimagining of the process of mourning as erotic engagement with the physical residue of the beloved is in many ways radical. It both offers an insight into *Drum-Taps* that is almost shocking in its simplicity, and it articulates a politics of mourning that defies the dictates of "normalcy" that Freud and his followers propose. At the same time, I am slightly uneasy with Moon's notion of the "traditional elegiac model." Some of the features of erotic lament that Moon outlines have (always) already been at the heart of the elegiac tradition.

Bion's *The Lament for Adonis*, for instance, which is always cited as one of classical sources of the elegiac tradition, offers little in the way of consolation and spends many of its stanzas in laments that are hardly less physical than those of Whitman:

> *Woe for Adonis, the Loves join in the lament!*
>
> A cruel, cruel wound on his thigh hath Adonis, but a deeper wound in her heart doth Cytherea bear. About him his dear hounds are loudly baying, and the nymphs of the wild wood wail him; but Aphrodite with unbounded locks through the glades goes wandering, —wretched, with hair unbraided, with feet unsandaled, and the thorns as she passes wound her and pluck the blossom of her sacred blood. Shrill she wails as down the long woodlands she is borne, lamenting her Assyrian lord, and again calling him, and again. But round his navel the dark blood leapt forth, and with blood from his thighs his chest was scarlet, and beneath Adonis's breast, the spaces that afore were snow-white, were purple with blood.[19]

It would be difficult to imagine the wounded male body more vividly displayed. Of course, Adonis is a beautiful youth and *his* wounded male body invokes almost universal desire. Even so, the careful attention to the white flesh and the bloody discoloration begins to insist that this is a special kind of lament, and the details of the description spell out what kind that is. If the imagery suggests a fetishistic fascination with dying form, then the imagined scene is one of intensely erotic, more precisely homoerotic, mourning. The poet expresses his desire through the lament of Aphrodite, to be sure; but he also expresses it through the broken body of Adonis. As the blood flows, Aphrodite wanders among the thorny glades, calling the name of Adonis, in a rendition of physical loss that is as vivid as the image of Adonis's "snow-white" breast covered in purple gore. It is impossible to imagine a consolation that can follow this extreme expression of grief. Indeed, this elegy offers no real consolation, certainly nothing as full of promise as the Christian vision of *Lycidas*.

Instead, it returns again and again to this pale and bloody form of the "languid" "thrice-desired" hero:

> He reclines, the delicate Adonis, in his raiment of purple, and around him the Loves are weeping, and groaning aloud, clipping their locks for Adonis. And one upon his shafts, another on his bow is treading, and one hath loosed the sandal of Adonis, and another hath broken his own feathered quiver, and one in a golden vessel bears water, and another laves the wound, and another from behind him with his wings is fanning Adonis.[20]

The fetishization of the bloody male figure as a form of bodily supplementarity is as vivid as anything Moon describes in Whitman. The body of Adonis is the subject here, and in its broken, bloody, castrated state, it represents tragic debilitating loss. This loss cannot be displaced with a consolatory gesture; rather in its aching physical pain, it defies consolation. "The delicate Adonis" comes to represent a kind of erotic loss that can only be measured in the frustrated cry of the Muses: "And *woe, woe for Adonis*, shrilly cry the Muses, neglecting Paean, and they lament Adonis aloud and songs they chant to him, but he does not heed them."

If the bloody, broken male is figured as loss in this originary lament, then it would not be an exaggeration to say that at the very heart of the elegiac tradition lies the blood-soaked figure of castration. Now this figure could represent, in a misogynist gesture, the threat that desire for the female represents. But this figure, Aphrodite, is no ordinary female; she represents desire itself. Adonis dies because of a desire for desire, and he is lamented in bloody, castrated form because desire cannot be fulfilled. This lament is melancholy because Adonis is dead; but it is doubly so because it is trapped in a desire that cannot be realized anywhere but in a figuration of a loss. This loss is physical, it is castrated, and it is male. The desire that is expressed for this castrated male is a desire that can only be realized in its very impossibility.

To claim that the elegy tradition, or the elegiac form itself, is about male-male desire is on one level so obvious that it hardly needs arguing. Even Milton needs to articulate a desire for Lycidas in order to mourn him properly. But how this male-male desire "fits into" the ideology of western culture is a far different question. In arguing about the dynamic of the concept of "interpellation," which is central to the working of ideology as explained by Althusser, Žižek claims that the "external 'machine' of State Apparatuses exercises its force only so far as it is experienced, in the unconscious economy of the subject, as a traumatic, senseless injunction." He also speaks of a "non-integrated surplus traumatism," which, in the process of interpellation, "confers on the Law its unconditional authority." For Žižek, this means that "ideological fantasy structures reality itself": "ideology is not a dreamlike illusion that we build to escape insupportable reality; in its basic dimension it is a fantasy construction which serves as a support for our 'reality' itself. . . . The function of ideology is not to offer us a point of escape from our reality but to offer us the social reality itself as an escape from some traumatic, real kernel."[21] I quote this argument at length because it seems to offer a possible explanation for the intense male-male desire that is central to the elegy tradition: by equating desire with loss, the elegy allows a public articulation of the inner workings of patriarchal, homosocial culture at the same time that it pushes the "traumatic, real kernel" of male-male erotic love so deeply into the cultural unconscious that these poems can be celebrated for their beauty at the same time that their erotic significance is ignored. Eve Kosofsky Sedgwick and others have argued the basic structure of homosocial culture, especially in the later nineteenth and early twentieth centuries.[22] The elegy tradition offers a particularly telling example of the ways in which transgressive desire can be articulated so as to foreclose the possibility of its realization. This explains something about the ways in which literary form and ideological control work so smoothly together.

Milton's *Lycidas* is a painful, angry poem. Sacks argues that in order to "rage against the conspiracy of those 'perfidious forces' that strike down the good while leaving the wicked in triumph," Milton "stages a displaced, verbal revenge, while also managing to conjure a transcendent context in which such vengeance is sanctified." Sacks describes this process in detail and suggests in general that the poem opens with an "intensifying exercise in making up or invoking a presence where there is none" and that consolation, which is "the achievement of a deflected sexual assertion," depends upon "the erection of tombs or stelae or indeed of a survivor's verse," which are "understandably associated with an invigorating liquid." "In 'Lycidas,'" he claims, "the imagery of a saving and surviving liquid" is "the figure for ongoing desire and creativity." Against the desolation of the "watery bier," that is, Milton evokes the "melodious tear" that with the aid of sacred springs transcends death in its figuration of "other streams" and "Nectar pure." [23] This is an impressively subtle reading, and its account of the transitional moments in the poem is persuasive.

But I want to question the effectiveness of the consolatory gesture here, as well as the sanctity of the sacred transcendence itself.

Lycidas suffers a watery, not a bloody death, and he is lamented in his absence, not his vivid, gory presence. But that absence measures loss in physical terms after all:

> But O the heavy change, now thou art gone,
> Now thou art gone, and never must return!
> Thee Shepherd, thee the Woods, and desert Caves,
> With wild Thyme and the gadding Vine o'ergrown,
> And all their echoes mourn.
> The Willows and the Hazel Copses green
> Shall no more be seen,
> Fanning their joyous Leaves to thy soft lays.
> As killing as the Canker to the Rose,
> Or Taint-worm to the weanling Herds that graze,
> Or Frost to Flowers, that their gay wardrobe wear,
> When first the White-thorn blows,
> Such *Lycidas*, thy loss to Shepherd's ear. (37–49)[24]

In this passage, Milton explains the physical dimension of his loss in language both painful and evocative. If it is "the harshly elaborated loss of that ideal, recollected world, whose images of freshness and nurture have given way to those of insidious disease and of a specifically premature ruin";[25] it is also an articulation of that ideal. This conventional lament of nature provides a "joyous" image of the "soft lays" that this lost poet sang, as well as the "gay wardrobe" of the flowers and the "weanling Herd" that are threatened by the absence of his song. The boyish intimacy that is evoked here only intensifies the loss that the "gadding vine" and "desert Caves" represent, of course, and the evils that beset delicate youth are brutal, violent, and victimizing. These lines articulate the loss of innocence as much as the loss of the friend, but the two are connected in the image of the shepherd that closes this section of the poem. The shepherd's own isolation, his own confrontation with the emptiness of the desire, becomes the subject of this elegy as well. The loss is personalized in order to render meaningful the consolation that follows.

Milton can only achieve consolation in this poem by transforming the specific physical ache to a transcendent vision of spiritual safety, to be sure. But that vision is hardly less physical than what has come before, and to some readers it might even represent unmediated erotic fantasy. For the Shepherds, the consolation is purely physical:

> Weep no more, woeful Shepherds, weep no more,
> For *Lycidas* your sorrow is not dead,
> Sunk though he be beneath the wat'ry floor,
> So sinks the day star in the Ocean bed,
> And yet anon repairs his drooping head,
> And tricks his beams, and with new-spangled Ore,
> Flames in the forehead of the morning sky.
> So *Lycidas*, sunk low, but mounted high,
> Through the dear might of him that walk'd the waves,
> Where other groves and other streams along,
> With Nectar pure his oozy locks he laves,
> And hears the unexpressive nuptial Song,
> In the blest Kingdoms meek of joy and love. (165–177)

This is visionary writing, but the vision is not simply otherworldly. For Sacks, this "act of substitution" replaces the physical Lycidas with a "troped, indeed apotheosized, version." For him this is a "spiritualization of the poet's own attachment, a refined reassertion of desire evident in the accompanying imagery (the emphasis on mounting, on repairing a drooping head, [on the bed?], on laving oozy locks, and finally on the nuptial song in the kingdom[s] of joy and love)"; and "the pastoral world is reinscribed in heaven."[26] I would argue, on the contrary, that heaven is reinscribed in the world of pastoral. The poet can only bring his song of mourning to completion, that is, if he eroticizes the very transfiguration toward which he directs the poem. Rather than call this a "spiritualization of the poet's attachment," I would call this a deeply physical rendition of spiritual regeneration. If I call it an erotic fantasy, that is only partly because of the specifics of imagery. It also seems to me to bring the poem to an excited (and excitedly visual) conclusion that answers the need that was best expressed in the searing lines:

> Look homeward Angel now, and melt with ruth:
> And, *O ye Dolphins*, waft the hapless youth. (163–64)

This is a physical ache, and it answered with a physical transfiguration. *Lycidas* brings consolation because of this power to eroticize an afterlife, to fetishize the body in such as way that it offers a kind of *jouissance* that defies mortality and eternalizes desire.

Ideologically, this transformation is not so simple. Desire can be refigured by means of fetishistic attachment, but the bodily supplementarity that Michael Moon describes in Whitman is here used to make desire function only on the level of fantasy. In the "dominant fiction," of course, male-male desire is proscribed. What better way to achieve this proscription than to remove it from the realm of the actual and inscribe it in the realm of fantasy. Male-male desire is rendered impossible precisely because of the degree to which the elegy commemorates desire as loss. The lost attachment between men insists on the impossibility of their love in the here and now. Lycidas may "melt with ruth" in Milton's poem, but he does so only in the world of imagination. The "nuptial song" of the heavenly transformation is finally "unexpressive" because the more fully male-male desire is expressed in the elegy, the more effectively it is placed in the realm of the unrealizable.

Thomas Gray demonstrates this effect even more vividly than Milton. As I have argued elsewhere, Gray's Latin elegies for Richard West commemorate desire in loss, and they do so in terms that make the erotics of male-male desire both vivid and debilitating:

> But you, blessed spirit, who do not need my grief, rejoice in the starry circuit of the heavens and the fire of pure ether whence you sprang. But, if, released from cares as you are, and no longer mortal, you should look back with pity on the labors which you yourself once suffered and have the time to acknowledge my trivial anxieties; if, by chance, you should look down from your lofty seat on the storm of human passion, the fears, the fierce promptings of desire, the joys and sorrows and the tumult of rage so huge in my heart, the furious surges of the breast; then look back on these tears, also, which stricken with love, I pour out in memory of you; this is all I can do, while my only wish is to mourn at your tomb and address these empty words to your silent ashes.[27]

The tears that Gray pours out at the tomb of his friend are the tears of sensibility that identify love and loss in modern culture. They are also tears of unrealized and unrealizable desire, the tears of accommodation that culture provides to those who feel. There is no consolation here that is separate from desire. And there is no desire that is separate from loss. The departed friend "look[s] back" not in anger but in love, and in the poet he recognizes his own "fierce promptings of desire" that have linked them in a transgressive bond and that locks them still in requited but unrealizable love. Gray does not attempt to render his love in a transcendent form that disguises erotic desire; instead he spells it out in painful physical terms. At the same time, however, he can do nothing with this physical desire but cry "vainly" at the tomb of his dead friend. Ramazani argues that "if the traditional elegy was an art of saving, the modern elegy is what Elizabeth Bishop calls an 'art of losing.' Instead of resurrecting the dead in some substitute, instead of curing themselves through displacement, modern elegists 'practice losing farther, losing faster, so that the "One Art" of the modern elegy is not transcendence or redemption of loss but immersion in it.'"[28] Gray's poetry is "modern" in this sense; and it is "modern" as well in its articulation of the discontents that culture imposes on the desiring self.

Gray articulates this discontent most memorably, of course, in *An Elegy Written in a Country Churchyard.* In that poem, as Sacks argues, Gray "mourns a particular death over and above those of the villagers. This individual death, albeit imaginary, is the death of the poet himself."[29] I have suggested that what the poet mourns is more (or less) than his own physical demise. Gray's *Elegy* mourns the death of desire—its very impossibility in the culture that the churchyard represents. In the final version of the poem, the tension surrounding the figure of Death is given voice. In this context, Gray attempts to confront the truth of his own tormented sensibility:

> For who to dumb Forgetfulness a prey,
> This pleasing anxious being e're resigned,
> Left the warm precincts of the cheerful day,
> Nor cast one longing lingering look behind? (ll. 85–88)

This stanza takes us from a flirtation with the "dumb Forgetfulness" of Death, that final repression, to a crucial assertion of Gray's own subjectivity. "One longing lingering look" begins to undermine the repression that has brought the poet to the graveyard in the first place and seems to open up the possibility of desire. The "pleasing anxious being" is a desiring subject, and the poet seems ready to cling to desire rather than accept the transformative displacement that transcendence represents:

> On some fond breast the parting soul relies,
> Some pious drops the closing eye requires;

Ev'n from the tomb the voice of nature cries,
Ev'n in our ashes live their wonted fires. (ll. 89–92)

The language of these lines insists on a residue of physical desire. At this point the poet takes no consolation in the possibility of transcendence. The poet turns from Death to the "fond breast" of companionship; in the tomb he hears the "voice of nature"; and even in the "ashes" he feels the "fires" of desire. I have said that Gray places himself at this turning point between the forces of life and death in the poem as a way of confronting his own abjection and opening the language of the poem to the cry of nature that he earlier silenced.[30] Now I would add that the resulting melancholy is the acknowledgment of loss and of the inability of the subject to realize the desire that he so painfully understands.

Gray seems to understand the ideological implications of his conflicted stance, and in the closing phase of the poem—the hoary headed swain and this picture of the solitary melancholy poet, the funeral precession, the epitaph—insists on the loss of desire and on the impossibility of the finding a "friend" anywhere but in death:

Here rests his head upon the lap of earth
A youth to fortune and to fame unknown.
Fair Science frowned not at his humble birth,
And Melancholy marked him for her own.

Large was his bounty and his soul sincere,
Heaven did a recompense as largely send:
He gave to Misery all he had, a tear,
He gained from Heaven ('twas all he wished) a friend.

No farther seek his merits to disclose,
Or draw his frailties from their dread abode,
(There they alike in trembling hope repose)
The bosom of his Father and his God. (ll. 117–28)

The poem ends, as Hagstrum so eloquently suggests, in the anxiety of sexual fulfillment and "trembling" desire.[31] This is not "consolation," even of the kind *Lycidas* offers. The "friend" he gained is (always) already lost. The pose of the "Melancholy" poet assures both that hope is "distant" and "trembling" and that the Father in whose bosom" he finds "repose" is not a friend, erotic or otherwise, or even a personal father whose embrace might (in

Gray's case certainly) have had private meaning. Instead, this "Father" is his "God," the paternal father, the representative of culture itself. If he embraces the poet, that is because he also negates desire. If he brings consolation, that is, it is the consolation that loss and repression provide.

The elegy form, then, promises consolation, release, resolution, but it brings these only in the form of loss. Male-male desire is posited in the elegy, only to be denied. Culture reasserts itself, however, even in these failed resolutions, because in the melancholic pose of the poet, quick to be diagnosed as a kind of "hypochondria," ideological control can finally be exerted so as to separate the mourning subject from his own body. Gray the poet stands back from the funeral in his *Elegy*, that is, precisely because the elegy form itself has separated him from the lamented, the elegized body. The result is isolation, repression, and loss.

Ramazani argues that "modern elegies, like modern art in general, according to Adorno, may be seen as the 'social antithesis of society,' negative responses to dominant social norms, in the sense that they resist the obliteration of the dead by the socioeconomic laws of exchange, equivalence, and progress. . . . Modern elegies betray in their difficult, melancholic mourning the impossibility of preserving a space apart, of grieving for the dead amid the speed and pressure of modern life."[32] I would argue that in the "traditional" elegies that I am discussing, the poets may attempt to establish a "social antithesis" to society, but they fail. Indeed Gray's melancholy desire for members of his own sex may begin to suggest such an antithesis, but its very expression renders it a cultural impossibility. Not only do these poets fail to "resist" the social pressure that would defy the very desire they are expressing, they reassert the power of repression both to circumscribe that desire and render it meaningless.

The final poem I am going to discuss, Shelley's *Adonais*, brings this transaction into surprisingly detailed relief.

> I weep for Adonais—he is dead!
> O, weep for Adonais! though our tears
> Thaw not the frost which binds so dear a head!
> And thou, sad Hour, selected from all years
> To mourn our loss, rouse thy obscure compeers,
> And teach them thine own sorrow, say: "With me
> Died Adonais, till the Future dares

Forget the Past, his fate and fame shall be
An echo and a light unto eternity!" (ll. 1–9)[33]

This opening is touching in its expression of loss and reminiscent of the earlier elegies, especially, as critics have noted, Bion's "Woe for Adonis," with which Shelley opens his own elegy.[34] The implications of this formal repetition places Shelley's lament in a long tradition of erotic mourning, but the shift from Adonis to Adonais transforms that mourning from the merely physically erotic to the spiritualization of the figure. Sacks claims that "the poem itself unfolds the very *process* of resignification, moving from the natural, sexual referents to their spiritualized successors."[35] The problem with this reading is the ease with which it claims that the poet moves beyond the physical. I would claim, on the contrary, here and in the other elegies that I am discussing, that the spiritual never fully displaces the physical, nor does "spiritualized" love ever completely replace the straightforward erotic longing that these poems express.

O weep for Adonais—he is dead
Wake, melancholy Mother, wake and weep!
Yet wherefore? Quench within their burning bed
Thy fiery tears, and let thy loud heart keep
Like his, a mute and uncomplaining sleep;
For he is gone, where all things wise and fair
Descend;—oh, dream not that the amorous Deep
Will yet restore him to the vital air;
Death feeds on his mute voice, and laughs at our despair. (ll. 19–27)

As in Gray's sonnet and Milton's *Lycidas*, Shelley's mourning insists on physical loss—the "burning bed," the "fiery tears," and the mockery that physically consuming death "laughs." Desire is once again expressed as loss, a kind of loss that requires an elaborate system of personified speakers to reflect its full range of erotic feeling. The "melancholy Mother," whom I discuss at greater length below, is an almost awkward personification for the poet's own deep and conflicted emotion. The maternal helps to describe the quality of his grief, and a desire for the mother gives it an uncanny depth and seriousness. The melancholy, however, is all the poet's own.

Grief made the young Spring wild, and she threw down
Her kindling buds, as if she Autumn were,

Or they dead leaves; since her delight is flown,
For whom should she have waked the sullen year?
To Phoebus was not Hyacinth so dear
Nor to himself Narcissus, as to both
Thou, Adonais: wan they stand and sere
Amid the faint companions of their youth,
With dew all turned to tears; odour to sighing ruth. (ll. 136–44)

The poet insists on natural mourning here, and grief has as usual the power to cast a shadow over the usually bright spring. But in reading the dew as tears, the poet begins to suggest a rationale for his mentioning Phoebus's love for Hyacinth and Narcissus's love for himself. Needless to say, these figures are coded as other than cross-gendered desire—Hyacinth and Narcissus are representative of male-male eroticism and excessive self-love—and as such they reinforce the overriding homoeroticism of the poet's lament. The grammar of the lines suggest that both Hyacinth and Narcissus were dear to Adonais, and that for him nature mourns in terms that are hauntingly familiar. These terms become even more vivid as the poet moves into his supposedly spiritualized transformation:

Stay yet awhile! Speak to me once again;
Kiss me, so long but as a kiss may live;
And in my heartless breast and burning brain
That word, that kiss, shall all thoughts else survive,
With food of saddest memory kept alive,
Now thou art dead, as if it were a part
Of thee, my Adonais, I would give
All that I am to be as thou now art!
But I am chained to Time, and cannot thence depart! (ll. 226–34)

The speaker in this passage is Urania—Urania is the name applied to Aphrodite "(Venus or Love) when she is associated with spiritualized love and beauty."[36] Spiritualized love, however, retains its physical power in the "kiss me" that structures this stanza. This love is poetic, transformative, even transcendent, but it is also physical. The poet here laments a lover who is lost to him, in other words, and Urania helps him to give that love not a spiritual but a burningly physical dimension. As the poet reaches out to his dead friend he gives his "spiritualized love" a specific erotic structure. "In my thoughtless breast and burning brain / That word, that kiss shall all thoughts else survive": these lines are reminiscent of Gray's Latin elegy, in which the poet urges his departed friend to "look down from your lofty seat on the storm of human passion, the fears, the fierce promptings of desire, the joys and sorrows and the tumult of rage so huge in my heart, the furious surges of the breast . . . while my only wish is to mourn at your tomb and address these empty words to your silent ashes."[37]

But in neither case are these words "empty": they are filled with the ideology that shapes them, the ideology that insists that male-male desire can be expressed, like this, only in loss. Žižek says that ideology works most effectively at the level of form. He argues that in the theories of both Freud and Marx, there is an understanding of the significance of form in the basic structures of psychological or political control. For instance, it is necessary to reveal the "secret" value of commodities not behind commodity-form, where classical bourgeois political economy looks for it: "classical political economy is interested only in contents concealed behind the commodity-form, which is why it cannot explain the true secret, not the secret *behind* the form but *the secret of this form itself*." For Žižek, dreams work similarly—"even after we have explained its hidden meaning, its latent thought, the dream remains an enigmatic phenomenon; what is not yet explained is simply its form, the process by means of which the hidden meaning disguised itself in such a form"—and form itself begins to have a power all their own. When the "forms" are followed, even if they are recognized to be hollow, the ideological effect takes its place.[38] The form of the elegy—the elaborate procedures of erotic mourning that I have described—has an implicit agenda as well. It promises consolation, transcendence, and the accommodation of loss. The poems I have discussed find the procedure lacking, and where consolation and transcendence belong, they reassert physical loss and erotic desire. But even this move can be accommodated in elegy form: instead of consolation, these poets face loss, the loss of desire and the impossibility of male-male love. The elegy bespeaks masculinist privilege at the level of form, of course, but it does this by means of an expression of male-male desire in works as disparate as the three elegies I have discussed. It would be disingenuous to claim that this desire is the same in all three works, but it would be equally disingenuous to disclaim, as it were, erotic desire in all but the case of the one poet of the three who can be proven to have harbored secret and not-so-secret erotic feelings for various friends and protégés.

In fact, I would go so far as to say that as different as the male-male desire is in each of the poems, there is a way in which it is the same. The erotic longing that they express, the need to embody their desire, and the recognition that male-male desire can finally be expressed only in loss—these features unite these poems in an ideological construct as vivid as it is inescapable.

The form of the elegy works, then, to put male-male desire at the center of the "dominant fiction" of this late and definitive phase of early modern culture.[39] For surprisingly enough, the love between men that is constituted in its very impossibility is, as Eve Kosofsky Sedgwick has repeatedly claimed, the very condition that defines western culture. The history of the closet that she describes has a lot to do with the formal articulation of the kind of proto-homophobia that elegiac mourning suggests. Sedgwick says that "same-sex desire is still structured by its distinctive public/private status, at once marginal and central, as *the* open secret."[40] I have said elsewhere that Gray understands implicitly how this mechanism works, and his attempts to articulate desire in loss create a closet-like structure from which he can utter his devastating pronouncements without the risk of public exposure. I would extend this observation to these other elegists precisely because they are not known to have been erotically interested in members of their own sex, at least not in the self-defining way that Gray was. The expression of same-sex desire as loss—physical, erotic loss—works to the advantage of culture in the very ways that Sedgwick has described. She says that in some eighteenth-century texts, "the desire that represents sexuality per se, and hence sexual knowledge per se, is a same sex desire. This possibility, however, was repressed with increasing energy, and hence increasing visibility, as the nineteenth-century culture of the individual proceeded to elaborate a version of knowledge/sexuality structured with its pointed cognitive *refusal* of sexuality between women, between men."[41] This contradiction—the inevitability of male-male desire and its concomitant cultural impossibility—is precisely where the workings of ideology are most vivid.[42] This contradiction is implicit in the articulation of desire in these elegies, and the debilitating melancholy that results from the tension between these two positions is of course the state that assures the smoothest working of culture. A love that is constituted in loss is a love that yields a longing that can never be fulfilled. It hardly needs to be silenced. Gray more than understands the consequence of the situation in which he finds himself: "I fruitless mourn to him that cannot hear, / And weep the more because I weep in vain."

Notes

1. Roger Lonsdale, ed. *The Poems of Gray, Collins and Goldsmith* (New York: Longman, 1969), 67–68.
2. Lonsdale, 67.
3. William Wordsworth, Preface, *Second Edition of the Lyrical Ballads*, in David Perkins ed., *English Romantic Writers* (New York: Harcourt, Brace & World, 1967), 323
4. The Gray *Concordance* (Cook) lists twenty uses of "vain"—mostly in this sense of "in vain"—in Gray's poetry. It is not an exaggeration to call this mood typical.
5. Wordsworth, 323.
6. For two (similar) readings of this poem, see Raymond Bentman, "Thomas Gray and the Poetry of 'Hopeless Love,'" *Journal of the History of Sexuality* 3 (1992): 216–17; and George E. Haggerty, "'The Voice of Nature' in Gray's *Elegy*," in *Homosexuality in Renaissance and Enlightenment England: Literary Representations in Historical Context*, ed. Claude J. Summers (New York: Haworth Press, 1992), 200–202.
7. Sigmund Freud, "Mourning and Melancholia," in *The Standard Edition of the Complete Psychological Works of Sigmund Freud*, ed. and trans. James Strachey (London: Hogarth, 1971), 14:244, 245.
8. Jahan Ramazani, *Poetry of Mourning: The Modern Elegy from Hardy to Heany* (Chicago: University of Chicago Press, 1994), 3–4.
9. Peter M. Sacks, *The English Elegy: Studies in the Genre from Spenser to Yeats* (Baltimore: Johns Hopkins University Press, 1985), 8.
10. Sacks, 9.
11. Sacks, 11.
12. Sacks, 16–17.
13. Slavoj Žižek, *The Sublime Object of Ideology* (London: Verso, 1989), 36–38; see also, Kaja Silverman, *Male Subjectivity at the Margins* (New York: Routledge, 1992), 15–51.
14. Michael Moon, "Memorial Rags," *Professions of Desire: Lesbian and Gay Studies in Literature*, ed. George E. Haggerty and Bonnie Zimmerman (New York: MLA, 1995), 235. For an extended and very thoughtful response to this essay and an alternative reading of Freud on mourning, see Douglas Crimp, "Mourning and Militancy," in *Out There: Marginalization and Contemporary Culture*, ed. Russell Ferguson, Martha Gever, Trinh T. Minh-ha, and Cornell West (Cambridge, Mass.: MIT Press, 1990), 233–45.
15. Moon, 234–35.
16. Silverman, 17, 21; see also, Žižek, 34.

17. Moon, 236.
18. Moon, 239.
19. Bion, *The Lament for Adonis*, in *Theocritus, Bion, and Moschus*, ed. and trans. Andrew Lang (London, 1924), rpt. in "*Milton's Lycidas*," ed. Scott Elledge (New York: Harper & Row, 1966), 22.
20. Bion, 24.
21. Žižek, 43–45.
22. Eve Kosofsky Sedgwick, *Epistemology of the Closet* (Berkeley: University of California Press, 1990), 1–63; Sedgwick also began the discussion of homosociability in early periods as well; see *Between Men: English Literature and Male Homosocial Desire* (New York: Columbia University Press, 1985).
23. Sacks, 93, 96-98.
24. John Milton, *Lycidas*, in *The Complete Poems and Major Prose*, ed. Merritt Y. Hughes (Indianapolis: Odyssey Press, 1957; rpr. 1975).
25. Sacks, 101.
26. Sacks, 114.
27. Lonsdale, 328; translation (adapted) 332; for a discussion of the context of this poem, see George E. Haggerty, "*O lachrymarum fons*: Tears, Poetry, and Desire in Gray." *Eighteenth-Century Studies* 30 (1996): 81–95.
28. Ramazani, 4; see Elizabeth Bishop, "One Art," *The Complete Poems, 1927–1979* (New York: Farrar, Straus and Giroux, 1983).
29. Sacks, 139.
30. See George E. Haggerty, "'The Voice of Nature' in Gray's *Elegy*."
31. "Hope trembles in the 'Elegy' because of guilt and the prospect of Judgment" (Jean Hagstrum, "Gray's Sensibility," in *Fearful Joy: Papers from the Thomas Gray Bicentenary Conference at Carleton University*, ed. J. Downey and B. Jones [Montréal: McGill-Queen's University, 1974], 10–11).
32. Ramazani, 14; see T. W. Adorno, *Aesthetic Theory*, trans. C. Ledhardt, ed. Gretel Adorno and Rolf Tiedermann (New York: Routledge, 1986), 23–67.
33. Reiman, Donald H. and Sharon B. Powers, ed., *Shelley's Poetry and Prose* (New York: Norton, 1977), 392; further references are to this edition.
34. Sacks, 146-47.
35. Sacks, 147.
36. David Perkins, ed., *English Romantic Writers* (New York: Harcourt, Brace & World, 1967), 1046, n. 10; see also Sacks, *The English Elegy*, 149–50.
37. Lonsdale, 328; translation (adapted) 332. See Haggerty, "*O lachrymarum fons*," 91.
38. Žižek, 19, 13–16; see also 28–30.
39. Silverman, 15–17.
40. Sedgwick, 22.

41. Sedgwick, 73.

42. For a useful account of this dynamic, see Elin Diamond, "*Gestus* and Signature in Aphra Behn's *The Rover*," *ELH* 56 (1989): 519–41.

George E. Haggerty, Professor of English at the University of California, Riverside, has just completed *Men In Love: Masculinity and Sexuality in the Eighteenth Century* and *The Encyclopedia of Gay Histories and Cultures*. He is currently working on a book project tentatively titled *Queer Gothic*.

Inchbald's *A Simple Story*: An Anti-Ideological Reading

Michael Boardman

Elizabeth Inchbald's *A Simple Story* is now being read by students as well as specialists. One finds, however, that while there are dozens of "ideological" readings of the novel, feminist, Marxist, and cultural, hardly anyone seems to have been interested in it as a novel. For reasons that are part of our recent critical heritage, unstable and uninviting as it may be for some of us who still study aesthetic experience, Inchbald's novel, which came into the canon only fairly recently, has been mostly a locus of speculation about gender matters. It seems to exist today only to invite an essay titled, "A Not So Simple Story" (for we love word play, no matter how painfully obvious), or the construction of one more anti-patriarchal argument. The metaphor is strained, I'm afraid, since a building at least rests on its site and most of these readings rest on very little at all, except, as Robert Storey called it, "the self-important penchant" of some English professors "for grand pronouncements."[1]

Inchbald's novel is so interesting, odd, and puzzling as an aesthetic object that you'd think someone, even some renegade feminist critic drooping from the ennui of detecting the dead hand of the Symbolic Law of the Father, would try to figure out what kind of story Inchbald was trying to write. After all, we've had Inchbald for over two centuries, and, as Terry Castle wrote in 1986, "We do not yet know, perhaps, how to read her fully."[2] At times Castle herself all too briefly recalls how innovative the novel is, and then offers valuable insights: "Much of [the novel's] tension grows out of the reader's persistent sense of obstacle—of the overwhelming ethical and psychic obstructions impeding the union of Miss

Milner and her guardian. The heroine's passion thrives on, indeed seems indistinguishable from, the barriers she faces." Yes. But then Castle, remembering her feminist readership and that it doesn't want affective or formalist readings, adds, ". . . [Miss Milner's] is a transgressive liaison par excellence."[3]

What is *A Simple Story*, read for its fictional experience and not as an "occasion" for "constructing" a "transgressive" political statement or some other, ahistorical, extrinsic purpose always already "elsewhere"? In this essay, I shall ignore as irrelevant to *A Simple Story*, viewed as a realistic fiction written in the late eighteenth century, such ideological readings. I don't think the novel's two-part structure is best explained by arguing, as Ty does, that "This tendency of female authors to postpone closure until the next generation may reflect their hesitancy in committing themselves to the finality of submission to the patriarchal order."[4] This is not how narrative decisions in realistic novels are made: innovations come out of the pressures of the storytelling moment and are modified much more by the weight of earlier innovations than by any "symbolic order." If culture "dictates" ideological adjustment to an innovative author, it is only as a provocation to further innovation.[5] None of these allegorizations of Miss Milner, including those dependent on the Great Simplifier, Sigmund Freud, has much to do with Inchbald's intention. By reading the novel as a symbolic statement, ideological critics avoid the hard work of figuring out where Inchbald's innovation fits into the development of the novel.

With these arguments and their shaky assumptions, I shall have only minor skirmishes here, reserving that properly metacritical critique. Nor shall I try systematically to refute the biographical readings offered by Littlewood, Kelly, Barker, and Inchbald's most recent biographer, Manvell, and tacitly accepted by many other critics.[6] Louis Joughlin, who examined the question as thoroughly as anyone, concluded that "none of [Mrs. Inchbald's] qualities" of character were to be found "in the heroine of her novel."[7] Nor did early readers who knew Inchbald react to the story as if it had a personal clef. They concentrate instead on its objective dramatic power. As Maria Edgeworth put it, in a letter to Inchbald, "I never read any novel that . . . so completely possessed me with the belief in the real existence of all the people it represents. I never once recollected the author whilst I was reading it."[8] Like *Wuthering Heights*, Inchbald's novel has its genesis in her personal history, but its structure is an act of mimesis with its own necessities independent of her psychic life. As Edgeworth's paean to the novel's "peculiar pathos," and her peculiar failure to remark on its contribution to the women's movement suggest, only critics who begin by assuming all narrative must be political can find political meaning in Inchbald.

What I offer here, in place of allegory and biographical speculation, is an analysis of the novel as a particular kind of innovative plot that develops a number of previously untried possibilities available to novelists since Richardson pioneered the form in 1740. Many of the more egregiously farfetched ideological readings of the novel would have been discouraged by an understanding of just how much like her predecessors, such as Richardson, Fielding, Lennox, and Burney, Inchbald really is. Like them, attacking the "patriarchy" was the furthest thing from her mind; she preferred instead to succeed independent of her gender by writing a complex, gripping, and therefore profitable story.

Inchbald's first novel is a serious action and, as Lytton Strachey wrote, "its subject is a group of two or three individuals whose interactions form the whole business of the book."[9]

Miss Milner is a young, beautiful, willful woman who falls in love with Dorriforth, a stern but attractive Catholic priest whose vows make him unavailable for dalliance. Even in the late 1770s, when Inchbald began the novel, the subject was daring, and she worked out a brilliant plot to take full but decorous advantage of the instability she created between the eighteen-year-old Miss Milner and her thirty-year-old guardian, Dorriforth. She shows them widely separated by his vows and caretaking role as her guardian, further estranged by his disapproval of her behavior and her resentful reaction, then magically betrothed, as he inherits a title and Rome releases him from his vows so he can marry. Theirs is a mutual passion repeatedly signaled by Inchbald's adroit, covert, dramatic representation. We then see them parted again when she refuses to obey an absolute command not to attend a masquerade. Just on the point of his leaving the country and renouncing her forever, his older tutor, friend, and fellow priest, Sandford, who has stood in the way of their union, has indeed scorned Miss Milner, recognizes the power of their love and marries them.

At this point, the first part of the novel ends and we leap forward to a Miss Milner now thirty-five, living out a tragic fate.

Then we hark back for the dismal history of "her fall."[10] After four years of happy marriage, Lord Elmwood had departed for the West Indies on business and in her husband's absence his wife had turned to an old admirer in resentment at being abandoned. With Elmwood set to return home, his wife casts herself out of his presence in shame and guilt,[11] leaving behind her infant daughter, Matilda, whom Elmwood soon sends after her mother and "refuses ever to see again, in vengeance to her mother's crimes" (195). Lady Elmwood lingers for ten more years before she dies. The rest of the novel shows Matilda, shunned by her father, persevering in both obedience and unflagging love, finally being kidnapped by an evil lord and rescued by her father, who then claims her as his daughter and marries her to her cousin. The conclusion is muted: Matilda's and her husband's "wedded life was a life of happiness" (337), unlike her parents', but absent is the joyous comic celebration of Fielding, Goldsmith, Burney, and Austen.

The novel's implicatory point of view is new too. The reader's chief joy is playing an elaborate game of inference, judging "by intelligible but simple signs" the "intensity of feeling" these characters repress with difficulty.[12] The reader soon recognizes Miss Milner's love for her guardian, and then must watch with her for amorous signs from him. Over Miss Milner's shoulder we try to see around the shield of "prudence" and "fortitude" (3) Dorriforth wears to protect him from a threatening world. As Gerard Barker puts it, "That Elmwood becomes conscious of his love only after he is assured of Miss Milner's love for him is indicative of the depth of his insecurity. It is his overriding sense of vulnerability, the risk of being hurt through emotional involvement, that has stifled his passions for so long behind the twin bastions of his priesthood and guardianship."[13]

Inchbald delineates the tension, sexual and otherwise, between her two characters with an innovative "hieroglyphic" method. Very little overt takes place between the two characters as they inch fearfully toward declaring their love. In its subtle but startling situations of suppressed passion, it manages to be both perfectly proper and perfectly sensational—something like what Inchbald herself was reputed to be: "perfectly modest; but arch, clever, and . . . interesting . . . a little of the coquette, but well disciplined, and well bred."[14] For example, Miss Milner's sham declaration of love for Lord Frederick, to prevent the duel, is clearly a gambit. We know it is because of her casual attitude toward him earlier, her readiness to give him up, and her almost overdeveloped sensitivity. So the power of the novel is crucially dependent on the ability of Inchbald's language to convey, covertly but clearly, her secret passion for Dorriforth. We see the same thing at work earlier, when Dorriforth precipitates a duel by striking Lord Frederick. He stands "silently by, with a manly scorn painted on his countenance" while Frederick continues to entreat Miss Milner to accept his love for her. It is only when Frederick "brought her hand to his lips, and began to devour it with kisses" that "Dorriforth with an instantaneous impulse, rushed forward, and struck him a blow in the face." Later, abject in apology, he "'entreated her forgiveness for the indelicacy he had been guilty of in her presence'" (61). Only the words "instantaneous impulse" and the very odd choice of "indelicacy" to describe slugging her would-be lover indicate what is previously unrevealed: that he loves her, and not as a guardian.

The novel shows clearly in what it essays and what it avoids the influence of other attempts, all the way back to Richardson, to construct serious plots out of romantic materials. Like *Pamela*, it is a story of branching alternatives, some of which are clearly preferable to others, although here the choices are revealed rather than created before our eyes, as Richardson does it. At one point, for example, Miss Milner confesses her hitherto hidden love for Dorriforth, in the most-often-quoted speech in the novel, one nicely expressive of her own and the novel's combination of the daring and the prim: "Oh, Miss Woodley! I love him with all the passion of a mistress, and with all the tenderness of a wife" (72). Miss Woodley, who is Miss Milner's confidante, Dorriforth's friend and domestic companion, like him a Catholic, and a kind of chorus for the reader, is shocked but agrees to keep silent for a time. Later, fearing nothing but sin and horror if Miss Milner stays under the same roof with her guardian, she insists, "Miss Milner . . . much as I respect the will of a dying man, I regard your and Mr. Dorriforth's present, and eternal happiness much more; and it is my resolution you shall part—if you will not contrive the means, that duty falls on me . . ." (88). Miss Milner actually goes to Bath, not to return until Dorriforth has acquired the title and the dispensation from Rome to marry so that the estate may be perpetuated.

Unlike so many earlier marriage plots, Inchbald's subject is conflicting character that ensures domestic strife, so it would have been absurd to try to give her story a comic power. The reader never believes that the pain, actual and potential, these two characters cause each other is only a brief barrier to their romantic aspirations, but it is not the mere seriousness of the differences between Dorriforth and Miss Milner that makes comedy inappropriate as a method of treating this story. In the intensely implicatory fictional game she invites us to play with these two possible people, Inchbald wants to try something Fielding and Burney did not: she explores the fictional potentialities of depicting two conflicted, attractive personalities who can't surmount their difficulties. So the emotions this plot evokes are those we associate with pairs of doomed lovers like Tess Durbeyfield and Angel Clare: clear recognition of the deserving nature of both, but with a compelling and anxiety-producing apprehension that they will never achieve permanent felicity. Unlike Hardy, however, this novel holds the reader suspended between desire for the lovers' union and fear for its consequences, and at the end of the first half, Inchbald refuses to resolve the tension, even with Miss Milner's death. This is clear immediately, not merely on a second reading, as Catherine Craft-Fairchild thinks.[15] We know as soon as the instability is established that these two will only cause each other pain, yet we go on desiring their union, uneasily, perhaps, but nevertheless wanting to see enacted the circumstances of their incompatibility.

Like the Richardson of *Pamela*, Inchbald begins her novel with external barriers. Dorriforth's vows of celibacy and his necessarily disinterested performance of his role as her guardian stand in their way, although not the difference in their ages, which would have struck readers in 1791 as irrelevant as it strikes me. The problem is not that Dorriforth is a father figure, any more than Squire B. is for Pamela; it's that they are both inflexible, egotistical men who insist on their prerogatives. So, as with Richardson, Inchbald creates a separate set of barriers, much more formidable, rooted in their radically different characters. The comparative premises are something like these: Pamela, rewarded for her moral resolve in resisting seduction, but also for her meekness and patience in adversity, discovers after marrying Squire B. that they face a great number of adjustments just to attain a modicum of marital happiness; indeed, they are so different that bliss seems out of the question, and Richardson makes sure the reader soon discerns that marriage is not the fairy-tale ending of this story.

Miss Milner, loving passionately and tenderly a man who is not just a priest but also a man with a priest's (merely plausible, not emblematic) moral absolutism and inflexibility, does not understand until her story is largely over that she has married a man as bad for her as she is for him.

Nancy Easterlin has argued that "play activities, including literature, serve two essential yet contradictory functions: They allow us to act out novelty within an arena that ensures control and safety."[16] *A Simple Story* affords a game of inferring powerful but hidden emotions and states of mind leading to the gradual joining of two people in a union defined as productive of at best only temporary happiness. The pattern could have been tragic, even without the second part, but Inchbald is not interested in representing the precise circumstances that lead to Miss Milner's complete estrangement from her husband. She doesn't do so because she expects her reader to realize that the doomed marriage will soon fall apart in bitterness. More important, it is Dorriforth who will be the center of tragic emotions, only after his wife's death. In fact, the first half of the novel is finished with the marriage, and Inchbald's remaining problem was not length but appropriate completeness. The "mourning ring" provides closure: Miss Milner's hopes are doomed, because what we have seen of her character makes her unlikely ever to avoid the kind of offense that would alienate Elmwood.[17] Her story, except in the sordid details of the mortal affront she gives her husband, is done. What remains is to reveal Elmwood's agony, which, given his moral inflexibility and masculine fortitude, cannot be done in a moment.

In this decision is the novel's strangeness, and its second innovation, its two-part structure, is best explained, not ideologically, but as an only partly successful solution to difficulties in resolving the instability resulting in Miss Milner's death. The first half of the novel repeatedly asks the reader to judge Dorriforth's state of mind—it is no accident that the novel begins with a statement of his character, not hers—but it does so largely by focalizing him through Miss Milner's eyes, as for example in the famous scene in which her passion for Dorriforth surfaces. Lord Frederick, smitten by Miss Milner but hardly ready to propose, hears from her that Dorriforth wishes him to "desist visiting." He replies, "By heaven I believe Mr. Dorriforth loves you himself, and it is jealousy makes him treat me thus." Miss Woodley is shocked at the "sacrilegious idea," but Miss Milner blandly replies, "Mr. Dorriforth sees and converses with beauty, and from habit does not fall in love" (20). She continues to argue that Dorriforth's feelings for her can be "never less pure . . . than those which dwell in the bosom of my celestial guardian," but when he unexpectedly enters the room, she looks all "her discomposure" (21). In the ensuing discussion, he contends he is too unimportant to be a subject of slander, and Lord Frederick replies, wishing to suggest more than his words will say, that the "man who has the charge of Miss Milner . . . derives a consequence from her." Now we are given one of those moments of delicious ambiguity with which the novel abounds: "'No ill consequence, I hope, my lord,' replied Dorriforth with a firmness in his voice, and an eye fixed so steadfastly, that his lordship hesitated for a moment in want of a reply—and Miss Milner softly whispering to him, as her guardian turned his head, to avoid an argument, he bowed acquiescence." We continue to watch him through her eyes, trying to decipher Dorriforth. Lord Frederick then sneeringly [mis]quotes Pope: "'From Abelard it came, / And Heloisa still must love the name.'" The shocking implication that Dorriforth and Miss Milner are like the tragic and illicit lovers Abelard and Eloisa makes her throw "open the sash" and hold "her head out at the window to conceal the embarrassment these lines had occasioned." Dorriforth, however, whether "from an inattention to the quotation, or from a consciousness it was wholly inapplicable . . . heard it without one emotion of shame or of anger" (22). Her love is clear, but what of his? By the time we know, they are married and soon after that, locked in misery.

The marriage doesn't seem a natural, felicitous result of mutual adjustments of character, but only a cessation of hostilities. Indeed, nowhere are the necessities of this plot more clearly revealed than in the way she uses Sandford to bring about the sudden marriage, a device open to the charge of artificiality. Betrothed, they continue warring. Indeed, she insists upon testing him to see if his love really equals hers, but in a way that challenges his moral authority. She goes to a masquerade, not because of its thematic significance but because in the eighteenth-century novel, as in society, masquerades are places for arranging assignations and not, therefore, fit places for betrothed (and passionate) eighteen-year-old women or ex-priests to be. Dorriforth's reaction at being invited to accompany Miss Milner is revealing: "Do you imagine I would play the buffoon at a masquerade?" (153) As usual in this novel, the reader sees them both as right and wrong: he is right not to want her to go, wrong in being so peremptory about it; she is right in wanting him to extend his generosity to her choice of activities (especially during their betrothal), but wrong to ignore his conviction that the masquerade is an indecorous place for her to go. There are "fashions in love," but no reader in 1791 would have failed to see that these two lack the "warmth" and "emotional commitment" that was for Lawrence Stone the "epitome of the new companionate marriage among the upper classes of the late eighteenth century."[18] Of course, she does go, and he decides to end the engagement.

Only at Father Sandford's urging do they reavow their love and four days later marry. Sandford, who disapproves of Miss Milner in morally unequivocal terms, makes the horrible mistake of equating rapture with the kind of confident generosity that makes domestic felicity possible. The marriage is brought about by the most unlikely of means and with a misplaced faith in the ability of "vows" to "constrain" Miss Milner "from offending" her husband, from doing, that is, what the reader knows her character will make her do (191). Like Foucault, Sandford thinks power and not good will runs relationships, not realizing that amicability flows only from generosity and forbearance, not rights and coercion. Nowhere in feminist discussions of this novel is Inchbald's intention missed more thoroughly than here. Spacks, for example, after quoting this passage, continues: "Marriage, the Jesuit reminds his immediate audience and the reader, implies immense social power for its male participants. It provides the definitive means to quell female insubordination."[19] Yet in the game Inchbald plays, it is crucial for the reader to see that Sandford is wrong, proven so by Miss Milner's character as already revealed, and by ensuing events. The very terms of Spacks's analysis—social, allegorical, adversarial—are misleading.

Elmwood and Miss Milner's mutual but doomed passion results in a marriage their own feelings of animosity and impatience, if heeded, would rightly have discouraged them from entering. Inchbald clearly wants us to recognize that these two people, unlike so many heroes and heroines from Fielding to Austen, do not hold their happiness in their own hands. Because Miss Milner is at the mercy of her impulses, her mortification will not open her way to self-appraisal as it will for Lizzy Bennet. While the ideological critics want the final rupture between her and Elmwood to be one more act of the unforgiving and inflexible patriarch, Inchbald gives us something explicitly quite different. Miss Milner is no Pamela, willing almost unceasingly to adjust her expectations as readily as her dress. Miss Milner, who "habitually started at the unpleasant voice of control," is quick to resent "injury or neglect" (15), "accustomed to receive the devotion of every man who saw her" (104), "pleased" when she is able to "irritate" Dorriforth, because it shows her power over him (153), and, most ominously, repulsed by his prudence, which causes "his understanding to get the better of his affection" (171). She cannot suspect any lessening of her husband's adoration without retaliating. Elmwood goes abroad to attend to his "very large estate in the West Indies," remains "near three years," the last months of which he suffers from "a severe and dangerous illness, which a too cautious fear of her uneasiness had prompted him to conceal" (196). In ignorance of his danger, Lady Elmwood, "at first only unhappy, became at last provoked; and giving way to that impatient, irritable disposition she had so seldom governed," starts to go out on the town again. Anger at her husband's absence gives way to "a degree of indifference still more fatal" (196). Thriving only on passionate love and attention, she fills the void with an illicit "love" more like a "delirium" (197). Fully conscious of her guilt, she flees into self-exile as he returns home to discover "his honour and his happiness" damaged beyond the remedy even of revenge.

The manner of representation of this bridging episode suggests that Lady Elmwood's fate is an expected event and a transition to the real subject of the continuation, the implacable misery of Lord Elmwood. It is summarized and saturated with a sense of witnessing something reluctantly expected: "To state the progression by which vice gains a predominance in the heart, may be a useful lesson; but it is one so little to the satisfaction of most readers, that it is not meant to be related here, all the degrees of frailty by which Lady Elmwood fell" (195). Here as elsewhere in this wise novel, Inchbald assumes her readers know how lovers sometimes conspire to doom each other, how an impatient, impulsive, openhearted woman would find a way to espouse a spartan rationalist addicted to keeping his own counsel.

The marriage that ensures Miss Milner's unhappiness also gives us an Elmwood whose despair opens his character for our examination and, finally, sympathetic understanding. The real humanity of Inchbald's novel inheres in how she estranges Elmwood from us at the beginning of the second part, then brings us back to seeing him as one of us in his suffering. The novel is a game in anticategorical thinking, and therefore beyond any critic who thinks in terms of "patriarchy." We may grasp something of the requirements of Inchbald's story at this point by asking why she did not continue the relationship between Lord and Lady Elmwood. If some sort of reconciliation is what Inchbald wanted as a conclusion, then why not bring the original pair together after many years of estrangement? The answer is not thematic but part of the irrevocable commitment of the story itself. They can't be reconciled—they couldn't even be married without Sandford—without changing Elmwood's character unbelievably. Elmwood's inflexibility "matches" him, unluckily, to his wife. Elmwood is a damaged, fearful, preemptory man incensed at a world in which love destroys happiness. Lady Elmwood's transgressions finish her story, but they leave her husband shattered. He closes up and, unrepentant and self-justifying, refuses to readmit the dangerous possibilities of affection, even for a daughter. Like Lear, Elmwood must be shattered twice to learn his lesson about love.

Since reconciliation could not take place until the second generation, Inchbald's choice is to portray Matilda finally gaining her father's heart and thus, in his clear identification of his living daughter with her dead mother, reconciling Elmwood to his wife. Elmwood, who once had greater depths of understanding than Sandford, only now learns to forgive. Doubtless closure of the second half of the novel is achieved artificially in the sense that, just as in the first half, someone has to interfere to bring about stability. Here it is Lord Margrave's abduction of Matilda. If the device is one of arid romance, it is at least in keeping with the implacability of Lord Elmwood's character. When he dismisses a kind and gentle gardener, of twenty years' loyal service just for mentioning Lady Elmwood's name, when he comes close to breaking with a lifelong friend merely for pointing out his inhumanity, it is clear that this story is still about a man so inflexible that he can rejoin humanity only through extraordinary grace.

Finally, something must be said about the didactic aims, shared with other novels of the time, of *A Simple Story*, what it says about the "proper education" Matilda has and her mother lacked. Critics since Boaden, with the marked exception of Gary Kelly, have dismissed the moral as at best not "integral" to the novel.[20] More recently, feminist critics have consistently read this part of the novel ironically, as they do almost anything in earlier literature that fails to echo late-twentieth-century feminist ideology. Thus Jane Spencer: "The novel has a feminist interest, not because it shares the contemporary advocacy of a rational education for women, but because it reveals what was repressed in order to make that case. . . . it is clear that education in this novel functions negatively, not adding wisdom but imposing taboos. The female desire which it is meant to stifle is the novel's more fundamental concern."[21] Since the novel is silent on these issues, someone needs to explain how gender platitudes could be what the story is really about, and so Craft-Fairchild argues, "Unlike her contemporary, Mary Wollstonecraft, Elizabeth Inchbald did not make a direct statement for the rights of women and against patriarchal oppression. Instead, in *A Simple Story* Inchbald constructs a complicated and disturbing narrative that exposes defects in the patriarchal system not through explication, but through enactment—showing troubling relationships between men and women and thereby forcing readers to examine the foundations, assumptions, and implications of masculine domination."[22]

No doubt Craft-Fairchild is right in one regard at least: novels are not statements, not even indirect ones. There is no evidence that, if Inchbald had wanted to make such a statement, she would have been more timid than Wollstonecraft. But there is evidence that, unlike Wollstonecraft, Inchbald could write a brilliant, realistic novel, one that was motivated by elements of thought that, while they did not seem to disturb her own contemporaries, either baffle more recent critics or throw them into paroxysms of denial.

First of all, when Inchbald's narrator refers to "education," she does not have in mind the general call for women to be educated as men were, as interesting as that question became in the nineties, but specifically a religious education with its beneficial moral effects. She motivates her novel in part by making Miss Milner the dutiful daughter of a Catholic father, and then brings her under the authority of a Catholic priest. The choice can't be adventitious, but not for the reason the gender critics think. Her father chooses a priest, a man he thinks unites "every moral virtue to that of religion, and native honour to pious faith" (5). What does he want from Dorriforth's guardianship? Clearly it is spiritual guidance for a daughter who has come from "a Protestant boarding school . . . with merely such sentiments of religion, as young ladies of fashion mostly imbibe" (4).

In short, it is her failure to be raised as a Catholic that has "left her mind without one ornament, except those which nature gave, and even those were not wholly preserved from the ravages made by its rival, Art" (5). It is that spiritual education that Dorriforth fears is missing when he tries "to warn her of her danger" and urges the "necessity of 'time not always passed in society; or reflection; of reading; of thoughts for a future state; and of virtues acquired to make old age supportable'" (18). Whether Inchbald believed in these values or merely used them as convenient elements of thought, along with others, to motivate her plot of attractive but faulty characters, they allow us to measure Miss Milner's failings and her temporary successes. When Dorriforth can give in to her, as a benign return for her concession, and ask her to attend the ball, she weeps "with gentleness and patience," and he is "charmed to find her disposition so little untractable." Their mutual amiability "foreboded the future prosperity of his guardianship, and her *eternal*, as well as temporal happiness from this specimen" (33, emphasis mine). In the novel, that is, their treating each other with consideration (even though of course it involves a guardian/ward relationship) signals a spiritual as well as worldly good. Had Miss Milner really learned the lesson of Christian patience, she would never have cheated on her husband and doomed her own happiness. Had Dorriforth learned to forgive as well as to judge, there had been no catastrophe.

These values are part of the reading, but they are also thoroughly, mundanely commonplace in their time, as much as the Christian stoicism of *The Vicar of Wakefield*, or the rejection in *Joseph Andrews* of the belief that virtue is always rewarded on earth. As ideas, they are as good as any to motivate a plot, to help define as unchristian the behavior of both Miss Milner and Dorriforth. Some of them might even be useful as ideas still, depending on who is doing the reading.

Second, although the plot of the novel clearly turns on the imperfections of both of these characters—Inchbald having learned from Richardson and, perhaps, Burney the problems of generating a plot with a paragon—ideological critics are quick to attack anyone who, like Gary Kelly, has the temerity to point out what is clearly a fully synthesized element in the novel's game of character.[23] But it is Inchbald, not Kelly, who gives us for the sake of this new kind of novelistic game with flawed characters a Miss Milner who is flippant (55), avid for cheap praise (50), habitually rebelling from control, instantaneous in resenting a slight, real or imagined; witty only in her manner of speaking (15), contemptuous of Catholic customs (17), impatient (104), "unthinking" in her desire to test Elmwood (139), needing to dominate (151). None of these traits of character, any more than Dorriforth's faults (and no more than the many good qualities of both), has the slightest allegorical function. Each is specified so that the reader can have a rich, innovative fictional experience, one that is highly implicatory, but in different ways for each of us, as is the case with all realistic fiction. To turn *A Simple Story* into political allegory is historically, epistemologically, and aesthetically naive. To teach it to our students as a lesson in gender politics is deceitful.

Notes

1. Robert Storey, "'I Am I Because My Little Dog Knows Me': Prolegomenon to a Theory of Mimesis," in *After Poststructuralism: Interdisciplinarity and Literary Theory*, eds. Nancy Easterlin and Barbara Riebling (Evanston: Northwestern University Press, 1993), 45. See in particular the readings of *A Simple Story* in Jane Spencer, *The Rise of the Woman Novelist* (Oxford and New York: Blackwell, 1986); Terry Castle, *Masquerade and Civilization: The Carnivalesque in Eighteenth-Century English Culture and Fiction* (Stanford: Stanford University Press, 1986); Patricia Meyer Spacks, *Desire and Truth: Functions of Plot in Eighteenth-Century English Novels* (Chicago: University Chicago Press, 1990); Mary Ann Schofield, *Masking and Unmasking the Female Mind: Disguising Romances in Feminine Fiction, 1713–1799* (Newark: University of Delaware Press, 1990); Catherine Craft-Fairchild, *Masquerade and Gender: Disguise and Female Identity in Eighteenth-Century Fictions by Women* (University Park: Penn State University Press, 1993); and Eleanor Ty, *Unsex'd Revolutionaries: Five Women Novelists of the 1790s* (Toronto: University of Toronto Press, 1993). All of these critics treat the novel essentially as a statement and not as a fiction, so what they end up "arguing" about is what the novel would have meant if Inchbald had written an essay. Since their "connections" of fictional character and event to ideology are arbitrary impositions on a realistic story that will neither support nor refute them, what looks to be disagreement about textual facts among these allegorizers is really a conflict of contemporary notions of what the novel ought to have meant if novels meant in the way they mistakenly think they do. Even so, Castle and Spacks are worth reading for occasional nonideological insights.
2. Castle, 292.

3. Castle, 297.
4. Ty, 95.
5. See my *Narrative Innovation and Incoherence* (Durham, N.C.: Duke University Press, 1992), where "ideology" means, not what authors fail to perceive, but what they both take in and create, accept and reject, and modify by the power of their stories.
6. See S. R. Littlewood, *Mrs. Inchbald and Her Circle* (London: Daniel O'Conner, 1921); Gary Kelly, *The English Jacobin Novel, 1780–1805* (Oxford: Clarendon Press, 1976), Roger Manvell, *Elizabeth Inchbald: A Biographical Study* (Lanham, Md. and London: Univ. Press of America, 1987); and Gerard A. Barker, *Grandison's Heirs: The Paragon's Progress in the Late Eighteenth-Century Novel.* (Newark: University of Delaware Press, 1985). See also G. Louis Joughlin, "The Life and Work of Elizabeth Inchbald," Ph.D. diss., Harvard University, 1932.
7. Joughlin, 305.
8. Maria Edgeworth, quoted in Kelly, 78.
9. Lytton Strachey, "A Simple Story," in *Literary Essays* (London: Chatto and Windus, 1948), 128. Originally published as the Introduction to *A Simple Story*. London: Henry Frowde, 1908.
10. Elizabeth Inchbald, *A Simple Story* (ed. J. M. S. Tompkins; Oxford: Oxford University Press, 1988), 196. Subsequent references to this edition will appear in parentheses within the text.
11. She is not "exiled," as Castle contends on 320.
12. Maria Edgeworth, quoted in Kelly, 78.
13. Barker, 93. Barker's reading of the first half of the novel is very astute. My only objections to his chapter are, first, that, after that fine beginning, Barker never even entertains the possibility that the second half may be there for a good storytelling reason; second, the novel is a completely inappropriate choice for inclusion in a book on fictional "paragons." No one in the novel is remotely a paragon, except in initial description soon proven suspect.
14. Spencer, ix.
15. Craft-Fairchild, 101: "On a second reading, knowing the outcome of the marriage, the reader realizes that the continually threatened dissolution of the engagement is a desirable event."
16. Nancy Easterlin, "Play, Mutation, and Reality Acceptance: Toward a Theory of Literary Experience," in Easterlin and Riebling, 116.
17. The overt symbolism with which the first half of the novel ends, with the happy Miss Milner noticing with "an excruciating shock" that Elmwood had "put upon her finger, in haste, when he married her . . . a—MOURNING RING" (193), is perfectly appropriate as a conclusion to the reader's powerful expectations of doom, although Tompkins, the novel's editor, thinks it "very unlikely that this omen of future unhappiness terminated the original version" of the story (344). Here is one of the many places where an understanding of the novel as a complete construction has been hindered by facile assumptions about its circumstances of

composition. Knowing that the novel was begun in the late 1770s and not finished until the early 1790s, critics are very ready to assume, in part on Boaden's word, that the second part of the story was created later and that it had to be grafted on to the earlier one. See James Boaden, *Memoirs of Mrs. Inchbald*, 2 vols. (London, 1833), 1:264.

18. Lawrence Stone, *The Family, Sex, and Marriage in England, 1500–1800.* (Abridged ed. New York: Harper and Row, 1979), 240.

19. Spacks, 198.

20. See Tompkins, notes to p. 338, p. 345.

21. Jane Spencer, quoted in Craft-Fairchild, p. 117.

22. Craft-Fairchild,120.

23. For example, Terry Castle refers Kelly's accurate presentation of Miss Milner's "lack of moral discipline" to his "pervasive antifeminism." See Castle 366–67, n. 15.

Michael Boardman is Professor of English at Tulane University, where he teaches and writes about novels and film. His most recent book is *Narrative Innovation and Incoherence: Ideology in Defoe, Goldsmith, Austen, Eliot, and Hemingway.*

The Feminization of Ideology: Form and the Female in the Long Eighteenth Century

Laura Brown

This essay is a sketch of a feminist formal history of the eighteenth century: it proposes that the dominant forms of English literary culture in the period between the English and the French revolutions are shaped by the representation of women. The priority of the woman in this literary discourse entails what I am calling a feminization of ideology—a permeation of cultural structures by the various, multivalent, discursive manifestations of the female. This formal history is revisionist in two ways. It asks that we reconsider the category of the domestic,[1] separating rigorously arguments about the social power or cultural position of women from arguments about a feminized ideology.[2] And it asks that we circumscribe our claims about the political significance of representations of women. The female does not automatically radicalize a formal structure or cultural mode; indeed, this history emphasizes the intimacy of misogyny, rape, commodification, and imperialism with the image of the woman.[3] On the other hand, this history concludes with the claim that the political movement that has come to be called feminism is formally shaped by the feminization of ideology. So this is a politicized, formal history, but its politics are located in the dynamic relation between radical and conservative that marks the feminization of ideology.

The radical discourse of the English revolution shaped a figuration of female autonomy that became the catalyst for the production of a complex set of images of women—misogynist, imperialist, libertine, reactionary—that came to constitute the feminized ideology of the eighteenth century. The sectarian movements offered a challenge to female subordination, within the family and the church, but also in society at large. Indeed, almost every attack on church authority was potentially an attack on patriarchy, family hierarchy, and even marriage. The sectaries' support of individual conscience and spiritual equality generated a series of accounts of women as God's mouthpieces, arguments in favor of female prophecy and preaching, claims for women's rights within marriage and rights to divorce, representations of sexual freedom, pleas for female education, descriptions of female pilgrims travelling independently, political actions in the form especially of women's petitions to Parliament, and even notions of a female deity and creator, superior to the male.[4]

These positions, images, actions, and rhetorics are vividly present to the literary culture of the late seventeenth century. Women writers from the second half of the century who have recently entered the canon—Margaret Fell, Margaret Cavendish, and Mary Astell—compress in their works some of the major discursive materials of the popular representation of women during the revolutionary period. Fell joins a heated and sustained debate about women preaching in *Womens Speaking Justified* (1667), a debate which attracts to itself representations of female prophecy, the ventriloquization of God, and the projection of a female deity. Fell, like others, sets out to explicate the injunction of St. Paul in First Corinthians against women preaching: women who are among the elect may rightfully speak "the Message and Word of the Lord God," and in fact, have a special right to do so, because "the Church of Christ is a Woman," because in the scriptures women know "more of the secret Power and Wisdom of God, then his Disciples did," and because the "Holy Jerusalem" of the millennium is the "free Woman that all the Children of the Promise are born of."[5]

Even though Margaret Cavendish and Mary Astell are Royalists, not radicals, their writing belongs, both in direct and mediated respects, to the figures and claims of these antipatriarchal precedents. Cavendish's diffuse and contradictory works mix misogyny with arguments against marriage and for female speech. Her closet drama *The Bridals* (1668) contains a call to a battle that the ladies will conduct through both speech and actions against a male assault to consummate a marriage. Astell's *Reflections Upon Marriage* (1706) and *Serious Proposal to the Ladies* (1696) also link, in a mutual relationship typical of this discourse, the attack on marriage, the advocacy of women speaking, and the evocation of insurrection. Astell's treatment of marriage raises those images of female liberty and community central to the revolutionary period, images of women leaving behind husbands and families, and living, teaching, and conversing independently from men. *A Serious Proposal* joins an attack on marriage with the advocacy of female education. But Astell's rhetorical investment in women's intellectual and economic autonomy creates another interesting female figure—the ignorant, fashionable, foolish woman who is the inevitable victim of unwise marital choice. The bitter ironies that characterize this ill-fated figure constitute a kind of feminist misogyny, a perverse consequence of the anti-patriarchal discourse of female liberty.

Misogyny channels the rhetoric of the sectaries into the cultural modes and literary tropes of the eighteenth century. In the backlash against assertions of female autonomy, the pamphlet attacks on women petitioners typically associate women's claims to political rights with sexual appetite: what they really want is not political rights but free love. By this means, the sexually threatening woman becomes the protagonist of the popular reactionary political discourse of the late seventeenth century, and she figures as a witch, a harlot, or as the Whore of Babylon. The problem of marriage remains a locus of rhetorical tension; the misogynist poetry adopts and repeats a conventional rejection of marriage, only to confront the question of how to effect procreation. Misogynist poetry is a prominent sub-genre of the 1680s and 1690s. We know it canonically and neoclassically from Dryden's translation of Juvenal's sixth satire (1692), but we must not let Dryden's canonicity overshadow the many other examples of this ideologically vital project.[6] In this poetry, with its obsessive troping of women's sexual appetite, the female body acquires a specific and connected collection of images. Dryden's touchstone, like that of Robert Gould in *Love Given O'er: or, a Satyr against the Pride, Lust, and Inconstancy, &c. of Woman* (1682), is the infamous Messalina, wife of Emperor Claudius, a familiar character in neoclassical anti-feminist discourse, who spends her nights in the "brothel-house" taking on one man after another and finally returning reluctantly to "Old Caesar's bed / The steam of lamps still hanging on her cheeks / In ropy smut: thus foul, and thus bedight, / She brings him back the product of the night."[7] This figure joins sexual voraciousness and autonomy with physical filth, emascu- lation or gender reversal, and a levelling operation in which the female womb, through its indiscriminate powers of consumption, reduces all male contributors to the same status. This social implication of female autonomy constitutes another crucial link between attacks on women and the liberationist positions of the revolution, when social levelling was the common cry.

Elsewhere in Dryden's poem this levelling produces a class anxiety, when the promiscuity of upper-class wives leads them to embrace "slaves and watermen, a race of strong-back'd knaves" (449–50), as well as a "fencer" (114) and an "Ethiop" (777). Significantly, in Gould's *Love Given O'er* this issue of levelling is generalized beyond class or even human objects: the womb is "as greedy as the gaping Tomb: / Take Men, Dogs, Lions, Bears, all sorts of Stuff,/ Yet it will never cry—there is enough."[8] Richard Ames in *The Folly of Love* (1691) describes the woman as a vast opening, a "fatal Gulph we call a *Common Whore*."[9] Rochester recites this trope for the female body in his poem *On Mrs. Willis*, a contemporary Messalina: "Bawdy in thoughts, precise in words, / Ill-natured though a whore, / Her belly is a bag of turds, / And her cunt a common shore."[10] Indeed, the sewer in the urban poetry of the eighteenth century—like Pope's *Dunciad* or Swift's *Description of a City Shower*—is still infected with this image of female sexuality.

In the negative vision of misogyny, then, the body of the woman contains claims to sexual equality and social autonomy, assertions of female power and gender reversal, and the engaging evocation of both social levelling and indiscriminate consumption. The evocation of consumption here, as we shall see, is a rhetorical precursor to the representation of female commodification and the connection of the female figure with accumulation, exchange, capital, trade, and the whole ethos of a new world of consumption. And this figural stew, brewed with the broth of the major historical forces of the age, receives its ideological urgency from the revolution, the ghostly ancestor of this vital misogynist trope, as Gould reminds us when he call up the threat of a parallel feminist revolution to match the recent one: "guard your Empire well; / For shou'd they once get power to rebel, / They'd surely raise a Civil-War in Hell." Anxiety about radical rebellion is never far from the surface in the misogynist poetry. Rochester's works illustrate the intimacy of the sexualized female figure with a challenge to a hierarchical status quo. The rhetoric of the radical sectaries, in the form of libertine antinomianism, is close to the surface in Rochester's pornographic texts, and gives their misogyny a more direct connection with political delegitimation.

Later misogyny condenses these tropes. Swift's female figures too are denizens of the sewers. Corinna in *A Beautiful Young Nymph Going to Bed* (1734) dreams that she lies in watch, "near *Fleet-Ditch*'s oozy Brinks, / Surrounded with a Hundred Stinks, / . . . / [to] snap some Cully passing by."[11] In Swift's misogynist poetry, the female body demonstrates its power by polluting the world. Celia, in *The Lady's Dressing Room* (1732), taints with her "excremental Smell" her own body, her "Pettycoats and Gown," and every room she visits (111–114). Swift's texts, though, are poised between the material presence and the absence of the female body. Celia is constituted by all the pieces of herself that she has left behind in her dressing room: her sweaty smock, her combs filthy with "Sweat, Dandriff, Powder, Lead and Hair" (14), her basin in which "she spits and . . . spues" (42), her grimy towels, her handkerchiefs "all varnish'd o'er with Snuff and Snot" (50), and of course her excrement encased in the decorated chest. Corinna, in undressing herself for the night, takes her body apart. And of course the "rotting" Celia of *The Progress of Beauty* (1719) gradually disappears altogether as "Each Night a Bit drops off her Face" (71).

Indeed, the disappearance of the woman is a prominent ideological feature of the latter day misogynist poetry. Pope's *Epistle to a Lady* (1735), too, leaves the ladies outside the scene of the text, and denies them, in its opening couplet, any claim to identity: "Nothing so true as what you once let fall, / 'Most Women have no Characters at all.'"[12] The dispersal, disintegration, or dissemination of the female body in the context of this troping of autonomous female sexuality represents a rhetorical generalization, in which the sewer's powers of indiscriminate incorporation are projected outward as a figure for all experience. But the more the woman is made absent in these texts, the more ubiquitous and omnipotent she becomes. In this sense, the disappearing woman thematizes the feminization of ideology, the moment at which literary culture finds the female figure indispensable. We can place that moment at the height of the misogynist tradition.

Misogyny is a vital channel, within which various streams from the discourse of the revolution merge and diverge, with each other and with the prominent topics and problems of the time. The poetry shows their merging; the misogynist drama, more conventionally known as the she-tragedy, gives a view of some of their divergences. These plays enact the same thesis of threatening, insatiable, female sexual autonomy, and they repeat many of the rhetorical conventions of the poetic attacks on women for inconstancy, tyranny, whoring, and pollution. But they focus this obsession with female sexuality on the representation and rape of a female victim, a figure through which the destructive anti-patriarchal woman can be punished and contained. Through her victimization, this drama generates, in a misogynist parallel universe, a pathetic and helpless female protagonist with the same identity as the figure of sexual autonomy.

In Otway's *The Orphan* (1680) Monimia is, on the one hand, a whore whose sexual appetite brings about the destruction of the world of the play: in this guise, she makes men her victims, like the sewer of the misogynist poetry. The consequence of her power is explicitly connected with the revolution in the play's summary account of the effect on the world of female sexuality: "Confusion and disorder seize the world, / To spoil all trust and converse amongst men; / 'Twixt families engender endless feuds; / In countries, needless fears; in cities, factions; / In states, rebellion; and in churches, schism."[13] On the other hand, Monimia is dovelike, tender, weak, and kind, a sympathetic victim, and a figure of pathos. In this guise, her sexuality is located in her breasts, and defined in terms of the pain that can be inflicted by beating them. This pain is the sadomasochistic source of the pleasure supplied in the play—both the sexual pleasure described by the male characters and the aesthetic pleasure proposed for the audience. And, just as Monimia's sexual identity is constituted by her victimization —her rapability—male sexuality in this drama is reciprocally constituted in terms of rape: men are those who rape women. The affective structure of the play, in which the audience joins with the male characters in the pleasurable contemplation of the suffering of a woman, proposes a community of fellow feeling in which sympathy, heterosexual identity, and a new structure of evaluative stability are merged. Out of this symptomatic and characteristic contradiction in the female figure, then, comes a rhetoric of suffering and a structure of affect that later in the eighteenth century is associated with sentimentalism. We can see in Monimia's two faces the intimate involvment of sensibility with violence against women, but also the coincidence of the angel and the whore. Though these figures subsequently diverge—the angel Clarissa is balanced by the devil Sinclair—they belong to the same dynamic engagement with a liberationist representation of female autonomy.

Rowe's *Jane Shore* (1714) follows the same pattern. Jane is similarly both a whore and an innocent victim. As a whore she is represented through the misogynist rhetoric of pollution and appetite. Female sexual power, in this case Jane's sexuality joined to that of her friend Alicia, brings on the disaster of the plot. But at the same time, Jane is an innocent victim threatened by rape and perhaps even originally raped by Edward. Like Monimia, she too is defined by images of cruelty and pain, blood and suffering. And she has a physical part, like Monimia's breasts, that condenses her sexual identity: her "lovely tresses"[14] are a signal of rape and cruelty, dishevelled in the final scene of her torture and death (5.1.142*sd*). In Rowe's play, though, the troping of the sexualized female body takes a significant turn from body parts—wombs, breasts, or tresses—to the fantastic substitution of objects of adornment for the body of the woman itself. At the end of the play, when Jane has been stripped, starved, and beaten, she is represented in terms of a string of pearls that her husband used to adorn her in happier days. At this point in the play, instead of the damaged female body that *The Orphan* offered the sympathizing audience, *Jane Shore* provides a mystified version of the body in the materiality of the pearl necklace. This substitution is a form of commodification, in which the body of the woman is replaced by the objects that adorn it.

In fact, if we posit a rhetorical trajectory from womb, to breast, to tresses, to the necklace, we can see a movement away from the representation of female body parts, though not from the female itself. The womb as we have seen is an image of female sexual autonomy and a monstrous material part and essence of the female body. Breasts are another essentially female part. But hair is a mediate image, ambiguously both a body part and an adornment. Both breasts and hair as we have seen are figures for female suffering, metonyms of female sexual identity. The necklace makes the female body disappear by absorbing all these images: the powerful woman, the rapable female victim, the suffering and sympathy produced by her victimization, and the sentimental community thereby constituted. This commodified female figure is a product of the troping of female sexual autonomy and its corollary violence against women, and belongs to the same discourse as the cult of sensibility. From the perspective of the feminization of ideology, rape is the aesthetic model for sentimentalism, and commodification is its alter ego.

Monimia and Jane are both whores and angels, but of course later in the period these contradictory qualities are kept separate. Defoe's Roxana is perhaps the period's most famous whore, and she provides another view of the transformation of sexuality to commodification that we saw in the misogynist drama. *Roxana* (1724) generates the commodified woman out of the connection of female sexuality and accumulation. If we place *Roxana* in the context of the misogynist tradition, we can see how the troping of female sexuality can lead away from sexualized images of women to a problematizing of female identity through commodification. In becoming a successful female merchant by selling her body, Roxana translates sexual into economic power. She is an Amazon, a "Man-Woman,"[15] a passionate critic of marriage, like the powerful anti-patriarchal figures of the sectaries. But even though Roxana maintains control of her profits, this process commodifies her. In selling herself, Roxana's body disappears beneath the things that adorn her: lavish dresses, costumes, disguises, and even a beautiful necklace like Jane Shore's. Symptomatically, then, this trope of female autonomy supersedes the sexual. Roxana has no body. In Defoe's dressing room scene, where she receives the diamond necklace from the French Prince, Roxana claims to be exposing her body by scrubbing her face to prove that she is not painted. But like Jane Shore, Roxana is transformed at just this point of undress by the necklace, and only thus adorned can she be pronounced complete. Defoe's dressing room, like those famous ones of Swift and Pope, is the site of this fetishizing of the female body. In Swift's poems the body disintegrates, dismembers itself, dissolves into pieces, excretions, and leavings of itself, and by that means pollutes the whole world. In *The Rape of the Lock* the female body becomes a trope of imperial expansion, and by consuming the whole world, pervades it. In Defoe's novel the female body occupies the powerful place of capital: it can be sold but it has no substance; it is a figure of accumulation and profit, but it has no identity.

Thus, through the versatile image of the prostitute, female sexual autonomy generates a representation both of the ideological crisis of commodification and of the cultural anxiety surrounding the expansionist ethic of economic self-interest. Roxana's argument for the connection of liberty and capital accumulation is an expression of the Lockean grounding of bourgeois liberty in private property. And this aspect of the text is readily interpreted as an extension of the argument for economic individualism and bourgeois liberty to women. But the unruly and threatening Amazon is not a Lockean figure of civil order; as we have seen, she is figure of revolutionary delegitimation. She functions, though, as a host for the feminist transmission of Locke. The novel ends in misogyny, with a formulaic punishment for the female protagonist reminiscent of the retaliatory violence against women in the misogynist drama. But here, since the female figure has accreted so many other significances, that punishment functions not only as a means of rejecting the autonomous woman, but also as a repudiation of the feminist extension of Locke, as a critique of commodification, and even as a demystification of economic individualism. The complicated politics of the representation of women in *Roxana* warns us against claiming a single political meaning for one image or another, or a single political origin for modern feminism, but it confirms at the same time the generative energy of the radical discourse of the sectaries.

Let me gather some of the strands we have been pursuing so far. The representation of female sexual autonomy is a trope of the powerful, speaking woman of the revolutionary period. But it is a proliferative, generative, and volatile trope, whose transformations we can best see through the extensive misogynist literary culture of the late seventeenth and early eighteenth centuries. Among its varied and politically multivalent forms are those images of the whore, the gulf, and the sewer; of disease, death, and emasculation; of sexual voraciousness, indiscriminate consumption, and social levelling; of the disintegrating or disappearing female body, the passive or innocent female victim, and the commodified or economically self-interested woman. These figures can be the basis of a radical attack on the status quo (Rochester); they can be objects of anxiety and political vengeance (she-tragedy); they can shape norms of heterosexual identity (she-tragedy); they can enact epistemological and political crises (commodification, mercantilism); they can ventriloquize class identity (bourgeois moral virtue), and they can generate forms of cultural expression (sensibility). In short, the troping of this powerful female figure acquires a versatility that makes it culturally ubiquitous, and ideologically indispensible.

The *Tatler* and *Spectator* papers are a kind of cultural encyclopedia, for which this ubiquitous female image is a mascot or a metonym, standing in for the larger cultural concerns that the papers seek to legislate. Women are the *Spectator* papers' ideological web, binding together various representations of capital and commodification, "Nature" and sensibility, gender and sexual identity through the representation of female energy and autonomy. The intimacy of women and capital is most evident in the extraordinary paper on Public Credit (No. 3).[16] Here in Addison's account the tremendous cultural impact of the growth of an international money market, public credit, and stock speculation is played out in a visit to the Bank of England. Publick Credit, who presides, is a nervous, hysterical woman, characterized as irrational, changeable, subject to fluctuations and fits, driven by desire and attracting rumor and opinion. She expresses, through the misogynist trope of female inconstancy, the anxiety about the new and unpredictable forces of capital. But her hysteria of course is the physiological term for sensibility, for the inclination to fantasy, passion, and imagination.[17] In this feminized figure, then, capital and sentiment are made synonymous. In fact, at the end of the essay when Mr. Spectator sees Publick Credit revived by political and financial forces, and "the Bags [of money] swell'd to their former Bulk, the Piles of Faggots and Heaps of Paper changed into Pyramids of Guineas," he is "transported" with an overflowing of feeling that obliges him to flee the scene.[18]

As a figure of commodification, the woman in the papers is often the slave of fashion. Steele and Addison would have her follow "Nature" instead; that is, adopt the "natural" adornments of imperial expansion, "the Product of an hundred Climates" (No. 69). Like Roxana or Belinda, Steele's female figure is an imperialist fetish, but a fetish with a rhetorical history. Female fashion emerges as a sign of women's sexual and reproductive autonomy, a translation of the discourse of the sectaries into the discourse of consumption, in the essays on the hoop petticoat (*Tatler* No. 116 and *Spectator* No. 127). In both essays this autonomy is felt as a threat. In Steele's *Tatler* essay the hoop is connected with a dangerous but unnamed female power, making women loom over men; in Addison's paper it liberates women entirely from male supervision. Like Swift's female figures, the hoop in Steele's account is itself punished by dismemberment, and like Jane Shore's tresses, through its mediate status it mingles commodification with sexuality and desire.

But with a revealing reciprocity. In connecting sexuality with the commodity, the hoop petticoat expresses a sexualization of the desire for commodities and accumulation; it gives capitalist desire a sexual genealogy. The relation between female autonomy and commodification can also be read backwards in this figure. Commodification itself seems to grant some form of power to the woman that it mystifies; concretely here, the fashion object—the hoop petticoat—supplants the female body but simultaneously makes it loom larger than life and gives it an unprecedented autonomy. This superimposition of female power and capital—conceived through commodity, consumption, and exchange—is a factor at other points in the papers. The ultimate anxiety here is that women, as exemplary figures of commodification and embodiments of capital, might acquire all the powers of capitalism to transform the world: female unruliness and capitalist dynamism might combine. This is the new face of the threat of the female figure, in the papers and at other major points in the literary culture of the period.

From this perspective, though the papers seek in their treatment of women and their use of the female figure to legislate women's cultural role, and, in large part, to create a domestic paragon, they also exceed these gestures of cultural regulation, representing occasions of the loss of control, or the failure of bourgeois hegemony. Capital, as we have seen, stands behind this excess. But so does the feminization of ideology itself. One of the ironic consequences of the ideological vitality of the female figure is the potential power of discursive centrality. The more indispensible the figure of the woman becomes in the self-representation of the culture, the more her cultural energy approaches excess, the more she becomes a locus of contradiction.

We have already seen in some detail in the misogynist drama and more briefly in the representation of hysteria in the *Spectator* the feminization of affective form, the central role of the representation of women in the constitution of the cultural mode of sentimentalism. The female figure brings to sensibility all of these complex aspects of her ideological significance: autonomy and misogyny, commodification and capital, sexuality and sexual identity, the body and its absence. We can trace the tensions of this ideological dynamic in the notorious ironies of the sentimental novel. The evocation of suffering and sentiment in Goldsmith's *Vicar of Wakefield* has a misogynist dimension in its commentary on marriage and its satire on female vanity and self-interest. It uses the foolish woman as well as the woman who suffers through sexual error to announce the value of love over property in marriage. Indeed, the project of the novel is the legislation of a separation of the female figure from capital, lest she become a "Man-Woman," or an Amazon, perhaps. Male identity, as in the she-tragedy, is defined in terms of this feminized project: the ideal man is someone who can control women, specifically by controlling their connection with capital. And he does so through the evocation of the affective aesthetic of sensibility, that is, by sympathizing with and relieving suffering. The "good man" pays out good money in an act of sympathy as a way of enforcing the woman's choice of love over money. In the *Vicar* then, sensibility is the constitution of a structure of affect that brings capital under control in the figure of and through the body of the woman.

Sterne's *Sentimental Journey* joins affect and capital through a more complex and even more fertile rhetoric of female sexuality. The diffuse sources of affect that this text describes along the way—the Franciscan monk, the dead ass, the caged starling—are focused in the figure of the suffering woman—Maria or Madame de C—with whom Yorick mingles his tears, and in the corollary figure of the sexually available woman—the Grisset, the *fille de chambres*—with whom Yorick mingles something else. At the same time, sensibility is represented in terms of buying, exchange, and commerce (33), and repeatedly enacted in the giving of alms or the financial exercise of charity. The sentimental category of "Nature," which calls forth Yorick's effusions of fellow feeling and proves "the existence of a soul within me,"[19] entails a specific kind of exchange, in which sympathy is the currency and the female figure is the ideal object. This rhetoric suggests a commodification of sympathy congruent with its feminization. That is, the female figure is both the cultural emblem of commodification and the prototypical object of sympathy, and these two dimensions of her role are not only compatible, but mutually constitutive. Thus Yorick's exemplary sensibility is generated both from his identification with these suffering and sexualized female figures, and from his engagement with exchange. Yorick represents the internalization of the woman as commodity and as affect.

Like that of the commodified woman, Yorick's identity is mystified: he is mistaken by the Count de B for the king's jester from *Hamlet*, on which basis he is granted a passport. So his travels are authorized by a falsehood. But this erroneous name is in another sense Yorick's most appropriate designation, as the Count de B sees when he catches him in a jest. The problem of identity is also raised in Yorick's attempts to demonstrate that he possesses a soul, a problem that could be seen as the underlying motive of the whole of the *Journey*. Yorick's interiority, like that of the commodified woman, is always in doubt, and the question of what lies within or beneath the surface is the motivating mystery of the cult of sensibility, just as it is the motivating mystery of the fetishism of the commodity. In *Jane Shore* or *Roxana*, the problem of commodification is located externally, in the necklace or the dress. In *The Sentimental Journey* fetishization is a problem of the subject itself: Yorick himself, or the reader who identifies and earns his sense of moral value from his fellow feeling with Yorick, seems to lack a name, a soul, a sense of confidence about his own interiority. The representations of the body in this novel are attempts to probe this mystery, by examining postures, blushes, and pulsations of the arteries. Here the body is dissected, dismembered, and examined like Swift's female bodies, as if by this means it can be grasped, named, and disciplined. But Yorick, like the woman, escapes this naming.

The project of *The Sentimental Journey* is not that of controlling the woman, as it is in *The Vicar of Wakefield*, but of controlling the internalization of that feminized figure of affect and capital. As we have seen elsewhere in the literary culture of this period, it is a figure of excess—excessive passion, excessive pain, excessive power, excessive appetite. It is a figure of unruliness—individualist, antisocial, self-interested, self-indulgent. And it is a figure of mystification—fetishized, elusively absent, disembodied, dismembered, dispersed, or disseminated. The various contradictions of sentimentalism—between excessive and appropriate passion, between a private, exclusive emotion and a community of moral virtue, between the legislation of a hegemonic bourgeois morality and the evocation of a challenge to hierarchy and convention, and even between the assumption of a normal heterosexuality and the evocation of an ambiguous, polymorphous sexual identity—can be understood in terms of the multivalence and vitality of a feminized ideology. Politically this view of the cult of sensibility helps to explain its ambiguous relation to the democratic and reformist movements of the late eighteenth century: the women's antislavery movement and the radical populist movements in particular. Sensibility, like the figure of the woman that shapes it, engages both with bourgeois hegemony and with liberation.

In Wollstonecraft's *Vindication of the Rights of Woman*, questions of politics, sentiment, and gender intersect in ways that reflect the dynamism of this multivalent female figure. As many critics have observed, female sexuality poses a special problem for the *Vindication*, and the female body—and the resulting cultural discrimination of the "sexual character"—is the locus of woman's subjection to commodification and fashion. Much of this text's rhetorical energy goes into the attack on the female body for its joint subjection to sensibility and fashion. To this end, the *Vindication* draws directly upon the misogynist tradition as well as upon the well-established representations of female commodification, and participates in the same feminist misogyny that we identified in Mary Astell. The representation of female sexuality in this text, then, is largely negative: "natural affection," or sexual love, even in marriage, is excessive, ephemeral, and perhaps even false.[20]

On the other hand, the *Vindication* sets up a vital positive image of the sexualized female body: that of the mother nursing her child. This is also the central figure of Wollstonecraft's *Maria*. In both works, this figure is shaped by the tropes of sensibility—the evocation of nature, the sympathetic emotion felt on the pulses, and the conventional affective power of the female breast. Like Monimia's breasts, the hidden, implied breasts of the *Vindication* are the objects of male affective identification: "Cold would be the heart of a husband, were he not rendered unnatural by early debauchery, who did not feel more delight at seeing his child suckled by its mother, than the most artful wanton tricks could ever raise" (142). So essential is the role of the male audience to the scene of affective female sexuality that in *Maria* the same image must have an imaginary observer. The horrible Venables, Maria's real husband, is replaced by an ideal alternative in her representation of her own sexual identity: "in my desolate state, I had it very much at heart to suckle you, my poor babe. . . . Of Mr. Venables I thought not, even when I thought of the felicity of loving your father, and how a mother's pleasure might be exalted, and her care softened by a husband's tenderness. . . . I imagined with what exstacy, after the pains of child-bed, I should have presented my little stranger, whom I had so long wished to view, to a respectable father, and with what maternal fondness I should have pressed them both to my heart!"[21]

Thus the representation of female sexuality in the *Vindication* is poised between a misogynist attack on the commodified female body and a sentimental affirmation of the woman suckling her child—a figure of domestic harmony and affective identification but also of sexual self-assertion. In *The Orphan* female sexual autonomy stands just behind the affective female protagonist, in her destructive role in the structure of the plot. In the *Vindication* that autonomy resides in the constitutive excess of affect, in the sentimental privileging of passion and in its translation to the political passion of a liberationist advocacy. Incidentally, or maybe not, the posthumous anti-Jacobin attacks on Wollstonecraft were based on the connection of women with the seventeenth-century radical movements, on female "magic," and on the notion of Wollstonecraft as a witch and a "false prophetess" like the prophesying and speaking women of the sects.[22]

We can trace that powerful image of female autonomy from the seventeenth century and see it emerging here, through the conjunction of the contradictory form of the cult of sensibility and the reactionary tradition of misogyny, and informing the radical discourse of this new age of revolution. And then receiving in turn its own reactionary reading. It is by simultaneously attacking women for their sensibility, and contradicting that attack, that Wollstonecraft imagines women's liberation. The attack comes out of the misogynist tradition provoked by the liberationist discourse of the previous century. It is contradicted by the sexualized figure of female affect and passion, another ghost of the revolution. In the *Vindication*, then, we could say that a radical critique is reconstituted when those two ghosts meet each other at another stage of sublimation.

This meeting is the basis of the political claims that I want to make for my argument about the feminization of ideology. I began with the caution that the notion of a feminized culture should not be confused with a claim for female power, authority, or autonomy in history, and in a corollary way, that misogynist or conservative figurations of women—as figures of commodification or tools of imperialism—should not preclude a radical reading of the female. In this sketch of a feminist literary history, the radical movement of the seventeenth century, through the formal intervention of misogyny, generates a series of vital images around the figure of the woman, which come to play a central role in cultural formations throughout the eighteenth century. In a new revolutionary period those images, produced by a common liberationist political logic, make the tropes of the radical discourse of one revolutionary period available to another. In this sense, the political movement that has come to be called feminism is formally shaped by the ideological vitality of the female figure—slippery, multivalent, susceptible over this long century to a variety of cultural uses and political readings, but retaining throughout a critical implication that gives it a political life beyond its time.

Notes

1. The seminal works in the account of eighteenth-century domesticity are Mary Poovey, *The Proper Lady and the Woman Writer: Ideology as Style in the Works of Mary Wollstonecraft, Mary Shelley, and Jane Austen* (Chicago: University of Chicago Press, 1984) and Nancy Armstrong, *Desire and Domestic Fiction: A Political History of the Novel* (Oxford: Oxford University Press, 1987).

2. Armstrong, for instance, equates women's ideological role with women's cultural position: if "the notion of the household as a specifically feminine space established the preconditions for a modern institutional culture," then "modern culture has empowered middle-class women" (254).

3. Catherine Gallagher in "Embracing the Absolute: The Politics of the Female Subject in Seventeenth-Century England" (*Genders* 1 [1988]: 24–39) documents Astell's and Cavendish's debts to absolutist ideas as an antidote to the kind of political optimism that assumes that woman is a radical force.

4. See, for these general issues, Elaine Hobby, *Virtue of Necessity: English Women's Writing 1649–88* (Ann Arbor: University of Michigan Press, 1989); Keith Thomas, "Women and the Civil War Sects," *Past and Present* (13: 1958) 42–62; Bridget Hill, introduction to *The First English Feminist:* Reflections Upon Marriage *and Other Writings, by Mary Astell*, ed. Bridget Hill (New York: St. Martin's Press, 1986); Phyllis Mack, *Visionary Women: Ecstatic Prophecy in Seventeenth-Century England*

(Berkeley: University of California Press, 1992); and *Women, Writing, History 1640–1740*, ed. Isobel Grundy and Susan Wiseman (Athens: University of Georgia Press, 1992).

5. Margaret Fell, *Women's Speaking Justified* (1667), 5 and 11.

6. For treatment of Dryden's poem and other misogynist works in the period see Felicity A. Nussbaum, *The Brink of All We Hate: English Satires on Women 1660–1750*, (Lexington, Kentucky: University Press of Kentucky,) 1984.

7. John Dryden, *Satires of Juvenal and Persius*, in *The Poetical Works of Dryden*, ed. George R. Noyes, 1909; rev. ed. (Cambridge: Houghton Mifflin, 1950), ll. 176–89. Subsequent references will be to this edition; line numbers will be given parenthetically in the text.

8. Robert Gould, *Love Given O'er*, in *Satires on Women*, Augustan Reprint Society (Los Angeles: William Andrews Clark Memorial Library, 1979), 5. Subsequent references to *Love Given O'er* will be to this reprint; page numbers will be given parenthetically in the text.

9. Richard Ames, *The Folly of Love*, in *Satires on Women*, Augustan Reprint Society (Los Angeles: William Andrews Clark Memorial Library, 1979), 13.

10. *The Complete Poems of John Wilmot, Earl of Rochester*, ed. David M. Vieth (New Haven: Yale University Press, 1968), *On Mrs. Willis*, ll. 17–20.

11. *A Beautiful Young Nymph Going to Bed*, in *Swift: Poetical Works*, ed. Herbert Davis (London: Oxford University Press, 1967), ll. 47–50. Subsequent references to Swift's poems, will be to this edition; line numbers will be provided parenthetically in the text.

12. *To a Lady*, in *Poetry and Prose of Alexander Pope*, ed. Aubrey Williams (Boston: Houghton Mifflin, 1969), ll. 1–2.

13. *The Orphan*, ed. Aline Mackenzie Taylor (Lincoln: University of Nebraska Press, 1976), 5:516–20.

14. *The Tragedy of Jane Shore* in *British Dramatists from Dryden to Sheridan*, ed. George H. Nettleton and Arthur E. Case (Boston: Houghton Mifflin, 1939), 5.1.24. Subsequent references to this play will be to this edition; line numbers will be included parenthetically in the text.

15. *Roxana*, ed. Ian Jack (Oxford: Oxford University Press, 1969), 171.

16. This feminization of credit is a period trope; for Defoe, the character is Lady Credit. On the history of the connection of women and money, specifically in regard to usury, see Ann Louise Kibbie, "Monstrous Generation: The Birth of Capital in Defoe's *Moll Flanders* and *Roxana*," *PMLA* 110 (1995): 1023–34.

17. For the physiology of sensibility, see John Mullan, *Sentiment and Sociability: The Language of Feeling in the Eighteenth Century* (Oxford: Clarendon Press, 1988).

18. *Spectator* papers, ed. Donald Bond (Oxford: Clarendon Press, 1965), No. 3 (March 3, 1711), 17.

19. *A Sentimental Journey through France and Italy*, ed. Graham Petrie (London: Penguin, 1967), 137.

20. The female body is reduced to the "nasty tricks" (127) of school girls, or the lack of "decent personal reserve . . . between woman and woman" (128). Mary Poovey argues that for Wollstonecraft female sexuality, rather than commodification, is actually the basis of woman's cultural objectification, and that her attack on the female body and her rejection of "natural affection" indicates a fear of female sexuality (138), a rejection of carnal lust and of the notion of women as "standing dishes to which every glutton may have access." Thus for Poovey Wollstonecraft's disgust with female bodies amounts to a general refusal to acknowledge female sexuality. Poovey, *The Proper Lady and the Woman Writer* (xx), 69–81. Mary Wollstonecraft, *A Vindication of the Rights of Woman*, ed. Carol H. Poston (New York: Norton, 1975).

21. Mary Wollstonecraft, *Maria or The Wrongs of Woman*, introd. Moira Ferguson (New York: Norton, 1975), 130.

22. See G. J. Barker-Benfield's account of this reception of Wollstonecraft. *The Culture of Sensibility: Sex and Society in Eighteenth-Century Britain* (Chicago: University of Chicago Press, 1992), chapter 7: "Wollstonecraft and the Crisis over Sensibility in the 1790s."

Laura Brown is Professor of English at Cornell University. Author of *Ends of Empire: Women and Ideology in Early Eighteenth-Century English Literature*, she is currently completing a study of literature and culture in the English eighteenth century.

Rebuttal

The Ends of Ideology: Politics and Literary Response

Lennard Davis

This collection of essays, assembled over time, allows us to observe the way that history influences any discussion about literature. David Richter's originating provocative essay, "The Closing of Masterpiece Theater," was written in 1991, while the respondents of the original *TECTI* issue wrote their responses in the mid-1990s. Richter's afterword comes closer to 1996, and now other responses including this one are being written toward the end of the century. So while the essays may all be discussing the value of ideology and theory, this book provides a series of frozen streaks in the cloud chamber of intellectual history concerning these ideas.[1]

Richter initially writes during a time when leftists had been assaulting the study of literature with the complex and shifting weapon of ideology. At the same time, conservatives had consolidated their hold on American and British political life, making formerly benign activities, like donating money to the American Civil Liberties Union, a sign of extremism. Lynne Cheney, then head of the NEH, had signaled a counterattack on "tenured radicals" by noting that "viewing humanities texts as though they were primarily political documents is the most noticeable trend in academic study of the humanities today. Truth and beauty and excellence are regarded as irrelevant."[2] While Richter's critique of ideological studies does not echo that of Cheney, the former nonetheless expresses similar concerns in a more measured way. Richter's concern is that ideological considerations "substitute a raw, crude vision . . . for the subtle and complex vision that Henry Fielding represented" (Richter, 11). While Cheney indicted leftists for neglecting truth, beauty, and excellence, Richter rued the lack of attention to the subtle and complex demands of form.

Richter's own ideology, if we may use that term, is born out of the educational structures that were dominant in the fifties and sixties—a legacy of New Criticism which draped an unassailable mantle over the notion of "form." Even though New Criticism was passé by the time people like Richter and me were in graduate school, the clear power of the ideas around formalism persisted. Indeed, that bellwether of intellectual enterprise of the sixties—the Twentieth Century Interpretation series edited by Maynard Mack and published by Prentice-Hall—invariably included at least one essay on form along with others on theme, symbol, myth, literary influence, Freudian analysis, and so on. Indeed, R. S. Crane's essay on the perfect plot of *Tom Jones*, in Martin C. Battestin's anthology, was one of those works that characterized academic study during this period.[2] If only we younger scholars could find and worship the perfection of that kind of form in other works, we could make our reputations. Form was the hidden god, and we were to be the revealers of its mysteries.

But one should recall that this emphasis on "enormous formal intricacy," to use Richter's term, was not always nor will always be so important to literary critics. Certainly, in the eighteenth and nineteenth centuries, critics of the novel spent their time looking at character and morality much more than they did at form. And when they discussed form, it was not so much to explicate the subtle and complex plan of the author as it was to make a snap judgment about the probability of the plot or other issues around verisimilitude, as did Coleridge in his brief statement praising the construction of *Tom Jones*. Indeed, Crane himself rues the previous lack of detailed interest in plot, saying that "in all the more extended discussions of Fielding's masterpiece since 1749 the consideration of the plot has constituted merely one topic among several others" (Battestin, 69). One imagines that critics like Dr. Johnson would have found an extended, detailed study of form an alien if not ludicrous activity.

It is only with modernism, coinciding as it did with the institutionalization of literary studies within the university, that we begin to see an interest in what we are calling the "formal" elements of literature. However, early academic study of the novel concentrated almost exclusively on literary history and influences. It was with novelists themselves—Henry James, E. M. Forster, Joseph Conrad, and D. H. Lawrence, to name a few—that we see more discussion of the craft, as they would have called it, of the novel.

During this period, both marxism and psychoanalysis were becoming dominant intellectual preoccupations, the two being combined by the Frankfurt School, so when New Criticism or Anglo-American formalism arose, it was perceived, correctly I would say, as a reaction against a leftist, subversive methodology. Rather than class, capital, and sexuality, the early New Critics, many of them Christians from the South with patrician values, focused on what seemed the most neutral and value-free aspects of literature—form. Their eschewal of literary history, influences, and biographical details indicates their rejection of the "old" criticism, but even more their lack of interest in the "new" criticism of Marx and Freud tell us that simple innovation was not their aim.

While I would not deny that looking at form gave literature professors and students a relatively new and interesting area of discussion, I want to point out that this area of study is by no means sacred or privileged. Indeed, form is not an object per se but the result of a process of analysis. Form comes into being only with formalists, to make the extreme argument. And therefore we must recognize form as the precipitate of a process of symbolic production—formalism—that itself is only one of many other types of symbolic production within culture including literature, art, criticism, and so on. So this process of formalism, as well as its virtual object—form, is therefore of a particular time and place, not a universal enjoyed by all human societies at all times.

Indeed, do we not perform an act of obfuscation by calling what is no doubt a multivalent and somewhat obscure concept—form—by this single, monolithic name? Richter discusses Fielding's form as if it were a self-evident object. But what is form? Form in literature, as well as other arts, is based primarily on repetition. Music gives us the most obvious model, since without repetition we would have no possibility of creating a recognizable theme, and without restatement of that theme there would be no form. But even the absence of form is form since we would call "formlessness" a kind of form. So Jackson Pollack's paintings might be said to be formless, which is their formal signature. Thus the repeated absence of a recognizable form could be construed as a form, as indeed chaos has recently seen to have a form. In literature form must appear in words. But we don't, for example, call the form of words "form." The shape or even the way words appear might be called style, although style is a kind of form established through repetition of phrases, rhythms, sounds, and so on. Richter says that Fielding's eclipse in popularity has to do with our current interest in "incoherence, disjunction, and *différance*" over "Fielding's Georgian valorization of tight economy of plot, coherence of tone, and elegance of expression"(Richter, 5). So, for Richter, form in a novel is the sum of these elements. But, then, would incoherence or disjunction not be a kind of form, as we might say that "formlessness" was a kind of form? Or, to turn the tables, why are Augustan notions of plot better or more formal than postmodernist notions of plot? Or asked another way, why is Fielding's definition of plot better than Kathy Acker's or James Joyce's? Or Lawrence Sterne's for that matter.

Let's take on the "tight economy" of Fielding's work. First, note that the phrase used by Richter makes certain assumptions about the value of a tight economy. Why would it be better to live during times of a tight economy versus a loose economy? Is tightness a value in itself—linking up, as it does, puritanical notions of sacrifice, utilitarian ideas of efficiency, regulation of interest rates, and female oppression through corseting? In what sense do we use the word "economy?" Richter seems happy that Fielding is economical—useful, prudent, measured, controlled—as opposed to uneconomical writers whose forms are wasteful, loose, spendthrift, sprawling, prodigal. But which cultural notions (can we call them ideological concepts) undergird the value of this kind of economic husbandry?

Second, why do we have to think of formal rigor when we think of *Tom Jones*? One might well consider it a baggy book. It may have the form of a three-act play or a Georgian mansion, but that form is superficial. Critics do not all agree with Coleridge's praise of the plot of *Tom Jones*. For example, F. R. Leavis thought "conventional talk about the 'perfect construction' of Tom Jones . . . is absurd," adding that Fielding's supposed "famous irony, seems to me mere hobbledehoydom (Battestin, 17–18). William Empson found "the basic impulse behind" Crane's praise of Fielding's perfect plot "trivial" (Battestin, 32). The actual text sprawls—like the raunchy supper at the very inn whose splattered menu we read on the first page of the novel. Its form is episodic to say the least, and its interpolated stories of the old Man of the Hill, Mrs. Fitzpatrick, and the King of the Gypsies are a violation of any sense of unity, as many critics have noted. Fine that it begins with the country and ends in London, better that Sophia's journey parallels Tom's, but there is so much else that makes poor structural sense. There is an unevenness of tone switching from patrician language to mock epic to farce. In reality what we might want to say is that Fielding's use of the rather static form of theatrical plays adapted to a novel made for certain kinds of rules (which he honored in the breach). But let's not elevate this theatrical symmetry to a divine level. Rather we might consider *Tom Jones* a dramatic wolf in a novelistic sheep's clothing. Parody and farce rely on form taken from elsewhere—and here too we might find another way of accounting for Fielding's use of form. Even Dr. Johnson had a well-known, low opinion of Fielding as an author, and it is interesting that Boswell had to argue against Johnson's pronouncement "that there was as great a difference between them [Richardson and Fielding] as between a man who knew how a watch was made, and a man who could tell the hour by looking on the dial plate."[3] To this Boswell replied, "But I cannot help being of opinion that the neat watches of Fielding are as well constructed as the large clocks of Richardson, and that his dial plates are brighter." (Boswell, 330). Boswell has to argue against Johnson's notion that Fielding's novel is not "well constructed," which makes us realize that even in the eighteenth century it was by no means seen as stately as a Georgian mansion; rather, it might have been viewed as rambling and drafty as Otranto's castle.

Form in plot is a tricky thing to call "economical" or "tight." Each generation will reshape what it sees as "form" in relation to plot. The very symmetry that Richter upholds was seen as old-fashioned by mid-to-late nineteenth-century writers, who sought less coherency in their plots and perhaps more in the way of the symbolic structure of a work. So we could say that in *Jane Eyre*, Bronte has spent much more time on the use of symbols than on the plot, the form being located in the symbolic structure. Indeed, we need to ask: is the form located in the symbolic structure, or in the plot points, the language, the tone, the character, or the harmonious arrangement of all of these? How can we tell the form from the formed? And, given an even somewhat twentieth-century tendency, do we not repeat the mind-body problem by separating form and content?

Even if one might disagree with most of what I've said just now concerning form, it is possible to concede that the notion of form is much more of a "muddle" than Richter's brief hypostatizing of it allows. So the next step in this argument is to say that perhaps the current renegotiation of ideas about the use and value of ideology is not so inappropriate or wrong—and certainly is not any less subtle or complex than discussions rooted in "formal" considerations. Indeed, it is fair to say that the subject of form is probably under-theorized from the point of view of the late twentieth century and for that reason is a less interesting subject than it might be as a result.

Here we should discuss the value and use of ideology as a way of thinking about literature. John Richetti, who in this volume does the most to amplify the concept of ideology, seems to have written his thoughts on this subject during the tumultuous period billed as "the fall of communism." Perhaps under the influence of these putatively apocalyptic events, Richetti finds himself thinking that ideology has become "a nearly useless notion for literary understanding," one that has "completely lost the positive and useful complexity it once possessed and degenerated into a term of abuse pure and simple" (Richetti, 32). The metaphorics of these statements bear some scrutiny. The notion of a "useful" or "useless" methodology is a somewhat mystified if not reified one. How do we judge the utility of any methodology? Is that utility inherent in the method or more likely must it be premised on the value or use of that methodology to a particular society? While Bentham or Mill might have fairly definite calibrations for their ideas of utility, standards for literary theory's utility are clearly dependent on what we must circularly argue to be ideological considerations. So the utility of a marxist term like ideology is really only as useful as is the marxism itself. The notion of a degeneration from positive complexity to simple abuse might be said to be the kind of language descriptive of the appropriation of the marxist project within the former Soviet Union. And by a simple elision, the fall of the Iron Curtain is seen as a repudiation of marxism, therefore of ideology. Indeed, the events that transpired in Eastern Europe and the former Soviet Union, seemed to have pulled the rug out from under the feet, if not the wool up from over the eyes, of many tenured radicals. While there was always much to criticize in the undemocratic governments that called themselves communist, the sheer force of the iconography of statues of Marx and Lenin tumbling down provided metaphorically and otherwise a blow to ideological theorizing. So, perhaps, Eagleton's book *Ideology: An Introduction* signaled, in its studied scholasticizing of the issue, a kind of death knell of ideology as a vibrant intellectual concept just as the plethora of critical studies on structuralism or deconstructionism proved the most effective silencer of those practices, covering them with a thick foam of extinguishing words.

Eagleton's earlier works *Marxism and Literature* and *Literary Theory: An Introduction* more optimistically synthesized and publicized the efforts of critics like Raymond Williams, E. P. Thompson, and Mikhail Bakhtin while combining their materialist insights into a more structuralist and deconstructionist framework provided by Adorno, Horkheimer, Althusser, Jameson, Greimas, and Barthes. Eagleton's early work on ideology served, as did the work of Althusser and Jameson, to heal a rift between marxists and structuralists in France in the early 70s. While we tend to see a convergence of these two schools from our perspective now, what was clear was that in post-1968 France, structuralism was seen as the opposing paradigm diverging from Marxism. But writers on both sides of the Atlantic, including Edward Said, Michel Foucault along with Eagleton and Jameson created a synthesis of continental thought and marxism, and it was the concept of ideology that permitted and contained that fusion. One of the major ways that marxism and structuralism could be fused was by the redefining of ideology as a language system, borrowing from the work of Saussure by way of Levi-Strauss and Barthes, that structured the false consciousness of a dominant elite. This notion then combined structural linguistics with the work of Marx, the Frankfurt School, and Sartre. Central to this fusion was the ambiguity of ideology as a system of signs and ideology as false consciousness. Added to this mix was Althusser's formulation that ideology was the site of symbolic class struggle—a site of contestation that had consequences for the side that lost and the side that won.

Richetti elides some of this jagged history of the term "ideology" in implying a rather smooth transition from a "scientific" term of the eighteenth century to a "polemical insult" during the nineteenth and twentieth centuries. This notion of ideology as a put-down of the belief system of one's opponent, described in most detail in Mannheim's work, is referred to by Richetti as "the bad[,] old sense." Richetti notes approvingly the rehabilitation of this bad, old usage by Eagleton's reformulation along Althusserian lines. But, as I hope I've indicated, the development of the concept of ideology was really not so simple. Marx's formulation of ideology as a concept was not designed in a limited or crude sense.

Rather, ideology for Marx expanded to include what Gramsci would call civil society—including government, religion, schooling, literature, art and so on. In other words, far from being a buzz word hurled at some cabal of capitalists, ideology very broadly encompasses virtually all of the visible, tangible aspects of the economic and social system.

The bulk of marxist cultural theory after Marx can be said to involve the refinement of a few references by Marx and Engels to the term "ideology." The work of Lukács, Bakhtin, Brecht, Benjamin, Adorno, Horkheimer, Sartre, and many others seeks to understand how economic structures and power relations are influences in the creation of an artistic work. That body of work is hardly a history of crude name-calling, nor is the idea of ideology a simple one. Try reading Adorno's *Aesthetic Theory* and see whether ideology lacks complexity or whether ideology's "bad, old sense" was really old or bad.

Richetti employs Eagleton's "refined or re-complicated notion of ideology" (although I would prefer to call it Eagleton's synthesized and inventoried notion) to show us that ideology, despite its bad, old baggage, really is a useful term. The aim is to demonstrate that such a reading of Fielding is not "crude" and does not "degrade" Fielding, as Richter had accused (11). This line of reasoning assumes that if *Tom Jones* was written by an author who uses ideology consciously in the creation of *Tom Jones*, then ideological studies have an upgraded use. So, Fielding is reconceived as someone who knows how to drive ideology rather than being driven by it. Richetti aims, by allowing for authorial agency, to rehabilitate ideology and thus to refute critics whose books about the novel see ideology operating "in the bad[,] old sense"(Richetti, 35–36).

> The question that always remains after reading these critics [McKeon, Bender, Armstrong, Warner, and myself] is how individual novelists fit into this larger picture. How much awareness is manifested in particular novels of the cultural and therefore the ideological role of fiction? (Richetti, 34)

Boardman makes a similar point more bluntly:

> I shall ignore as irrelevant . . . such ideological readings. . . . This is not how narrative decisions in realistic novels are made: innovations come out of the pressures of the storytelling moment and are

> modified much more by the weight of earlier innovations than by any "symbolic order." (Boardman, 206)

This is Richter's point as well: that authors make decisions based, perhaps, on some element of cultural imperative but, more likely, on the level of individual genius, the demands of plot, the exigencies of storytelling. If not, then the big, bad computer of history is the one writing novels and humans are mere ink-jet printers spewing out that which they are commanded. Therefore, people who set ideology over individual creativity are robbing authors of their birthright to be artistic, innovative individuals.

Perhaps it is over this point more than any other, in the eyes of critics of ideology, that this concept turns into a kind of tourniquet limiting freedom of movement and killing the limb while attempting to save the life of art and society. It is true that ideological studies, or rather marxist-inspired critique, becomes the bearer of bad news—news so bad that it has to be used to wrap fish because if taken as gospel it savages the unquestionable fundamentals of bourgeois art. Among these are: 1) authors write literary works; 2) in doing so authors use their creative freedom to construct masterpieces; 3) masterpieces make up the enduring tradition of a national literature and by extension world literature; 4) literature is a civilizing moral force that in turn shapes national character by providing pleasure, example, and ambiguity through high-quality entertainment. In this essay, it would be impossible to talk about all these factors at length, but suffice it to say that first two fundamentals present a cherished notion of authorship. However, an ideological critique sees these assumptions not as freestanding universals but conditioned to very specific historical periods and attitudes toward culture. That is, probably most of these assumptions would not appear self-evident to person living in Europe before 1600. The idea of authorship is one dependent on a cult of individuality, a divorce of art from communal forms of expression, the invention of various techniques of mechanical reproduction, and so on. The role of nationalism in the formation of literary canons has been well documented over the last twenty years, and the necessity for a distinction between high culture and low culture has also been widely discussed. So, ideological studies question what are deeply held beliefs of authors and critics, and an attack on these is the equivalent of a narcissistic wound to the aesthetic tradition of western, bourgeois art. Therefore, it is no wonder that even progressive academics might feel that a methodology that downplays what appears to be individuality, choice, "freedom," and so on is in effect a "bad" system.

On the other hand, there is a major political point at stake with major consequences. If we pretend that the art or literature is freely self-creating, we may feel better about life under late capitalism. But there is a cost. The cost is that we ignore the mechanisms and systems of oppression at work in the world that are dependent on citizens doing this kind of feel-better thinking. We may feel better thinking that Fielding is driving ideology, but, in so doing, we are forgetting who made the roads and the maps. The aim is not to blame the analysis but the mechanism that creates the problem.

And do we really resuscitate ideological studies by seeing Fielding, the gentry politician, manipulating and using symbols of culture to his own ends? In eighteenth-century Britain, it is surely not his class that lacks agency. So to ascribe him the power to manipulate ideological markers seems to turn the argument about ideology in the wrong direction. Would people feel better knowing that Dick Morris, or Phillip Morris for that matter, has the power to spin ideology the way they want to? Recuperating individuality seems the exquisitely wrong direction in which to steer ideology.

The point I am trying to get to is that ideology is not a methodology or a concept that one adopts from among several others in the supermarket of ideas. Rather, one is drawn to it because it reveals and elaborates how a system of oppression and domination operates. Ideology, as a concept, comes out of a tradition of thinking concerned with the specific role of capitalism and allied forms of oppression in controlling and limiting the lives of billions of people over the past century. The fact that "communism" has fallen does not eliminate the need for an analysis and a praxis that elucidates and opposes the workings of this kind of power. So if mere world-weariness or millennial angst is what is making us tire of ideology, then we need to fight those impulses. It may be tiresome to have this bad news written over and over again, and indeed it is a challenge for leftist critics to rethink and retool their work to appeal to that portion of the population who is not totally conditioned by the good news of the corporate world. But, as I think I've made clear at the risk of mounting the soap box, an aesthetic or utilitarian judgment about the concept of ideology is inappropriate, just as an aesthetic judgment about the holocaust would be. In this sense Patricia Meyer Spacks is more than right in noting the wistfulness of some academics in wishing for a world in which aesthetic concerns were all.

Since I've tried to place some of contributors to this volume in their historical moment, I need to account dialectically for my own. I am writing this in early 1998. Now the realities of "fall of communism" are apparent. Rather than capitalist havens arising in the former communist countries, what we are seeing is increased unemployment, criminality, homelessness, and so on. In trying to comply with the imperatives of the World Bank and to reassure would-be investors, free-market mentality is plunging the general populace of these countries into desperate straits. So my perspective is that socialism, or at least social and financial justice, still seems a viable alternative to rampant capitalism. As I write this line, the Pope and Castro shake hands in Havana and also agree on this last point. Marxism still remains the only concrete and capacious analysis of capitalism, other than the one that is promulgated by capitalists. And ideological studies in its many forms—cultural, feminist, multicultural, queer, and disability studies—still seems to be the best and current way to use scholarship in the service of justice.

So, to blame ideological studies for the decline of interest in Fielding's work is perhaps to shoot the messenger. Fielding's decline, if we can chart his rise and fall like the morning stock market reports, may simply be a phenomenon of observation. Perhaps, had Richter been checking the popularity of Fielding from the 1920s on, he might have discovered the current fall to be a mere blip in the larger cycles of interest and lack of interest in any author. And, of course, we must note that the desire to graph the popularity of an author comes out of what we must call an ideological impulse, based as it is around statistics, marketing, and polling—all of which, while pretending to be value-free methods, owe much to the mind-set and assumptions connected to positivist and materialist ways of envisioning human life.

But there may be another answer than the one Richter comes up with for the decline in the sales of Fielding products. The past twenty years has seen the recovery of a lost canon—that is the novels of female authors of the eighteenth century. When the cavalcade of Defoe, Richardson, Fielding, Goldsmith, Sterne, and Smollett were the only hits in the parade, the steady gaze of scholars was not diverted from these top six. But with the work of

Aphra Behn, Mary Delariviere Manley, Fanny Burney, Mary Wollstonecraft, Sarah Fielding, Sarah Scott, and others, the stars of the show have been increased. Logically, then, Fielding would end up getting short shrift, shorter when we consider that the rollicking, macho antics of Tom might be considerably less interesting to contemporary female readers than to the tweedy, pipe-smoking dons who were chuckling into their after-dinner port.

So, in the end, if one decides to analyze the popularity of literary works based on a statistical model, one still has to leave the realm of quantities to ascribe qualities to explanations. Those explanations can be as various as their ideologies. If one wants to cling to form, or style, or irony as the ultimate arbiter of value, one has to acknowledge that these seemingly enduring monuments to unaging intellect may turn out to be little more than a mirage of concepts in the shifting sands of critical fashion. And if the enemy is ideology, then, as Pogo used to say, the enemy is us. So, one must, I think, avoid objectifying the study of ideology, which itself is a process that continues an enduring attempt to understand the rather complex *pas de deux* between creativity and historical demands, between the author's intention and the possibilities of genre and market, between freedom and necessity. In this sense, rather than reifying ideology as an object that then needs to be reviled, we might see it as a tradition of hermeneutics tied to types of political practice. In that way, we may consider the ends rather than the end of ideology.

Notes

1. Not so ironically, Richter sees Richetti's work on ideology in *Tom Jones* as one that serves to "degrade" the novel, substituting "a raw, crude vision of sexual, social, political life in Georgian England for the subtle and complex vision that Henry Fielding represented" (11). Richter says that Richetti's marxism "degrades" Fielding's text, and in turn Richetti says that the problem is that ideology has "degenerated" to inutility.

2. *New York Times*, 13 September 1998, 15.

3. Martin C. Battestin, ed., *Twentieth Century Interpretations of Tom Jones* (Englewood Cliffs, N. J.: Prentice Hall, 1968). Further references will be cited in the text.

4. James Boswell, *The Life of Johnson* (Boston: Charles E. Lauriat, 1925), 330. Further references will be cited in the text.

Editor's Note: Davis correctly encapsulates the history of this project. The "epilogue" to the 1996 edition of *TECTI* to which Davis alludes, for which I substituted the "afterword" that follows, ran thus:

Having instigated this brawl with my not-so-innocent essay on ideological misreadings of Henry Fielding, it is nice to get in a brief last word. I am delighted to have stimulated essays that seem so representative of the major critical languages we now speak: historicism, marxism, feminism, cultural studies, as well as a new formalism striving to be reborn. Predictably, the invited contributors have taken up too much space in this special issue for the editor to indulge his usual privilege of summarizing and distorting them.

Nevertheless, the reader will surely be able to infer from my own position paper my essential agreement with John Richetti's richly dialogical vision of Fielding's ideology ("the ongoing history of a large variety of changing institutions") as uneasily contained by form ("the patterns and symmetries of comic romance and universalized moralism"). Or my archly raised eyebrow when Patricia Meyer Spacks defined the age-old category of the aesthetic entirely out of existence as something the "literary-academic world" of today has learned to do without. Or my Johnsonian mutterings ("too, too, too"), provoked by Carol Houlihan Flynn's reduction of Henry Fielding's discourse to "structures of surveillance and oppression," to some standard Foucauldian example of early-modern gridlock.

When I wrote my own piece nearly five years ago, I was fretting about Fielding's place in the literary canon, endangered, I feared, by crudely resistant readings coming from armed camps of ideological critics. Much more than that seems at stake today. Whatever Fielding's place in it, that canon itself has largely lost its authority by now, and there is a growing sense that literature itself is not just an essentially contested concept but an overvalued aspect of the broader cultural scene. Those of us who are interested in the eighteenth century might just as well study midcentury manuals of midwifery as lyric poetry, or investigate other sorts of documents like John Rocque's map of London. I have myself been guilty of working on the broadsides and biographies sold at Tyburn holidays. Where we once spoke of ourselves as literary scholars, we now tend to claim to be politically engaged cultural historians, and of literature as merely one space where culture is embalmed.

Meanwhile, we may also note out of the corner of our eye the rapid implosion of our profession, where retirees' tenure-track jobs simply vanish, or are replaced by part-time or temporary lines, while the students we have nurtured through the doctorate are forced to decide whether to continue subsisting within the lumpen-intelligentsia long into their thirties or to give up and find a real job in some other field. Can it be a pure coincidence that positions in literature departments are disappearing precisely when the profession as a whole has become dubious about the significance and value of literature? Deciding to study cultural history is our privilege, of course, but it puts us into direct competition with history departments, who are already doing that. It should be no wonder that universities with scanty resources decline to invest in departments with such vague responsibilities, whose fields of study as well as methods seem to change from year to year.

One of the contributors characterized me as nostalgic for the innocent time of the 1950s, when Fielding's reputation was highest (and when I was five years old). But I suspect that many besides me are becoming nostalgic about the early 1970s, when the era of Grand Theory had us thinking more seriously than ever before about what literature was and did, and when our profession was expanding instead of imploding. Today the bell that tolls for Fielding is tolling for us as well.

Lennard J. Davis, author of *Factual Fictions: The Origin of the English Novel,* is Professor of English at Binghamton University (State University of New York). He is currently at working issues concerning disability and novel theory.

Afterword

Form and Formalists, Ideologies and Ideologues: A Polemical Conclusion

David H. Richter

Out of the Sack

Scorched by the hot breath of Lennard Davis, who has sentenced me to be sewn into a sack together with a monkey, a viper, and Lynne Cheney, and dropped into the nearest river—the mandatory punishment for recrudescent formalism—I nevertheless rise to reply—though not perhaps to reply in kind. Despite my tutelage in the 1960s at that bastion of reactionary ideas, the University of Chicago, and his at Columbia, that radical cell lurking on Morningside Heights, I suspect that Lenny and I agree on a great many more things than we disagree about, including the vision of professional history that he offers as part of his essay, though I would probably inflect that vision somewhat differently.

Both of us think of the era in which we were trained in the study of literature as a dreadful period, and agree that things got better for a while before they got worse again. Lenny may be surprised to learn that I haven't the least twinge of nostalgia about the New Criticism or the era of its hegemony, since the Chicago school of neo-Aristotelians that trained me loathed the New Criticism the way Trotskyites loathed Stalinists. For us Trotskyites, the new-critical notion of form as a function of tropes like metaphor or irony seemed almost as absurdly oversimplified as Lenny's characterization of form as "based primarily on repetition" (p. 241). In particular I used to be perplexed by the paradox that, although the New Critics viewed poetics as a function of language, none of them ever bothered to learn the first thing about linguistics, a field then being revolutionized by Noam Chomsky and his cohorts.

The fact is that, despite all the lip service paid to the notion, derived from I. A. Richards, that literature spoke not in statements but in pseudostatements, and the endless quotation of Archibald MacLeish's dictum that a poem "should not mean / But be," most of the followers and fellow-travelers of New Criticism were deeply focused on the special things tropes could get language to say. As a result, criticism became in practice a thematics of literature, rather than a poetics. Given the pressure recently imposed to publish or perish in a university system swelling with baby-boomers, assistant professors of literature in the late 1960s were forced to rake exhaustively through the then-canonical texts in the hope of discovering new thematic links demonstrating their unity. This hope was, by the nature of the venture, always rewarded, since it is difficult to find any text that cannot be made, properly coaxed, to speak about the commonplaces of human existence: love and hate, innocence and experience, life and death, the individual and society, changelessness and mutability, and, in the last resort, appearance and reality. A sardonical student of R.S. Crane's, Richard Levin, once satirized the practice in an essay titled "My Theme Can Lick Your Theme," illustrating the rhetorical ploys, ranging from the Retort Circumstantial to the Lie Direct, by which practitioners of literary thematics wedged their own favored analysis of a particular text into the already-existing discourse.[1] It was not, as Davis suggests, Crane's admired but seldom-imitated analysis of how Fielding constructed the arc of desire in "The Plot of *Tom Jones*" that characterized formalist criticism in this period. It was rather essays like Martin C. Battestin's thematic study of prudence and Providence, "Fielding's Definition of Wisdom: Some Functions of Ambiguity and Emblem in *Tom Jones*," although, owing to Battestin's superior historical grasp of the period, his essay is as superior to the average thematic study as Chateau Petrus is to Bulgarian merlot.[2]

American literary studies was saved from the lingering brain death of thematic pseudoformalism by the concussive arrival of an era of Grand Theory, as structuralism and semiotics, deconstruction, Lacanian psychology, Althusserian marxism, Russian formalism, phenomenology, and reception theory, rode successive waves into our awareness. The turbulence and clash of ideas had begun decades before on the continent, of course, but those of us on this side of the Atlantic, who read French and German haltingly and Russian not at all, probably didn't experience the explosion of theory until the mid-1970s. A profession that a few years before had been hacking out dozens of progressively less plausible ways of misreading *The Turn of the Screw* was suddenly lit up with a rush of ideas, a dozen disparate systems with enormous philosophical reach and scope. To academics like me who were fed up with the stifling donnish atmosphere of literary studies, the sense of intellectual liberation was palpable: one felt like echoing Wordsworth's sentiments about a much more significant revolution two hundred years past: "Great it was in that dawn to be alive / But to be young was very heaven."

In those days staying abreast of what was going on required catching up on a half century of philosophical, psychological and linguistic speculation from the continent, and just trying to keep up with whatever was the flavor of the month led to intellectual vertigo, while not trying meant letting the parade pass you by. Over the last decade or so, however, things have calmed down. There has been a consolidation of elements of these theories around a number of specific issues—issues of gender and sexual orientation, class, nationality and race—but although there have been some changes in what texts we favor talking about, and although some new rhetorical moves have surfaced (as when Bhabhian liminality replaced Spivakian confrontation between colonialist and subaltern), the fundamental terms of the conversation have remained remarkably constant over the past few years.

Grand Theory and Its Discontents

Things are still changing today in the sense that the energy that a dozen years ago was devoted to promoting women into the canon or into resistant readings of texts by patriarchal males seems now to have passed into a more diffuse "gender theory," with lesbians, gays, and bisexuals resisting incorporation into any essentialized dialectic of man and woman, femininity and masculinity. The impetus that fed what was called Black Studies in the 1970s appears now to be invested in a more generalized multicultural vision incorporating, in addition to works by African Americans, other marginalized literatures like those of Latinos and Latinas, Native Americans, and the "subaltern" writings of former British colonies in Africa, the Caribbean, and the Pacific islands. The searchingly dialectical methodologies through which we used to read the social text, based on a variety of forms of neo-marxism exemplified in Gramsci and Althusser, Eagleton and Jameson, have by and large been superseded by a poststructural ideological critique based loosely on Foucault. (This may be one reason Lennard Davis's essay may be sporting an embattled tone: even though all the old and new formalisms have been decisively defeated, the current vogue seems to have shifted away from the dialectical devotees of European marxism.) But while the conversation has changed in any number of ways, the basic issues that surfaced on the critical horizon around the time the hegemony of the New Criticism was breaking down—gender, sexual orientation, race, nation, and class—are the ones still in the forefront.

In the clear light shared by all Monday morning quarterbacks, it is obvious that the period of Grand Theory had to be short-lived. Part of the problem was the sheer speed with which a critical practice based on an elaborate philosophical theory could move into and out of the charmed circle of favored methods. That made us deeply wary of investing too much time and intellectual energy in any theoretical enterprise. But even an enterprise not too maddeningly philosophical, even one reasonably safe from standing trial at a reconvened Nuremberg Tribunal (as de Man and deconstruction did), imposes heavy production costs on scholars trying to retool. Traditional historical critics attempting to adapt to the "new historicism" needed to read a great many difficult texts: not just Stephen Greenblatt but Clifford Geertz and Hayden White and Michel Foucault. And doing the job right would include reading these people's primary influences: not just Clifford Geertz but Levi-Strauss, not just Hayden White but Derrida and Wittgenstein, not just Foucault but Heidegger and the later Nietzsche. . . . The impatience to find a way out of this thicket of theory and to be getting on with a critical practice can only have been overwhelming.

The process of consolidating and simplifying the elaborate and difficult Grand Theories happened in the same way people manage to communicate across barriers of natural languages, by creating a lingua franca for trade and barter during interludes between hostilities. This critical pidgin was unwittingly encouraged by the way universities traditionally operate in this country, which generally avoids creating "schools" of like-minded thinkers such as those you find on the Continent, and instead fills slots so as to create the greatest possible diversity. Departments who acquired a Lacanian or a reception theorist to be au courant didn't feel the need for a breeding pair. This tendency to isolate individuals speaking a particular critical language from each other meant that you could talk your chosen critical language in all its purity in your own classroom and at conferences but you had to find some other sort of common ground to talk with your colleagues. And as you talked, you learned a few of their moves and they learned some of yours. In the carnival of jostling jargon that resulted, purity of rhetoric took second place to the pragmatics of discourse. A theorist like Judith Butler could derive her notions about sex and gender from Foucault, but her rhetorical ploys might be taken straight out of Derrida, and never mind that the two Frenchmen might otherwise be strange bedfellows. In the long run we became no longer feminists or marxists or poststructuralists but, more likely than not, a combination of all three at once.

One result of the rapid consolidation was the absorption of new languages of Grand Theory in the form of dumbed-down "pidgins" with near-total loss of higher features. An old friend interviewing candidates at the MLA convention told me, "Everybody I talk to seems to know precisely one sentence of Lacan, one sentence of Althusser, and so on." The fact is that knowing one sentence would be a major achievement. As Wittgenstein puts it, "Einen Satz verstehen, heisst, eine Sprache verstehen. Eine Sprache verstehen, heisst eine Technik beherrschen."[3] If we knew even one sentence in Wittgenstein's sense, we would be able to compose a new one that is well-formed. But we don't. What we know is a few words and a few combinations of words formed into slogans. "The unconscious is structured like a language." "Ideology has no history." "Always historicize!"

The result is that, when we try to say something for ourselves, the result is often gobbledegook composed of different and irreconcilable terminologies, a farrago of incomprehensible nonsense. Let me cite a single proposition from a book which wasn't primarily theoretical at all, an otherwise brilliant study of Victorian Gothic fiction: "Bakhtin's reading of the process of self-realization is the opposite of Lacan's. If for Lacan there is an inevitable dismemberment of a total self, for Bakhtin there is a continual movement toward a self that is never total but always capable of further realization."[4] It would take a long time to explain everything that is wrong with this formulation, though one might begin with the fact that in Lacan there is no "total self" to be dismembered except as an imaginary construct. But the main problem is not in such details but in the unexamined assumption that Bakhtin's use of the word "self" and Lacan's have enough in common to allow them to be juxtaposed in this fashion. And it is not only the terminology, the lexical component. The philosophical "grammar" of Lacan's system—the way its ideas fit together—is as different from Bakhtin's as the vocabulary is. Possibly someone who had learned both languages and mastered both techniques might make a disciplined stab at relating dialogics to poststructural psychology with the aid of a metalinguistic grid such as Richard McKeon's philosophical semantics—but it isn't clear that the results would be worth the bother. The "languages of criticism," as R. S. Crane called them forty years ago, work most effectively when we use them carefully one at a time.

Cultural Studies as Solution and Problem

But of course we don't speak a coherent language: we speak pidgin. The prevailing pidgin of the moment, "cultural studies," contains our collective response to two decades of theory that had produced a vital set of competing ideas about literature, society, and the mind, but failed to coalesce into any coherent rationale for textual and literary study. Cultural studies is not a new paradigm so much as a way of making do temporarily without a paradigm. Or as Vincent Leitch put it, cultural studies "aspired to be a new discipline but served as an unstable meeting point for various interdisciplinary feminists, marxists, literary and media critics, postmodern theorists, social semioticians, rhetoricians, fine arts specialists, and sociologists and historians of culture."[5] It is not a theory as such or a combination of theories; it is a practice, or rather a set of related practices. Nevertheless, essays in cultural studies must desperately situate themselves in relation to theory to make comprehensible the questions raised, the texts chosen, and the methods followed.

Cultural studies has in fact stimulated a certain amount of interest in theories of practice such as those of Michel de Certeau and Pierre Bourdieu. But it is usually distrustful of pure theory in almost any form. We could call this "Theory Lite" as long as we are willing to live with the consequences, which are not limited to cynical sloganeering. For it is at this point that the danger is raised of theoretical "pidgin" turning into a "creole": a linguistic hybrid cut off from its origins in separate schools of thought and with those higher features indefinitely suppressed. Once this happens, the next generation of the theory-damaged will have no refuge from the internal contradictions of this hybrid discourse, formed from some elements that are "scientific" and positivistic, like Saussurean linguistics, with others that are deeply hostile to science, like Foucauldian Theory; some elements that are humanistic and pluralistic, others that are profoundly distrustful of these relics of the Enlightenment.

I resist labeling "cultural studies" a Kuhnian paradigm of scientific research because, despite its wide acceptance, it reverses the structure of the frameworks Kuhn felt typically operated in the hard sciences. Kuhn's paradigms defined worthwhile problems and useful methods for solving them, but left the results open to the vagaries of experiment.[6] In one popular version of cultural studies, at least, the problems and methods may be selected almost at random but the results of the research are preordained. One example is Carol Houlihan Flynn's essay in this volume, which explores the relationship between Fielding's last novel, *Amelia*, published in 1752, and the John Rocque map of London, proposed in 1740 and published in 1746.

Flynn's essay is brilliant about the Rocque map, whose large scale (1"=200') made the physical map itself an unmanageable thirteen feet wide by seven feet high, needing to be opened and closed with a system of pulleys; about what it includes (like Westminster Bridge, which had not yet been built at the time of publication) and what it leaves out (including the street of Rocque's own publishing firm, which is mysteriously missing); about the way the map, despite its ostensible neutrality, presents as ripe for development the open spaces of Westminster, contrasting with the narrow alleys of East London, with even the placement of shadows proclaiming the light streaming from the West; about the ideological assumptions implicit in the way the limits of the map extend to include aristocratic places of pleasure south of the Thames, Ranelagh and Vauxhall.

But fascinating as all this is, Flynn presents not a shred of direct relationship between the Rocque map and *Amelia*. Rocque's map is not mentioned in Fielding's novel, and Flynn presents no evidence that Fielding ever saw the map or indeed even heard of it. The connection between the Rocque and Fielding is that they shared the same streets and therefore, given the assumptions of cultural studies, the same ideology. As Flynn puts it, "The Foucauldian implications of [Rocque's] project, enthusiastically endorsed by ward beadles, are almost too obvious. . . . The Rocque map promises comprehensive understanding of the networks of a city, which no doubt particularly interested the author not only of *Amelia*, and the *Enquiry into the Causes of the late Increase in Robbers*, but of the Bow Street runners, the prototypes of the police force. What both the map and the novel attempt to do is fix, comprehend, 'know' its subjects, placing them on grids topographical and cultural" (95).

Almost too obvious is right. The meeting place of Rocque and Fielding lies not on the London streets but in the pages of Michel Foucault's *Les Mots et les choses*, in his topos of the Enlightenment episteme. Never mind that Foucault himself eventually abjured this totalizing "archaeological" approach for a more supple "genealogical" one: this is still the Foucault one is likeliest to hear appealed to in cultural studies. The connection with *Amelia* is through that novel's reportage of "the structures of surveillance and oppression, which Fielding himself keeps in play as magistrate, part of a system which sends debtors [like Billy Booth] to sponging houses and unpaid servants [like Amelia's] to Monmouth Street where they pawn stolen dresses" (100).

While no reader could have predicted the unlikely history of the John Rocque map project (which seems to have sent Rocque himself into bankruptcy), practically anyone who had read *Les Mots et les choses* or *Surveillir et punir*, or D. A. Miller's *The Novel and the Police*, written under their influence, could have written Flynn's conclusions about Fielding, whether they knew about his activities as a magistrate and penal reformer or not. That Fielding was part of the power/knowledge mafia, using the discourses of the day, including his novels, to contain and confine any rebellion against the tenets of Georgian society goes almost without saying, just as it goes without saying that Fielding's desire to promote law and order in the dangerous London streets he considered "a wilderness of vice and roguery" was the social conservatism of a hanging judge. What the essay could not have concluded and have still counted as a piece of respectable cultural criticism was that Fielding's terror of urban disorder was understandable in a society that had not yet learned to police itself, and where pervasive unemployment, lacking even an inadequate conception of a social safety net, bred misery and crime. Nor would one expect gender theorists to endorse Fielding's comic vision of Tom's sexual education at the hands of more experienced women like Molly Seagrim, Mrs. Waters, or Lady Bellaston, or to note that Fielding's notion of "women's place," though nothing like our own, was rather liberated for its day.

Any method whose conclusions are always already foreknown is sterile. The popularity of high-Foucauldian cultural studies is owed to the way it allows us to hang personal social agendas on hostile, resistant readings of once-canonical literary texts. Not that I see anything wrong with having a political and social agenda: I too would like to make my world more tolerant of racial and sexual differences, less exploitative of the poor. But it strikes me as a pathetic fantasy—what Fredric Jameson would call a product of the political imaginary—to think that the politics we bring into the classroom or the pages of an academic book is going to reshape a world in need of transformation. Only a worldly politics of the sort few academics have the stomach for will achieve that. I'd be surprised if Davis disagreed.

Endangered Species

Finally I need to return, at least briefly, to the issue with which I began my provocation piece—the notion that the canonical texts of English literature were becoming endangered species, snail darters in a hostile environment. Davis is certainly right that some of the attention that is getting directed away from authors like Fielding is being focused instead on other authors, many of them women, who had previously languished in the shadows of masterful males like Defoe, Richardson, Fielding, Sterne, and Smollett. Surely we are the richer for having cheap and easily available editions of *Behn's Letters between a Nobleman and His Sister*, Haywood's *History of Betsy Thoughtless*, Sarah Fielding's *David Simple*, Lennox's *Female Quixote*, Sheridan's *Memoirs of Miss Sidney Bidulph*, Inchbald's *A Simple Story* and all the rest. But these texts don't constitute a countercanon, nor have they simply been added to an existing canon. By this point the very idea of a canon of texts embodying the great tradition, the notion of a center and a periphery, is no longer tenable in academic circles. It is an article of faith within a religion whose devotees are dying out, or at least retiring from their posts.

At the time I wrote my provocation piece, in 1991, the "canon wars" were pitting cultural conservatives defending a literary tradition of texts primarily written by dead white European males against radicals attacking both the idea and ideal of a canon as a way of espousing neglected perspectives by women and minorities. By now (autumn 1998), the action has quieted down to a bit of sniping from entrenched positions. For both sides, the battle has been both lost and won.

Harold Bloom's *The Western Canon: The Books and School of the Ages* (1994) prophesied with the canonical voice of Jeremiah that "what are now called 'Departments of English' will be renamed departments of 'Cultural Studies' where Batman comics, Mormon theme parks, television, movies and rock will replace Chaucer, Shakespeare, Milton, Wordsworth and Wallace Stevens. . . . This development hardly need be deplored; only a few handfuls of students now enter Yale with an authentic passion for reading. You cannot teach such love."[7] Yet the publication of Bloom's book by Harcourt rather than some university press, and its immediate bestsellerhood, suggests that the American public, or that part of it that still buys trade hardbacks, is still firm in its commitment to a canon based on Homer, Dante, Shakespeare, and all the rest, and is happy to read *about* those texts as a preface to, or more likely as a substitute for, actually reading them. But Bloom's weary tone and flabby prose suggest that he has tired himself out preaching to the unconvertible, and that the students at Yale, New York University, and all the other schools where this indefatigable shaman teaches are considerably more eager to read Bloom the untraditional theorist than the texts of the tradition that made Bloom the reader he is. The moral is that the canon of Western literature is entrenched and secure in the eye of the greater public—and largely unread. Meanwhile academics like me have, in defiance of Bloom, turned to reading ephemeral texts (like my Tyburn biographies) as texts worth understanding on their own terms and not just as a way of appreciating the greatness of canonical novelists like Henry Fielding.

This paradox is explained by John Guillory's *Cultural Capital: The Problem of Literary Canon Formation* (1993), which interprets the canon wars as a symptom of a slow but massive shift in the class structure of the Western democracies.[8] Guillory views the function of the school as central to the class structure of capitalist society. Schools not only train the young in the specific information and skills they need to operate in a utilitarian society under capitalism, they also reproduce the structure of that society by creating young heirs to take their places within the social hierarchy. The class basis of culture requires the reproduction of "cultural capital" from one generation to the next, and in a society based on inequalities the distribution of such capital must be unequal: some people must get more than others. The acquisition of a certain quantity of cultural capital is needed to produce the vision and discourse of a member of the ruling class and to distinguish him or her from social inferiors.

But there is no rule that would allow one to predict precisely which forms of cultural capital will be valued in a particular time and place: The mandarins of the Ming Dynasty were required to know literary classics from the previous millennium, the aristocrats of the Enlightenment were required to be able to compose Latin and Greek verses, and the upper bourgeoisie of the nineteenth century were required to know and revere the classics of Western literature from Homer and Virgil through the early modern period. Needless to say, that is no longer the case. As Guillory puts it, "At the present moment, the nation-state still requires a relatively homogeneous language to administer its citizenry, but it no longer requires that a distinctive practice of that language identify a culturally homogeneous bourgeoisie. That class has long since been replaced by a culturally heterogeneous New Class, which has in turn been fully integrated into mass culture, a media culture mediating the desires of every class and group. In this 'new phase of civilization' the historical function of the literary curriculum—to produce at the lower levels of the educational system a practice of Standard English and at the higher levels a more refined bourgeois language, a 'literary' English—is no longer important to the social order" (63). Guillory's point is that the one thing English departments do that still has genuine value for contemporary capitalism is training the university's students in composition and rhetoric. The art of incisive expository writing with "proper" diction and syntax, almost universally neglected at the primary and secondary levels of schooling, is still a necessary component of the education of the professional-managerial elite, one that in fact differentiates those who will rise to executive management positions from those who will stay at the lower sales and technical levels of the corporate structure.

The warfare over the canon represents, for Guillory, the thrashing about of a profession whose central preoccupation, literature, no longer has the significance for society that it once did. The humanities professoriate imagines that it could retain its usefulness within the educational system if it could only redefine the traditional canon, or replace it with other objects of study. The problem, Guillory argues, is that the noncanonical texts that multiculturalists want to substitute for the Western canon do not in fact constitute a different form of cultural capital. It thus no longer matters whether students read Sarah Fielding instead of Henry Fielding or, indeed, any novels at all. The training in literature we give our students is a vermiform appendix attached, without any culturally significant function, to the training we give them in rhetoric and in writing.

If Guillory is right, then the growing practice of cultural studies might allow former students of literature to retool themselves for a new type of relevance to an era when knowledge of "media culture" is far more useful than knowledge about the printed literature of ages past. Cultural studies—practiced in the spirit of genuine critical inquiry, including a critical attitude toward the tools of theory one employs—might be an essential survival skill.

Nevertheless I hope that Guillory is wrong about the value of reading and analyzing literary texts, and that such practices can have value other than the reproduction of a technomanagerial elite. I entered this poorly paid profession, instead of making millions performing quadruple bypasses, as my working-class parents wanted me to do, because I was one of the people Bloom can't find at Yale any longer. I thought it might be more rewarding to spend my life reading old novels and teaching and writing about them—novels by radical women like Elizabeth Inchbald as well as by conservative men like Henry Fielding. If it upsets me when literary texts two centuries old are judged and found wanting against our current beliefs and prejudices (superior as these may be), it is because such a "presentist" procedure short-circuits the arch of desire the artists painstakingly wove into their linguistic fabric. That arch of desire can carry us, as both Michael Boardman and George E. Haggerty have shown in their very different essays, into regions of human behavior where we may never have traveled, and if we make the journey without blinders on, we cannot help but be changed and enlarged by it. But if we should die to the pleasures Inchbald's story or Gray's elegy offered, those artists themselves will be dead beyond hope of resurrection and the world will have lost something beyond price.

Notes

1. See Richard Levin, "My Theme Can Lick Your Theme," *College English*, 37 (1975), 137–52

2. See R. S. Crane in *Journal of General Education* 4 (1950): 112–30, and Martin C. Battestin in *ELH* 35 (1968): 188–217. My claim is that Battestin's essay is methodologically more typical than Crane's of the sort of critical work that was being done in this period, though it is far superior to the average specimen that was published in the late 1960s. The appalling mindlessness of much of the thematic criticism of this period can be sampled best by going through old volumes of *PMLA* and other "generalist" journals of the period or casebooks on popular college texts like James's "The Turn of the Screw" or Salinger's *The Catcher in the Rye*.

3. Ludwig Wittgenstein, *Philosophische Untersuchungen* I, (New York: MacMillan, 1953), 199: "To understand a sentence is to understand a language. To understand a language is to master a technique."

4. Joseph Wiesenfarth, *Gothic Manners*. (Madison: University of Wisconsin Press, 1988).

5. *Johns Hopkins Guide to Literary Criticism and Theory*. (Baltimore Johns Hopkins University Press, 1994), 188.

6. Thomas S. Kuhn, *The Structure of Scientific Revolutions*. (Chicago: University of Chicago Press, 1970).

7. Harold Bloom, *The Western Canon: The Books and School of the Ages* (New York: Harcourt Brace, 1994), 484–5.

8. John Guillory, *Cultural Capital: The Problem of Literary Canon-Formation* (Chicago: University of Chicago Press, 1993), 263.

Index